THE X FILES™
ORIGINS

COVER ART BY **Chris Fenoglio, Corin Howell, and Matthew Dow Smith**
COVER COLORS BY **Chris Fenoglio**
COLLECTION EDITS BY **Justin Eisinger and Alonzo Simon**
PRODUCTION BY **Chris Mowry**
SERIES EDITS BY **Denton J. Tipton**
EXECUTIVE PRODUCED BY **Chris Carter**
PUBLISHER: **Ted Adams**

THE X-FILES CREATED BY **Chris Carter**

IDW®

Special thanks to Joshua Izzo and Nicole Spiegel at Twentieth Century Fox, Gabe Rotter at Ten Thirteen Productions, and Jul Mae Faustino and Kristoffer Ivan Carl D. Pagaduan.

Ted Adams, CEO & Publisher
Greg Goldstein, President & COO
Robbie Robbins, EVP/Sr. Graphic Artist
Chris Ryall, Chief Creative Officer
David Hedgecock, Editor-in-Chief
Laurie Windrow, Senior Vice President of Sales & Marketing
Matthew Ruzicka, CPA, Chief Financial Officer
Dirk Wood, VP of Marketing
Lorelei Bunjes, VP of Digital Services
Jeff Webber, VP of Licensing, Digital and Subsidiary Rights
Jerry Bennington, VP of New Product Development

For international rights, please contact licensing@idwpublishing.com

Become our fan on Facebook **facebook.com/idwpublishing**
Follow us on Twitter **@idwpublishing**
Subscribe to us on YouTube **youtube.com/idwpublishing**
See what's new on Tumblr **tumblr.idwpublishing.com**
Check us out on Instagram **instagram.com/idwpublishing**

ISBN: 978-1-63140-845-8   20 19 18 17   1 2 3 4

Originally published as THE X-FILES: ORIGINS issues #1–4.

MULDER

STORY BY **Jody Houser & Matthew Dow Smith**
SCRIPT BY **Jody Houser**
ART AND COLORS BY **Chris Fenoglio**
LETTERS BY **Dezi Sienty**

SCULLY

STORY BY **Matthew Dow Smith & Jody Houser**
SCRIPT BY **Matthew Dow Smith**
ART BY **Corin Howell**
COLORS BY **Monica Kubina**
LETTERS BY **Dezi Sienty**

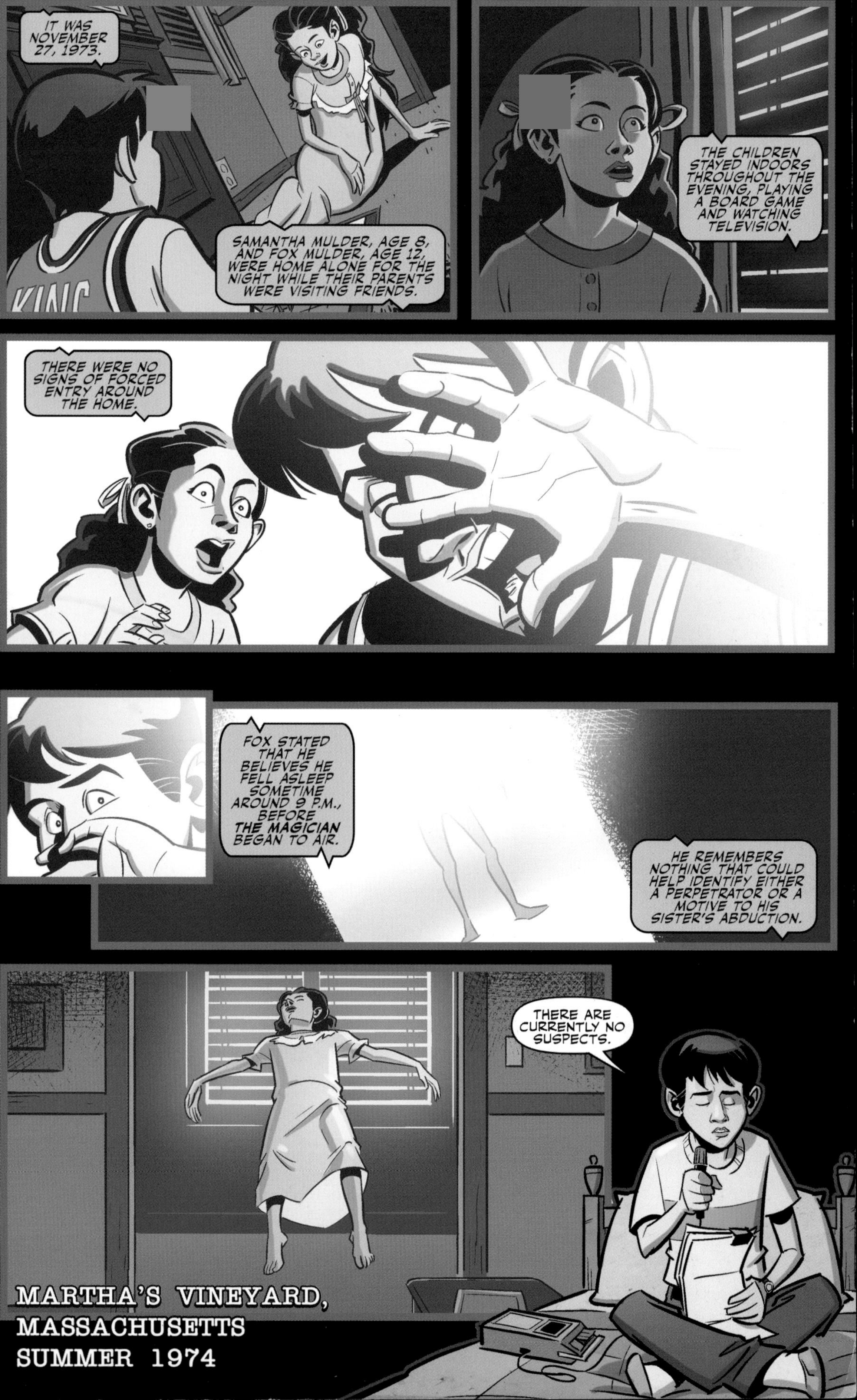
IT WAS NOVEMBER 27, 1973.
SAMANTHA MULDER, AGE 8, AND FOX MULDER, AGE 12, WERE HOME ALONE FOR THE NIGHT WHILE THEIR PARENTS WERE VISITING FRIENDS.
THE CHILDREN STAYED INDOORS THROUGHOUT THE EVENING, PLAYING A BOARD GAME AND WATCHING TELEVISION.
THERE WERE NO SIGNS OF FORCED ENTRY AROUND THE HOME.
FOX STATED THAT HE BELIEVES HE FELL ASLEEP SOMETIME AROUND 9 P.M., BEFORE THE MAGICIAN BEGAN TO AIR.
HE REMEMBERS NOTHING THAT COULD HELP IDENTIFY EITHER A PERPETRATOR OR A MOTIVE TO HIS SISTER'S ABDUCTION.
THERE ARE CURRENTLY NO SUSPECTS.
MARTHA'S VINEYARD, MASSACHUSETTS SUMMER 1974

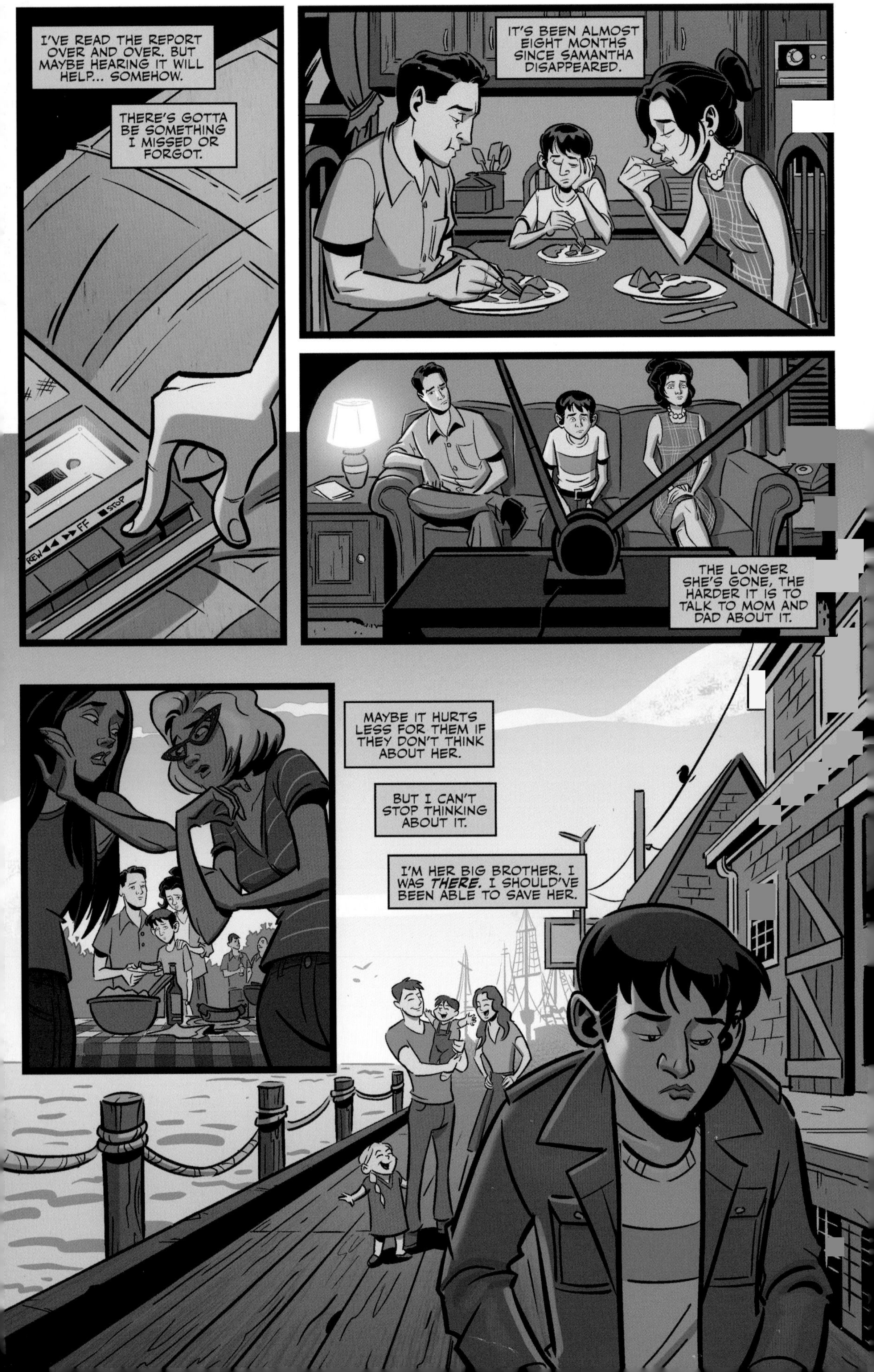
I'VE READ THE REPORT OVER AND OVER. BUT MAYBE HEARING IT WILL HELP... SOMEHOW.
THERE'S GOTTA BE SOMETHING I MISSED OR FORGOT.
REW◀◀ ▶▶FF ■STOP
IT'S BEEN ALMOST EIGHT MONTHS SINCE SAMANTHA DISAPPEARED.
THE LONGER SHE'S GONE, THE HARDER IT IS TO TALK TO MOM AND DAD ABOUT IT.
MAYBE IT HURTS LESS FOR THEM IF THEY DON'T THINK ABOUT HER.
BUT I CAN'T STOP THINKING ABOUT IT.
I'M HER BIG BROTHER. I WAS *THERE.* I SHOULD'VE BEEN ABLE TO SAVE HER.

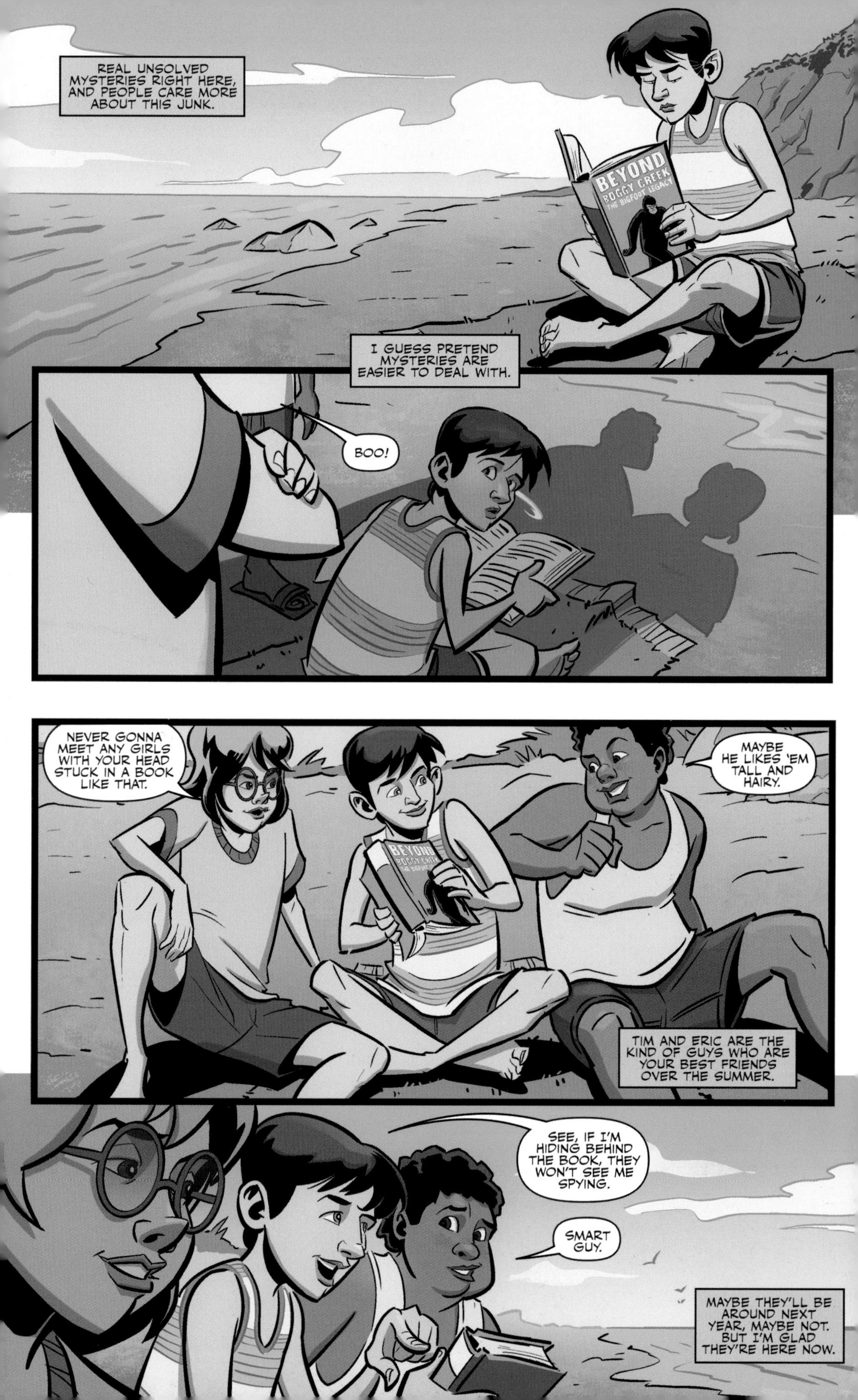
REAL UNSOLVED MYSTERIES RIGHT HERE, AND PEOPLE CARE MORE ABOUT THIS JUNK.
BEYOND BOGGY CREEK THE BIGFOOT LEGACY
I GUESS PRETEND MYSTERIES ARE EASIER TO DEAL WITH.
BOO!
NEVER GONNA MEET ANY GIRLS WITH YOUR HEAD STUCK IN A BOOK LIKE THAT.
MAYBE HE LIKES 'EM TALL AND HAIRY.
TIM AND ERIC ARE THE KIND OF GUYS WHO ARE YOUR BEST FRIENDS OVER THE SUMMER.
SEE, IF I'M HIDING BEHIND THE BOOK, THEY WON'T SEE ME SPYING.
SMART GUY.
MAYBE THEY'LL BE AROUND NEXT YEAR, MAYBE NOT. BUT I'M GLAD THEY'RE HERE NOW.

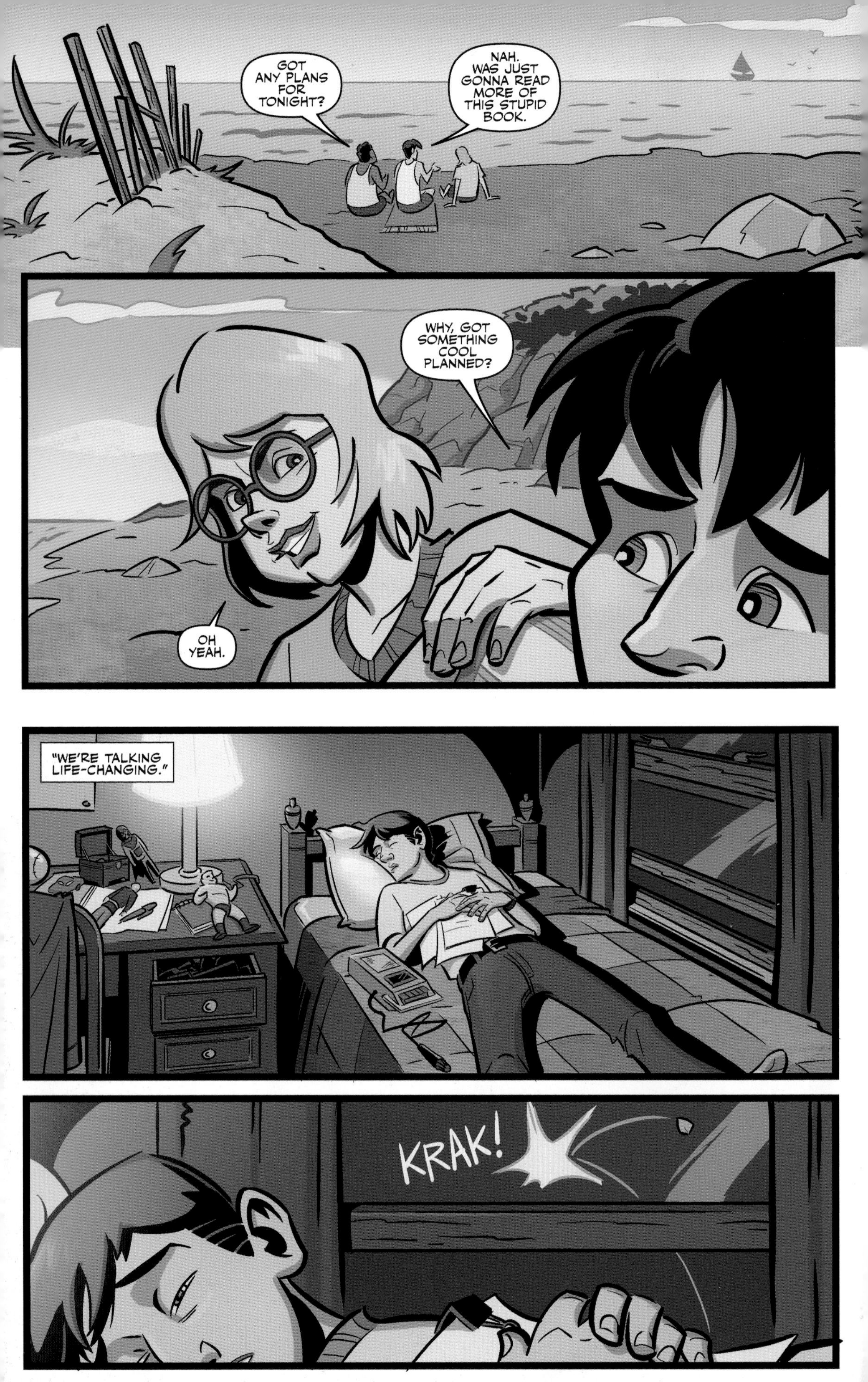
GOT ANY PLANS FOR TONIGHT?
NAH. WAS JUST GONNA READ MORE OF THIS STUPID BOOK.
WHY, GOT SOMETHING COOL PLANNED?
OH YEAH.
"WE'RE TALKING LIFE-CHANGING."
KRAK!

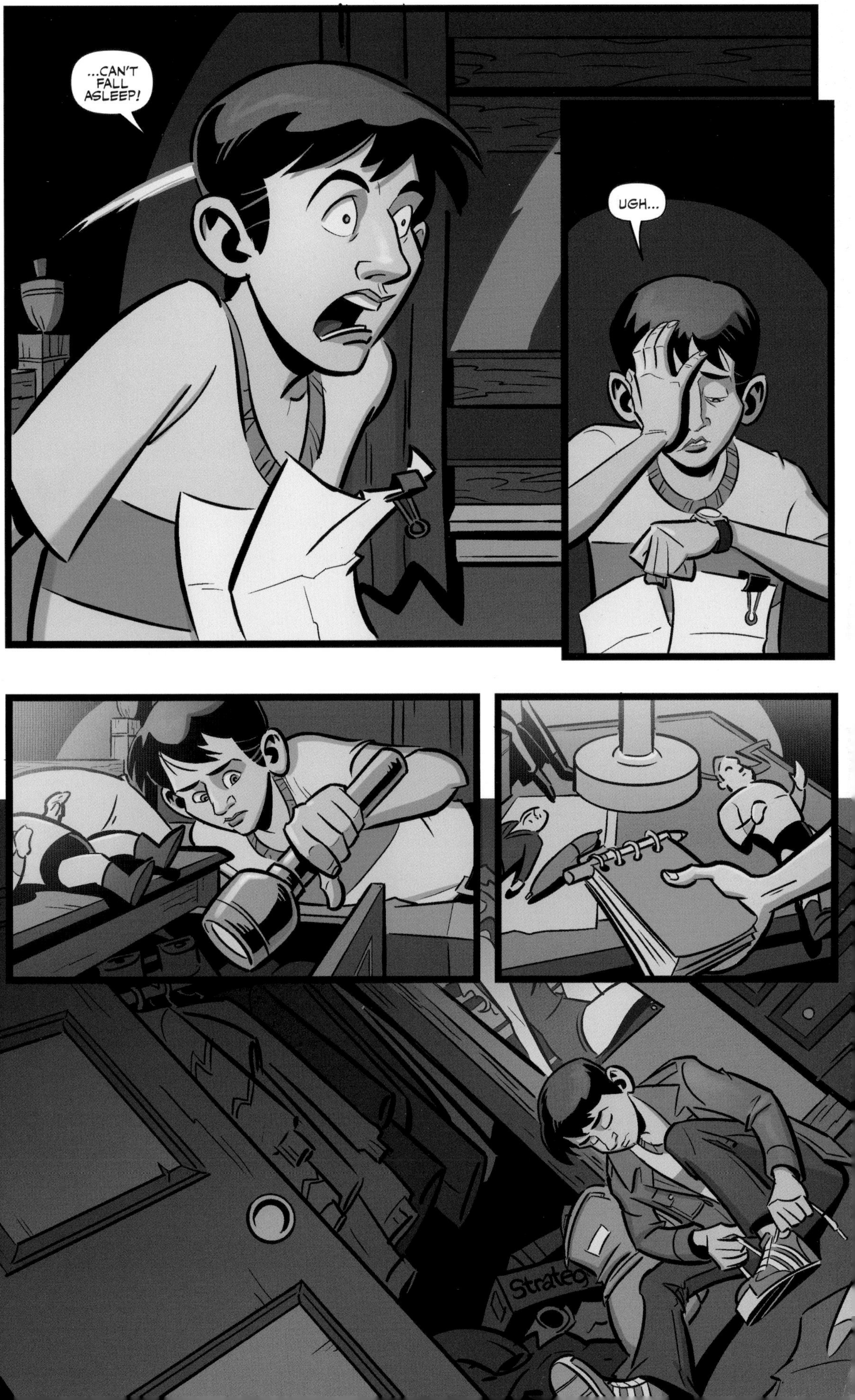
...CAN'T FALL ASLEEP!
UGH...
Strateg

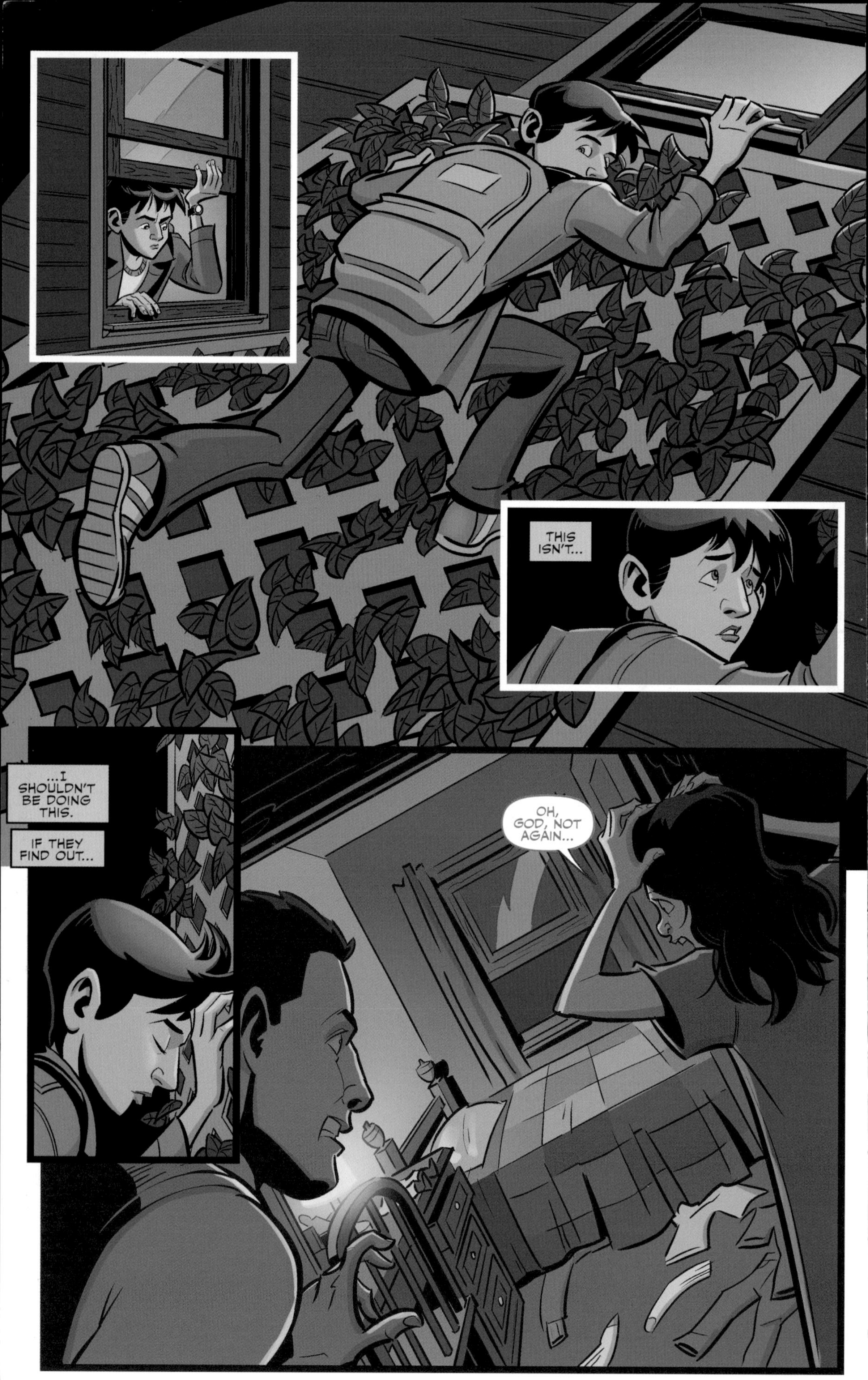
THIS ISN'T...
...I SHOULDN'T BE DOING THIS.
IF THEY FIND OUT...
OH, GOD, NOT AGAIN...

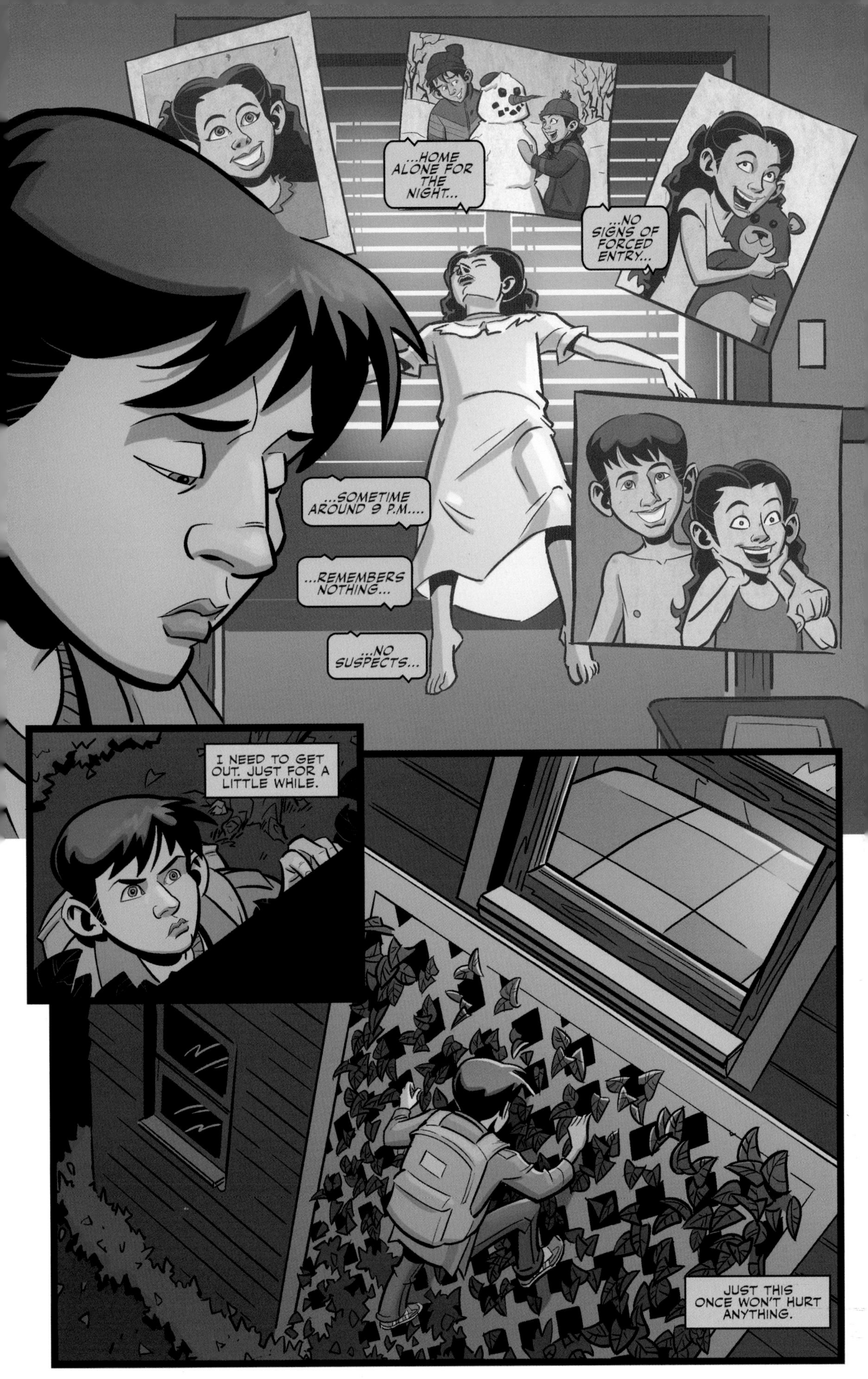
...HOME ALONE FOR THE NIGHT...
...NO SIGNS OF FORCED ENTRY...
...SOMETIME AROUND 9 P.M....
...REMEMBERS NOTHING...
...NO SUSPECTS...
I NEED TO GET OUT. JUST FOR A LITTLE WHILE.
JUST THIS ONCE WON'T HURT ANYTHING.

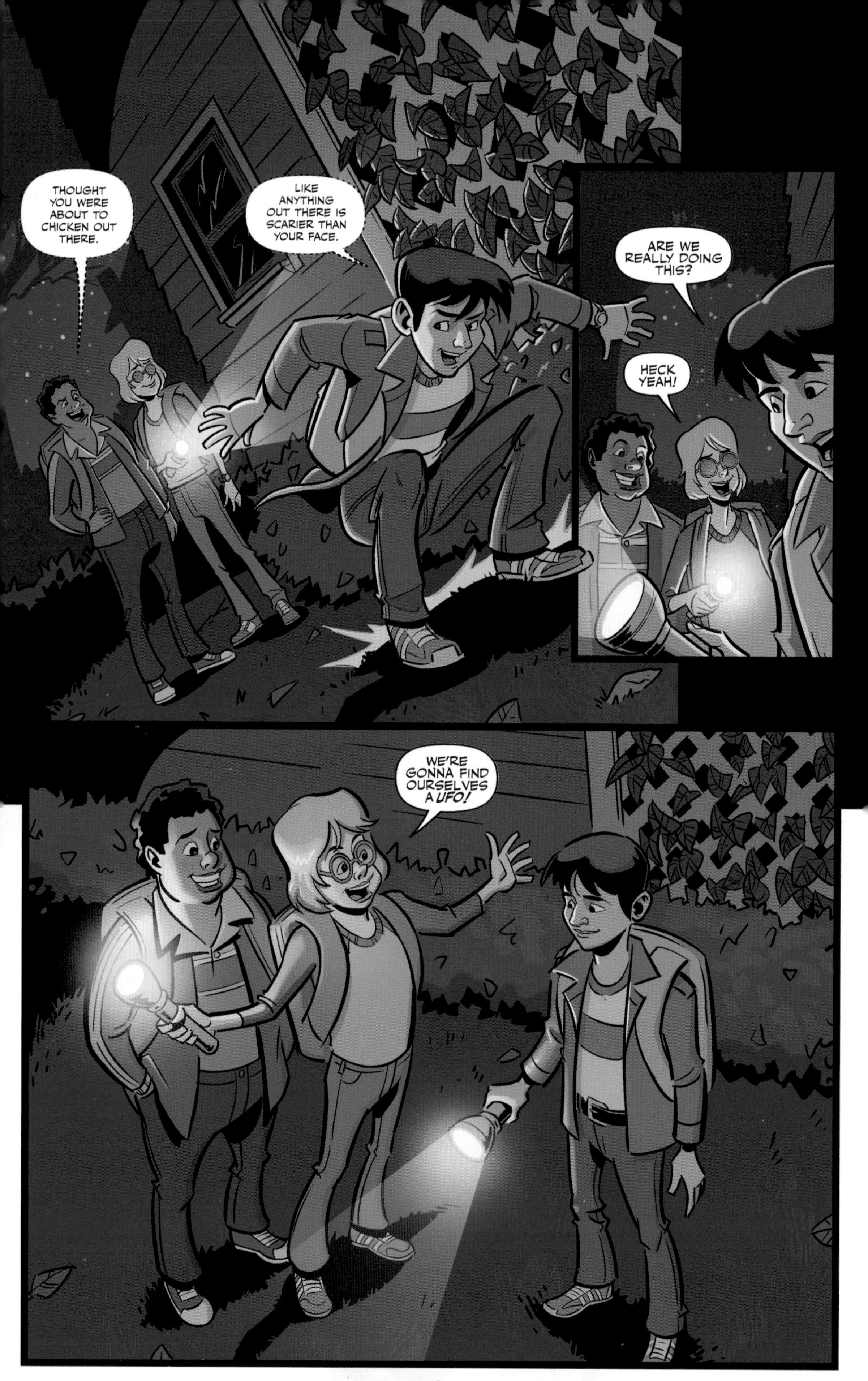
THOUGHT YOU WERE ABOUT TO CHICKEN OUT THERE.
LIKE ANYTHING OUT THERE IS SCARIER THAN YOUR FACE.
ARE WE REALLY DOING THIS?
HECK YEAH!
WE'RE GONNA FIND OURSELVES A *UFO!*

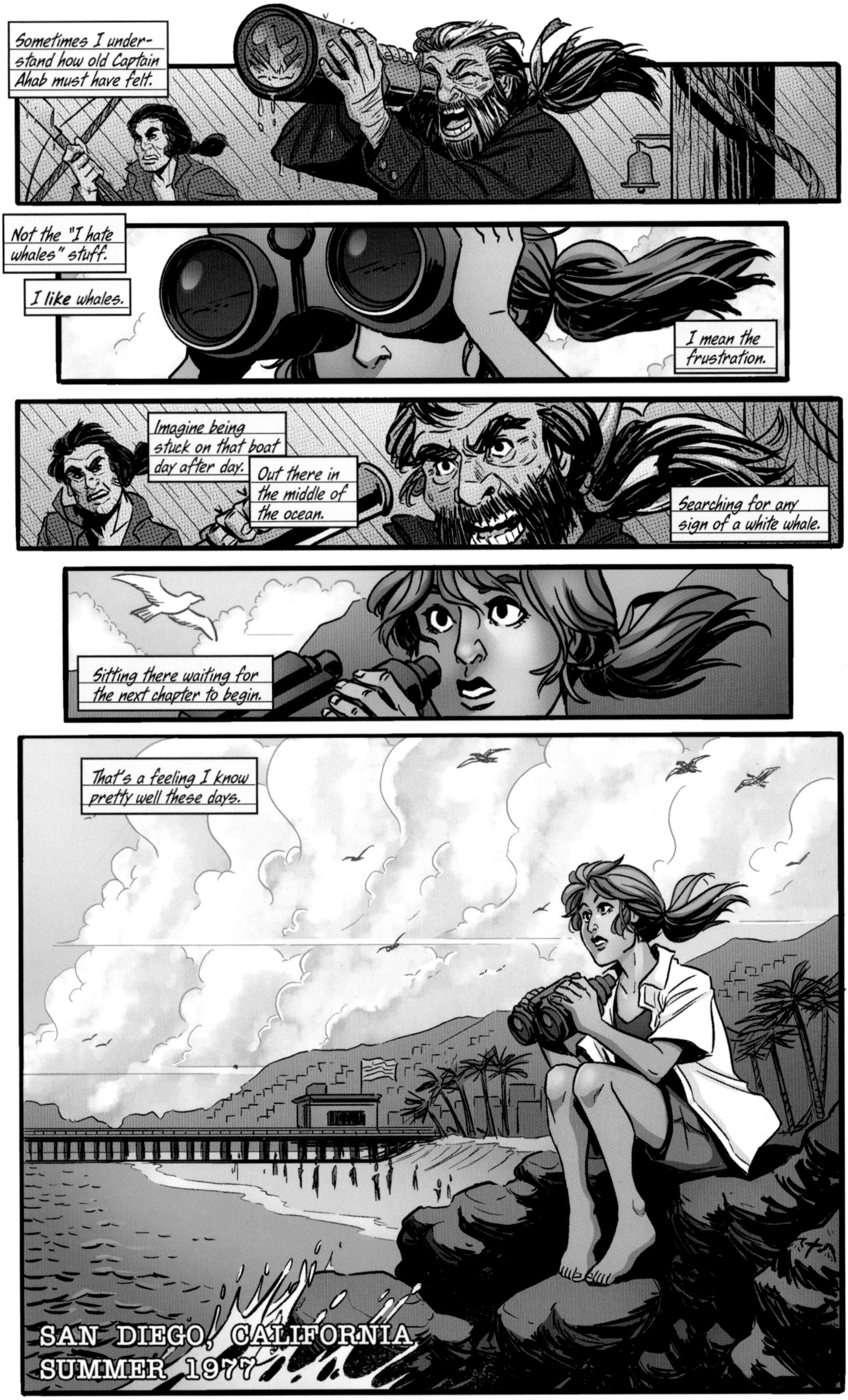
Sometimes I understand how old Captain Ahab must have felt.
Not the "I hate whales" stuff.
I like whales.
I mean the frustration.
Imagine being stuck on that boat day after day.
Out there in the middle of the ocean.
Searching for any sign of a white whale.
Sitting there waiting for the next chapter to begin.
That's a feeling I know pretty well these days.
SAN DIEGO, CALIFORNIA
SUMMER 1977

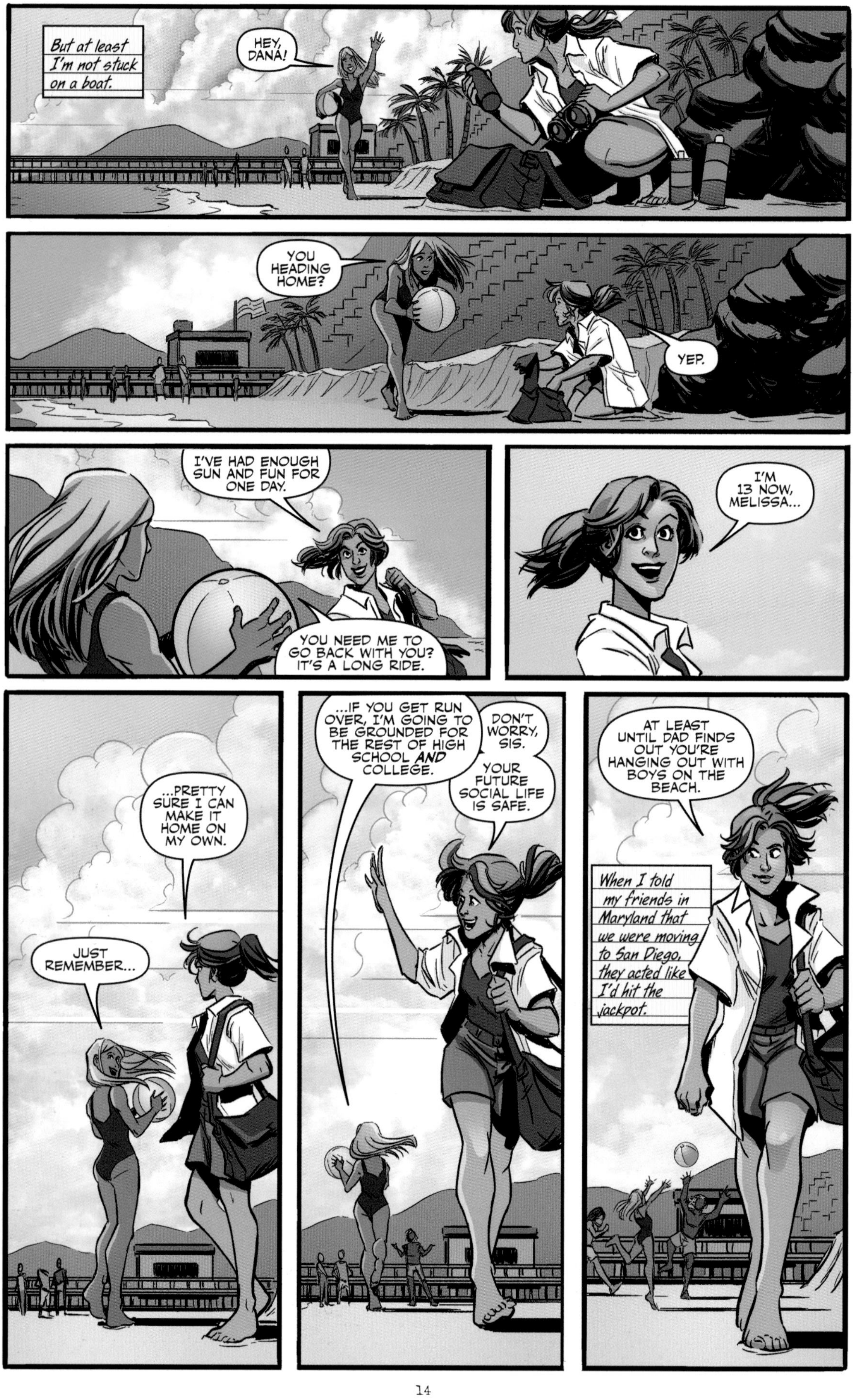
But at least I'm not stuck on a boat.
HEY, DANA!
YOU HEADING HOME?
YEP.
I'VE HAD ENOUGH SUN AND FUN FOR ONE DAY.
YOU NEED ME TO GO BACK WITH YOU? IT'S A LONG RIDE.
I'M 13 NOW, MELISSA...
...PRETTY SURE I CAN MAKE IT HOME ON MY OWN.
JUST REMEMBER...
...IF YOU GET RUN OVER, I'M GOING TO BE GROUNDED FOR THE REST OF HIGH SCHOOL AND COLLEGE.
DON'T WORRY, SIS.
YOUR FUTURE SOCIAL LIFE IS SAFE.
AT LEAST UNTIL DAD FINDS OUT YOU'RE HANGING OUT WITH BOYS ON THE BEACH.
When I told my friends in Maryland that we were moving to San Diego, they acted like I'd hit the jackpot.

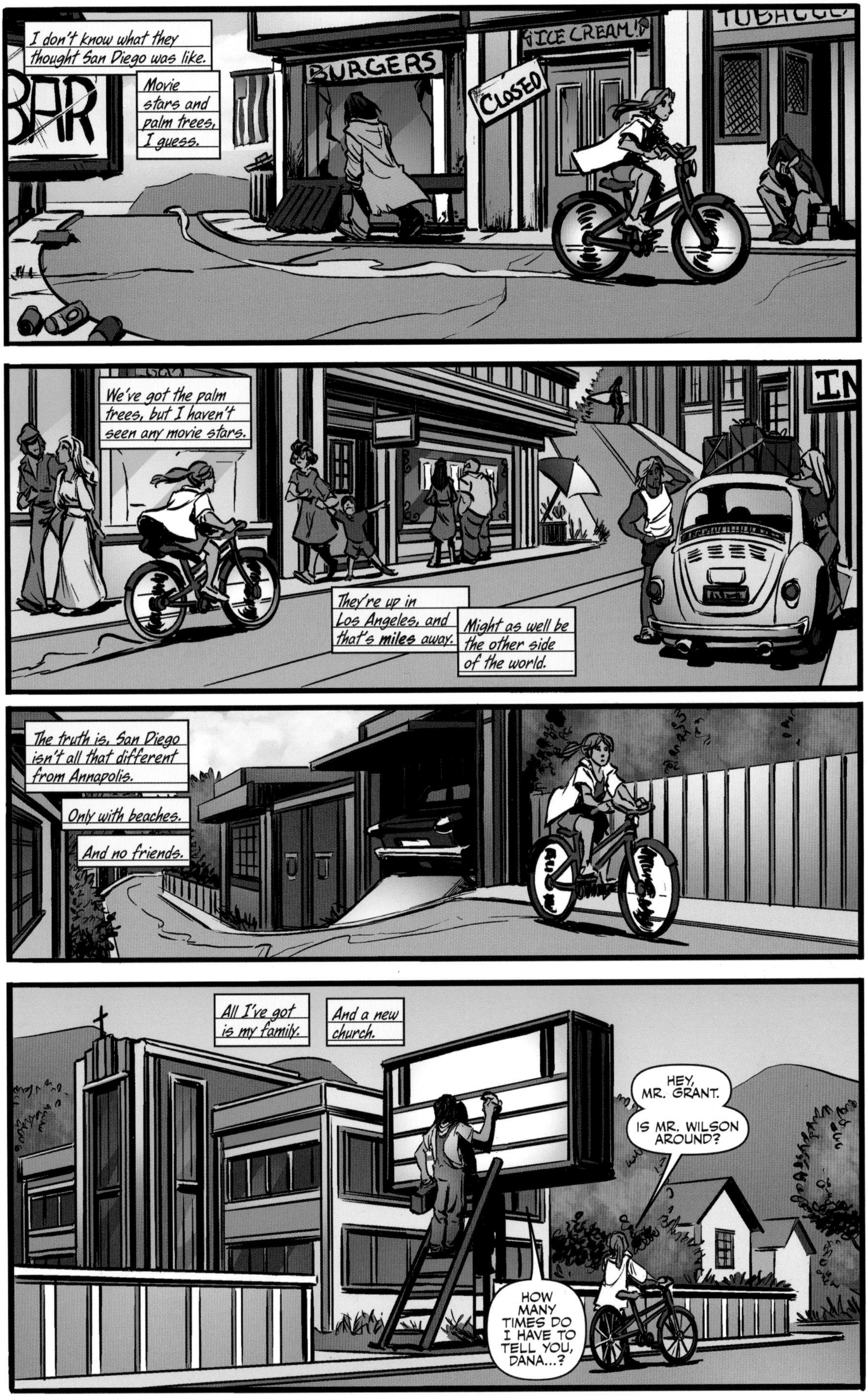
I don't know what they thought San Diego was like.
Movie stars and palm trees, I guess.
BAR
BURGERS
ICE CREAM!
CLOSED
We've got the palm trees, but I haven't seen any movie stars.
They're up in Los Angeles, and that's **miles** away.
Might as well be the other side of the world.
The truth is, San Diego isn't all that different from Annapolis.
Only with beaches.
And no friends.
All I've got is my family.
And a new church.
HEY, MR. GRANT.
IS MR. WILSON AROUND?
HOW MANY TIMES DO I HAVE TO TELL YOU, DANA...?

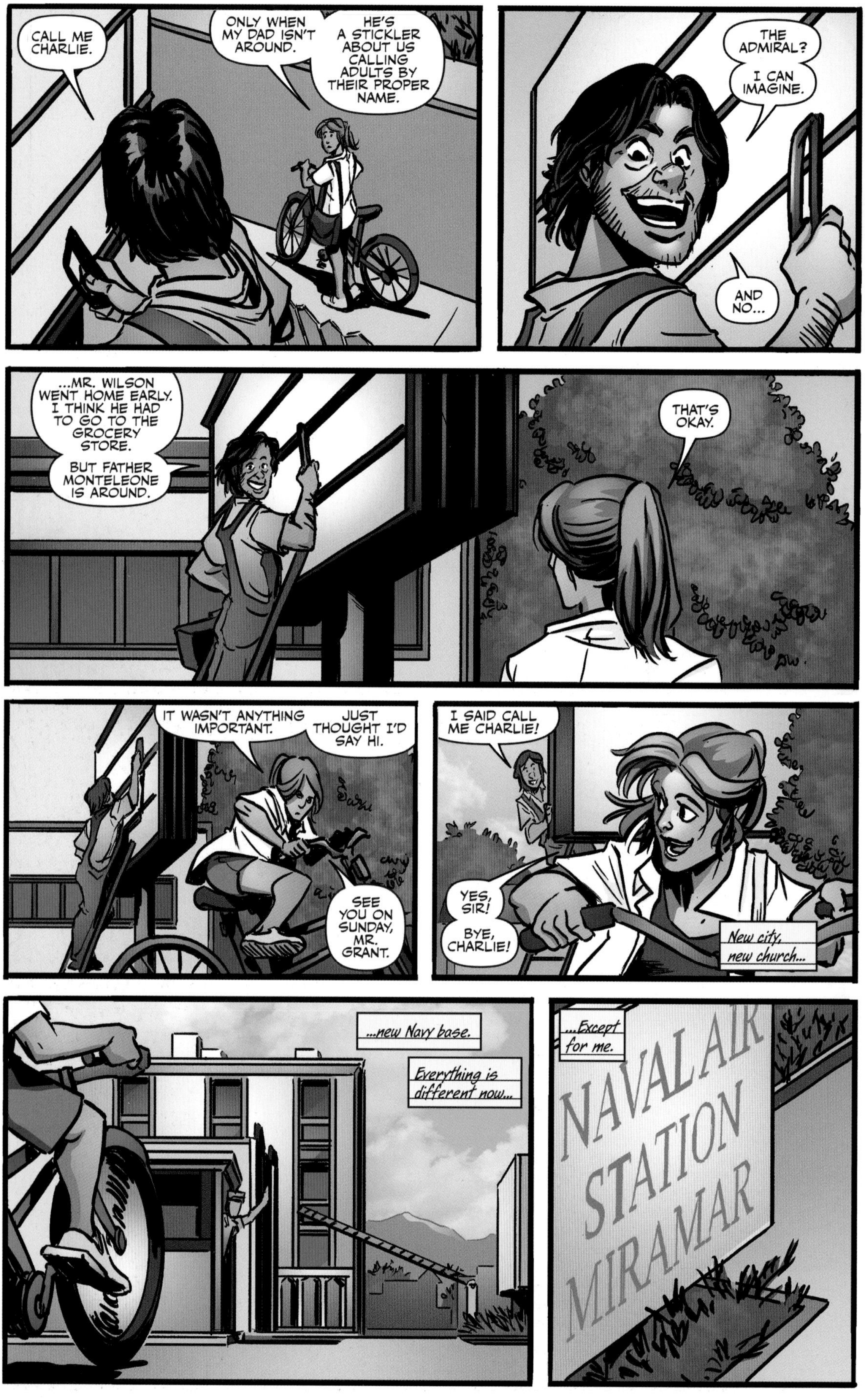
CALL ME CHARLIE.
ONLY WHEN MY DAD ISN'T AROUND.
HE'S A STICKLER ABOUT US CALLING ADULTS BY THEIR PROPER NAME.
THE ADMIRAL?
I CAN IMAGINE.
AND NO...
...MR. WILSON WENT HOME EARLY. I THINK HE HAD TO GO TO THE GROCERY STORE.
BUT FATHER MONTELEONE IS AROUND.
THAT'S OKAY.
IT WASN'T ANYTHING IMPORTANT.
JUST THOUGHT I'D SAY HI.
SEE YOU ON SUNDAY, MR. GRANT.
I SAID CALL ME CHARLIE!
YES, SIR!
BYE, CHARLIE!
New city, new church...
...new Navy base.
Everything is different now...
...Except for me.
NAVAL AIR STATION MIRAMAR

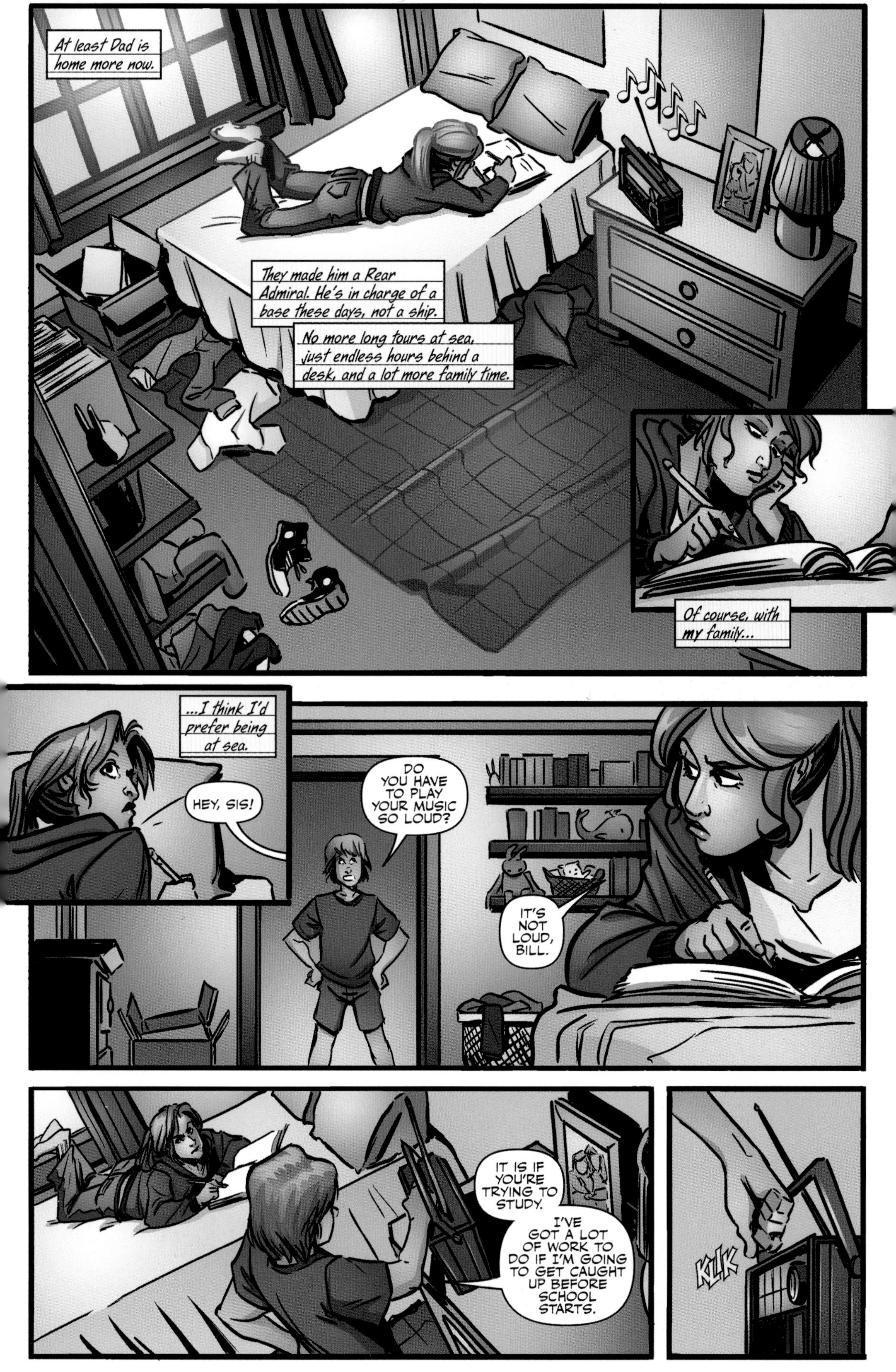

At least Dad is home more now.
They made him a Rear Admiral. He's in charge of a base these days, not a ship.
No more long tours at sea, just endless hours behind a desk, and a lot more family time.
Of course, with my family...
...I think I'd prefer being at sea.
HEY, SIS!
DO YOU HAVE TO PLAY YOUR MUSIC SO LOUD?
IT'S NOT LOUD, BILL.
IT IS IF YOU'RE TRYING TO STUDY.
I'VE GOT A LOT OF WORK TO DO IF I'M GOING TO GET CAUGHT UP BEFORE SCHOOL STARTS.
KLIK

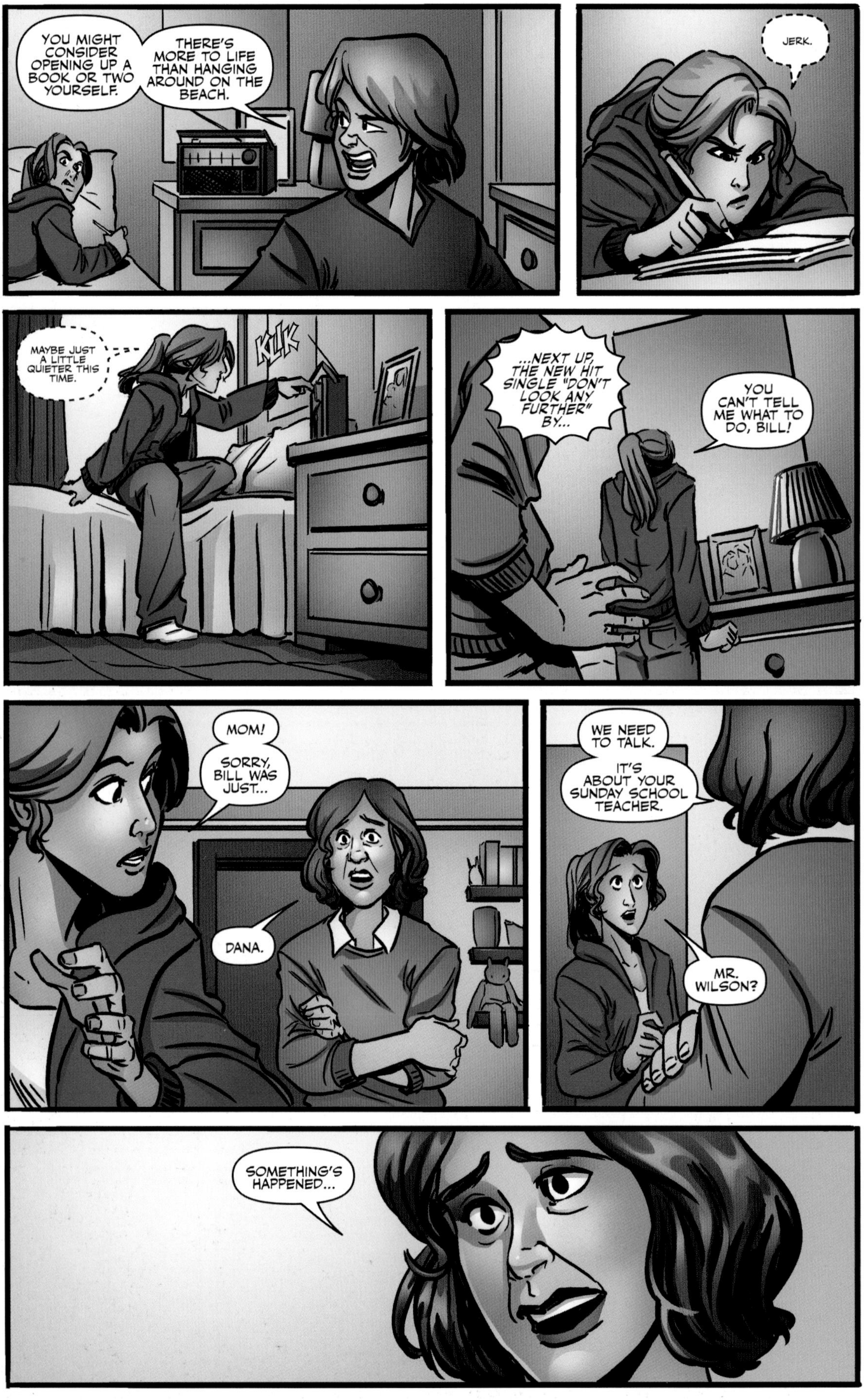

YOU MIGHT CONSIDER OPENING UP A BOOK OR TWO YOURSELF.
THERE'S MORE TO LIFE THAN HANGING AROUND ON THE BEACH.
JERK.
MAYBE JUST A LITTLE QUIETER THIS TIME.
KLIK
...NEXT UP, THE NEW HIT SINGLE "DON'T LOOK ANY FURTHER" BY...
YOU CAN'T TELL ME WHAT TO DO, BILL!
MOM!
SORRY, BILL WAS JUST...
DANA.
WE NEED TO TALK.
IT'S ABOUT YOUR SUNDAY SCHOOL TEACHER.
MR. WILSON?
SOMETHING'S HAPPENED...

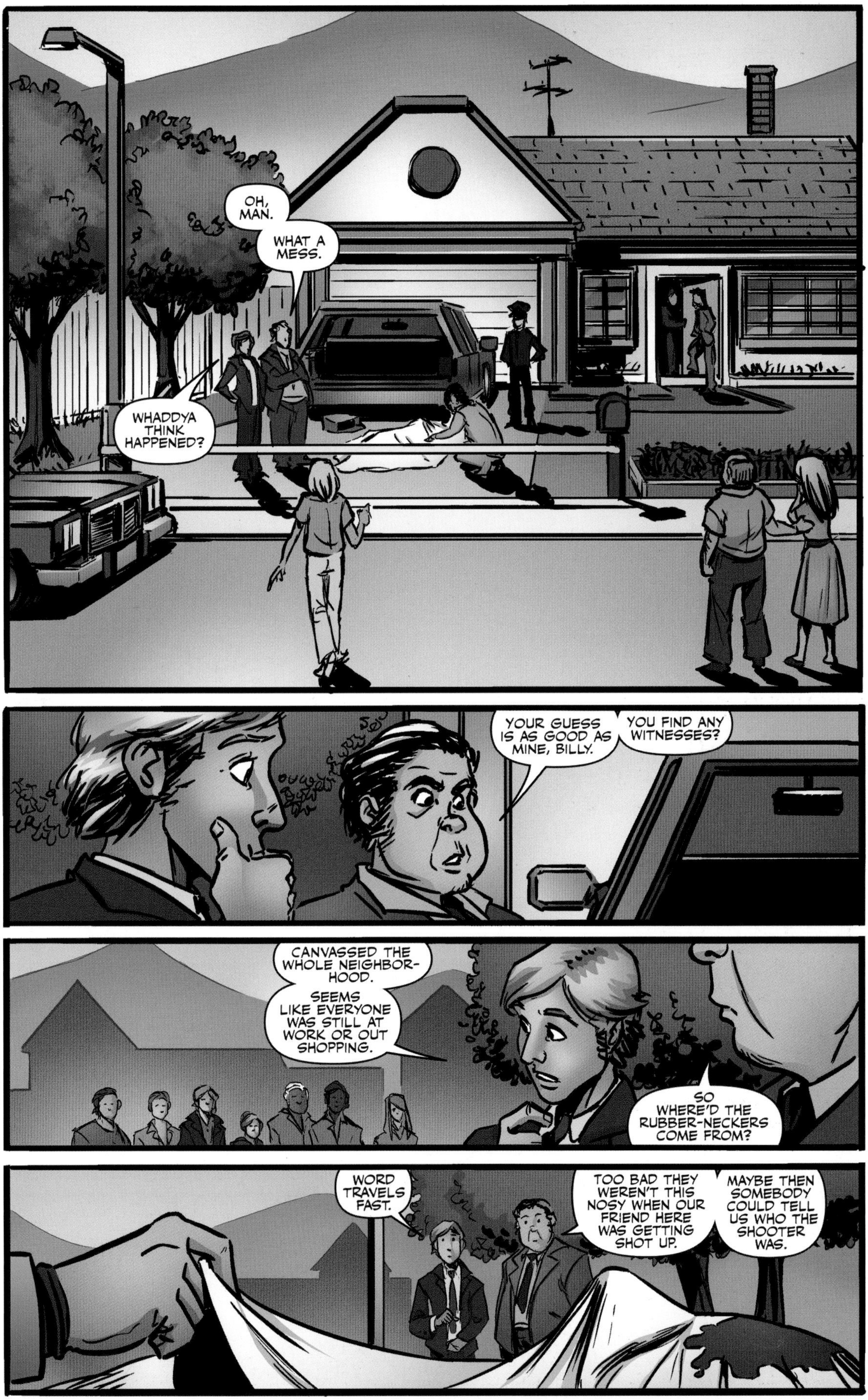
OH, MAN.
WHAT A MESS.
WHADDYA THINK HAPPENED?
YOUR GUESS IS AS GOOD AS MINE, BILLY.
YOU FIND ANY WITNESSES?
CANVASSED THE WHOLE NEIGHBOR-HOOD.
SEEMS LIKE EVERYONE WAS STILL AT WORK OR OUT SHOPPING.
SO WHERE'D THE RUBBER-NECKERS COME FROM?
WORD TRAVELS FAST.
TOO BAD THEY WEREN'T THIS NOSY WHEN OUR FRIEND HERE WAS GETTING SHOT UP.
MAYBE THEN SOMEBODY COULD TELL US WHO THE SHOOTER WAS.

VICTIM WAS A FRANCIS WILSON.

ACCORDING TO THE NEIGHBORS, HE TAUGHT SUNDAY SCHOOL DOWN AT ST. THOMAS'S. NO FAMILY, NO REAL FRIENDS ANYONE KNOWS ABOUT.

NEVER BEEN IN ANY TROUBLE.

ANYONE SAY IF THE GUY WAS A DRUGGIE?

YOU THINK THIS IS A DRUG THING?

THIS CLOSE TO THE BEACH?

THAT WOULD BE MY GUESS.

GUY PROBABLY TRIED TO BUY FROM THE WRONG SCUMBAG.

YOU WANT ME TO BRING IN THE USUAL FREAKS?

DON'T BOTHER.

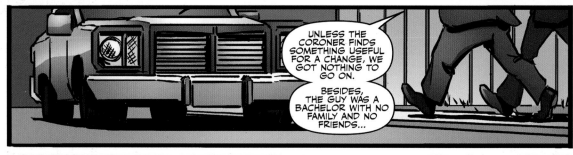

UNLESS THE CORONER FINDS SOMETHING USEFUL FOR A CHANGE, WE GOT NOTHING TO GO ON.

BESIDES, THE GUY WAS A BACHELOR WITH NO FAMILY AND NO FRIENDS...

IT'S NOT LIKE ANYONE REALLY CARES WHAT HAPPENED TO HIM.

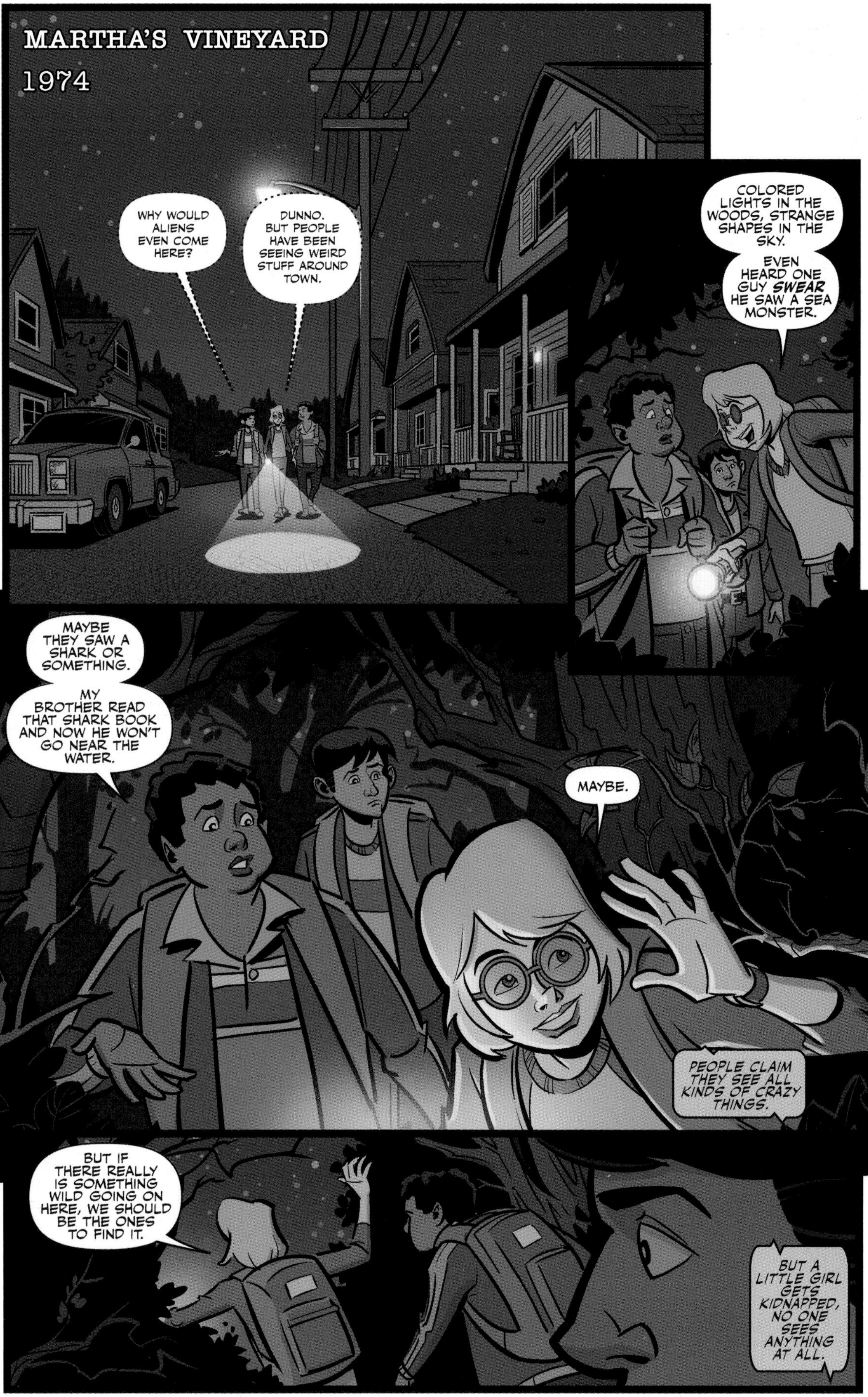
MARTHA'S VINEYARD
1974
WHY WOULD ALIENS EVEN COME HERE?
DUNNO. BUT PEOPLE HAVE BEEN SEEING WEIRD STUFF AROUND TOWN.
COLORED LIGHTS IN THE WOODS, STRANGE SHAPES IN THE SKY.
EVEN HEARD ONE GUY SWEAR HE SAW A SEA MONSTER.
MAYBE THEY SAW A SHARK OR SOMETHING.
MY BROTHER READ THAT SHARK BOOK AND NOW HE WON'T GO NEAR THE WATER.
MAYBE.
PEOPLE CLAIM THEY SEE ALL KINDS OF CRAZY THINGS.
BUT IF THERE REALLY IS SOMETHING WILD GOING ON HERE, WE SHOULD BE THE ONES TO FIND IT.
BUT A LITTLE GIRL GETS KIDNAPPED, NO ONE SEES ANYTHING AT ALL.

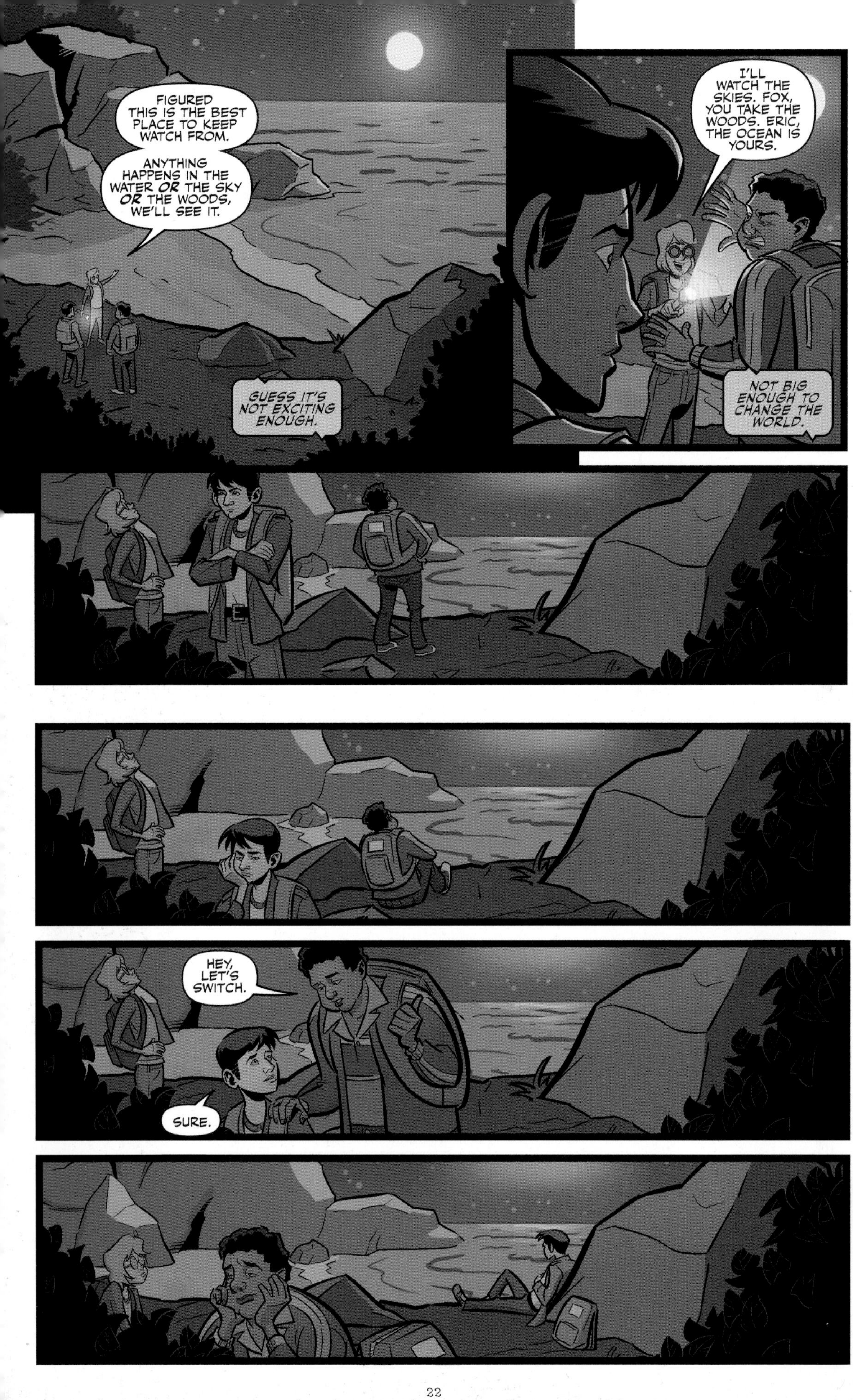
FIGURED THIS IS THE BEST PLACE TO KEEP WATCH FROM.
ANYTHING HAPPENS IN THE WATER OR THE SKY OR THE WOODS, WE'LL SEE IT.
GUESS IT'S NOT EXCITING ENOUGH.
I'LL WATCH THE SKIES. FOX, YOU TAKE THE WOODS. ERIC, THE OCEAN IS YOURS.
NOT BIG ENOUGH TO CHANGE THE WORLD.
HEY, LET'S SWITCH.
SURE.

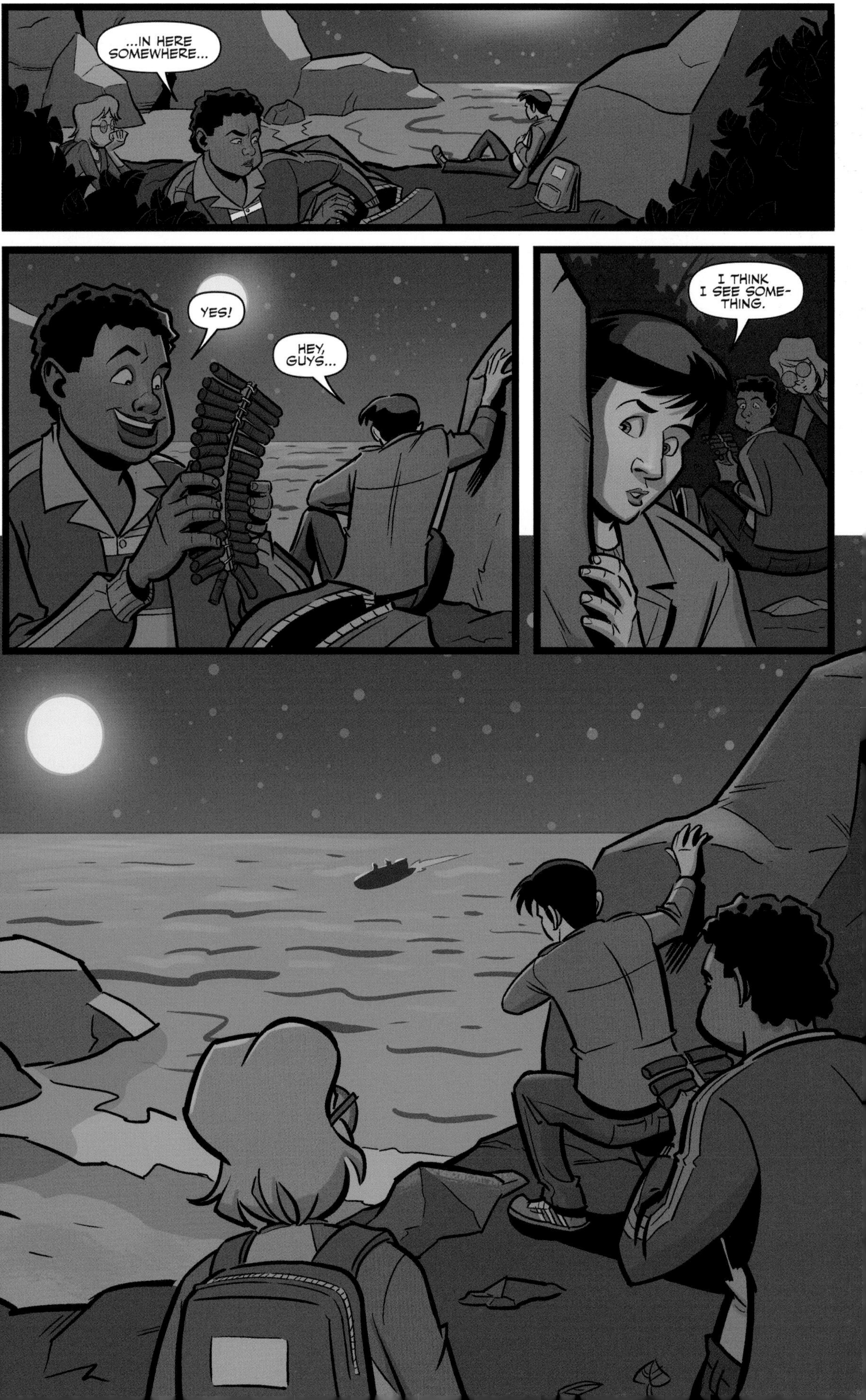
...IN HERE SOMEWHERE...
YES!
HEY, GUYS...
I THINK I SEE SOME-THING.

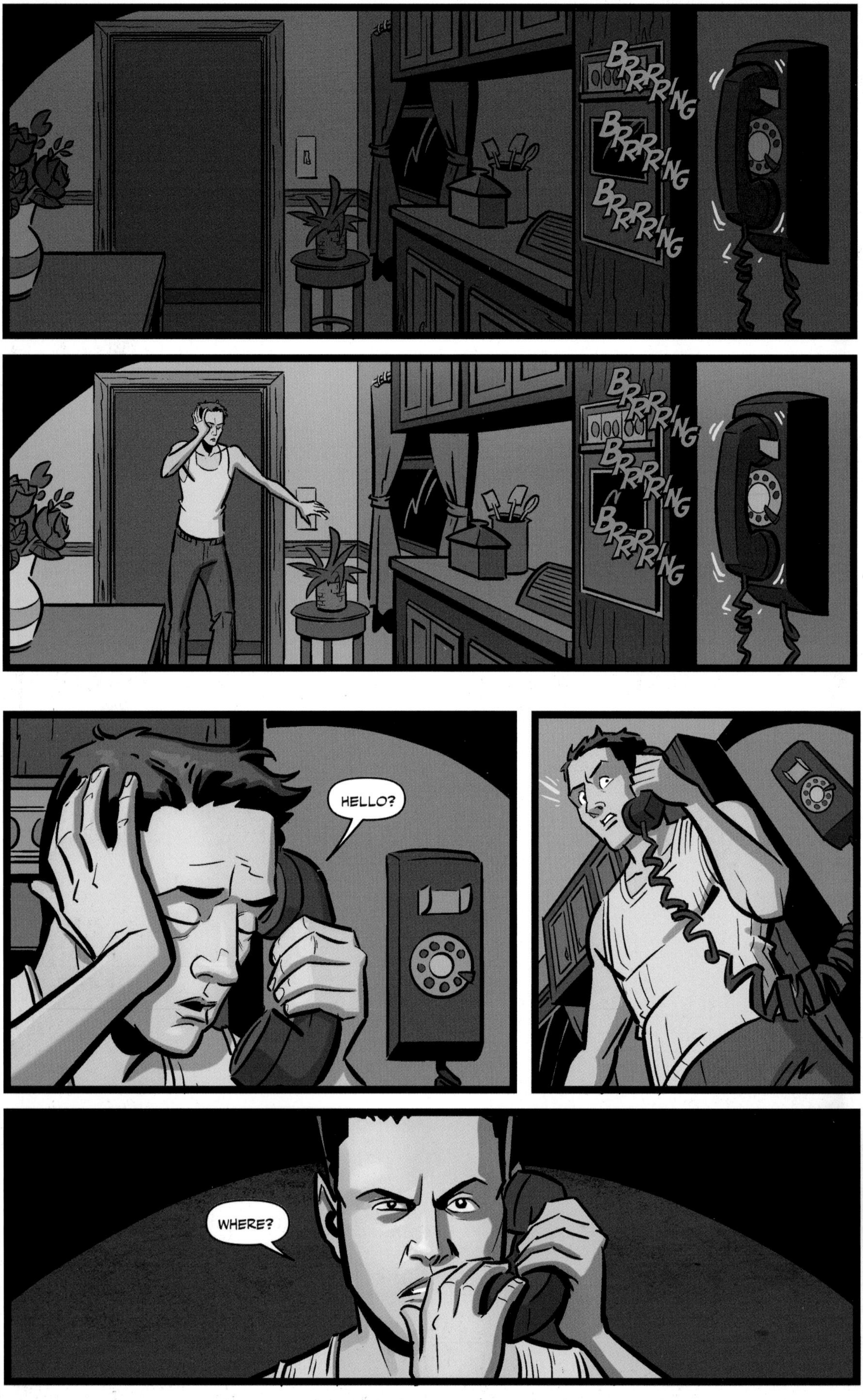
BRRRRING
BRRRRING
BRRRRING
BRRRRING
BRRRRING
BRRRRING
HELLO?
WHERE?

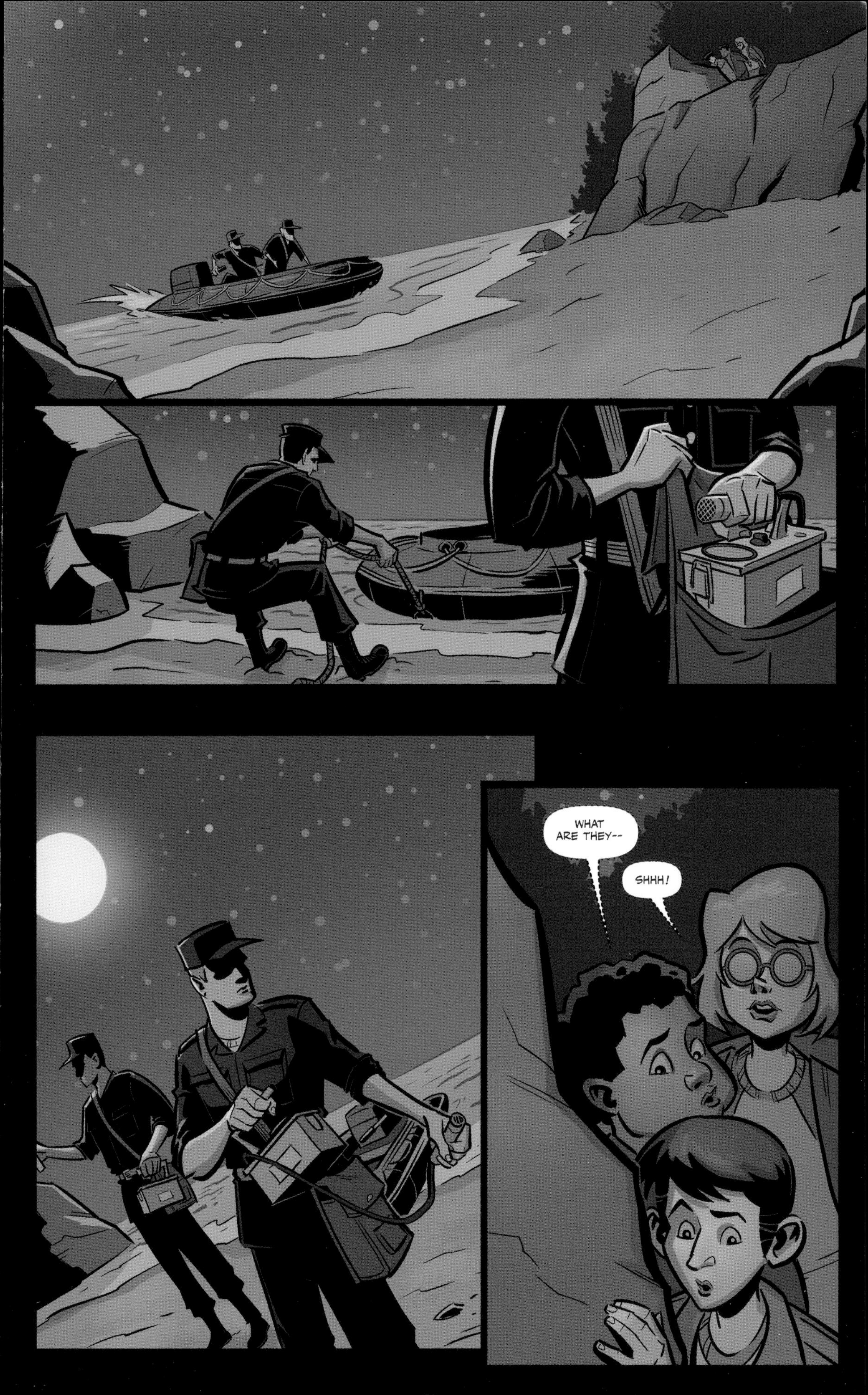
WHAT ARE THEY--
SHHH!

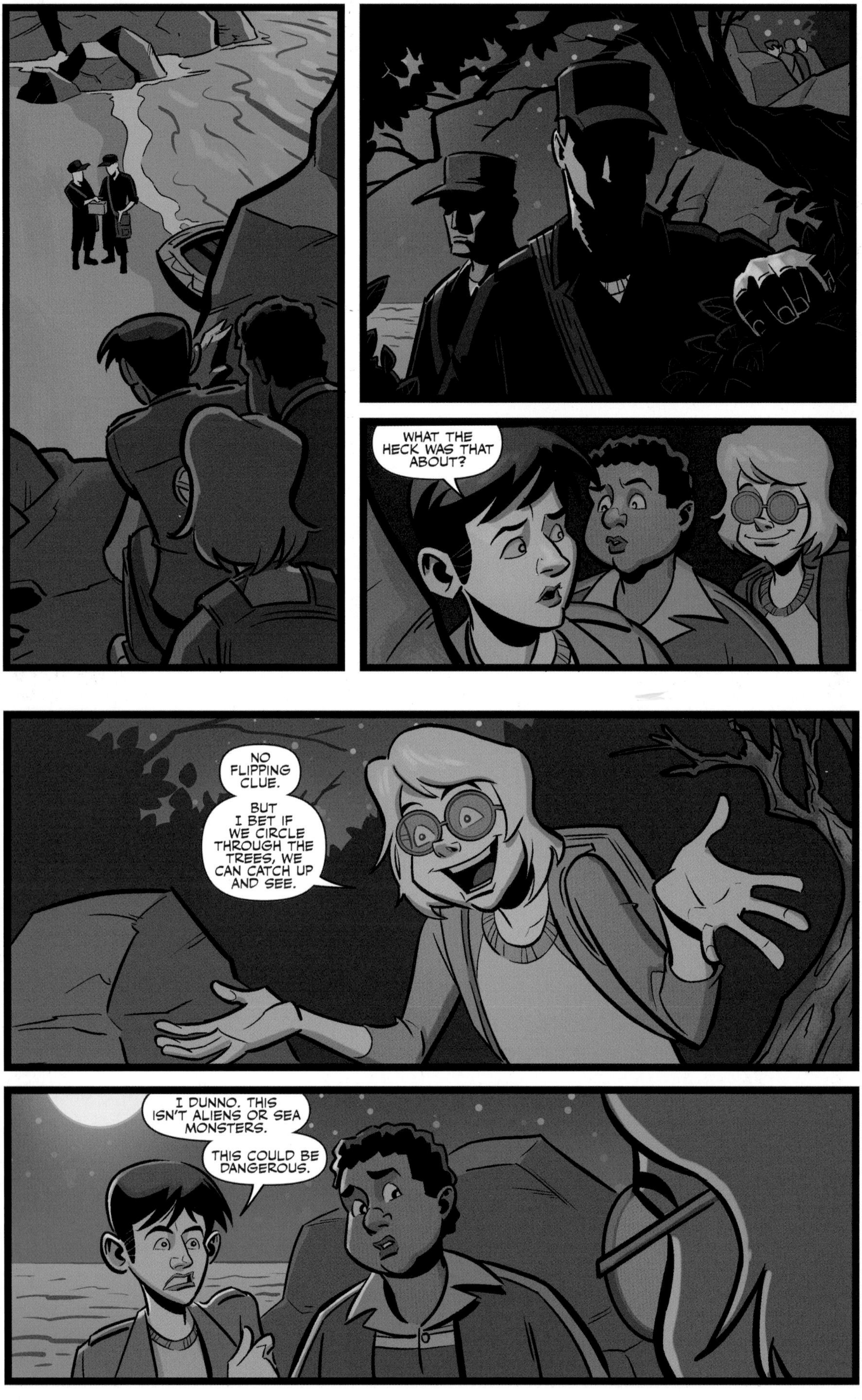
WHAT THE HECK WAS THAT ABOUT?
NO FLIPPING CLUE.
BUT I BET IF WE CIRCLE THROUGH THE TREES, WE CAN CATCH UP AND SEE.
I DUNNO. THIS ISN'T ALIENS OR SEA MONSTERS.
THIS COULD BE DANGEROUS.

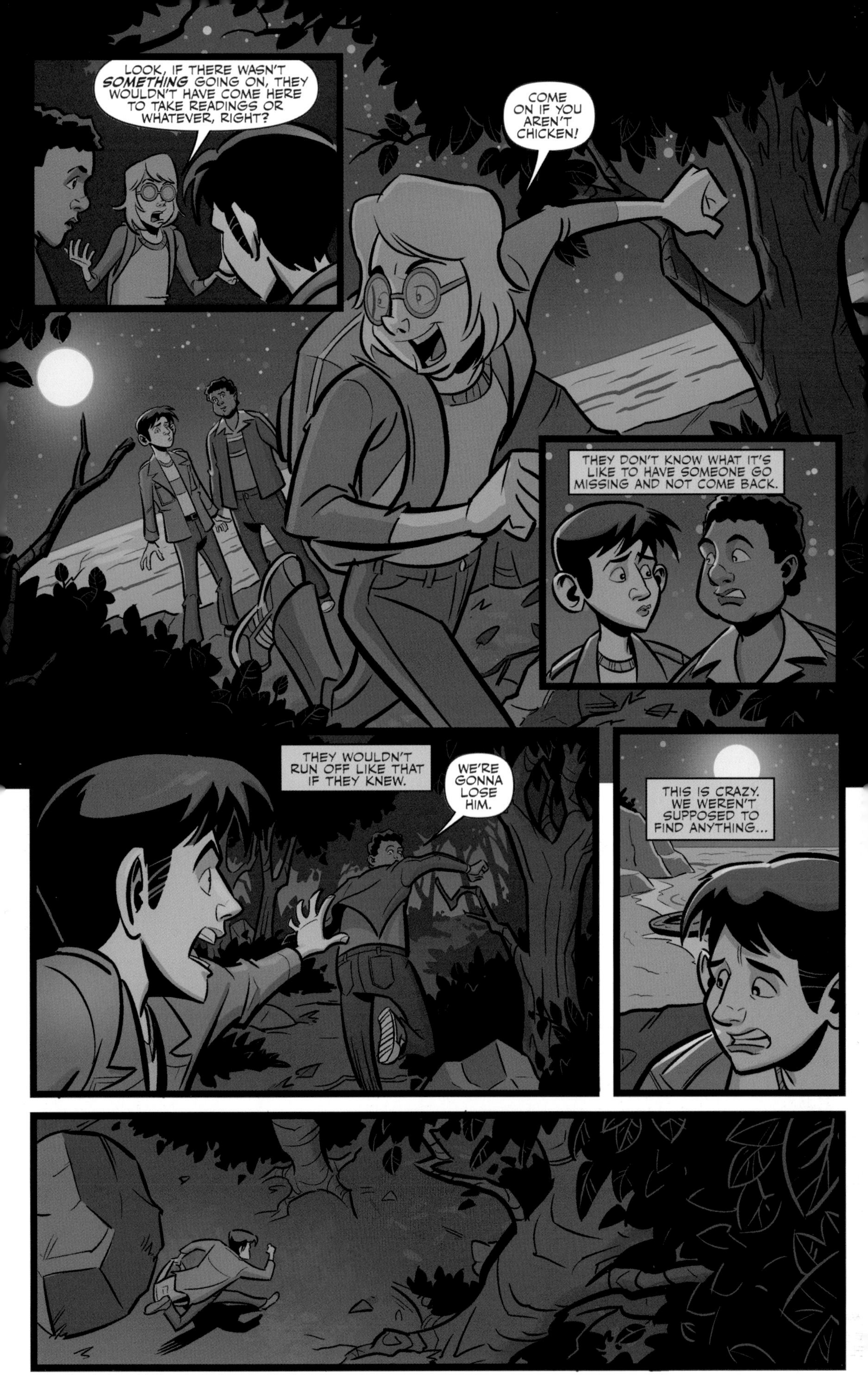
LOOK, IF THERE WASN'T *SOMETHING* GOING ON, THEY WOULDN'T HAVE COME HERE TO TAKE READINGS OR WHATEVER, RIGHT?
COME ON IF YOU AREN'T CHICKEN!
THEY DON'T KNOW WHAT IT'S LIKE TO HAVE SOMEONE GO MISSING AND NOT COME BACK.
THEY WOULDN'T RUN OFF LIKE THAT IF THEY KNEW.
WE'RE GONNA LOSE HIM.
THIS IS CRAZY. WE WEREN'T SUPPOSED TO FIND ANYTHING...

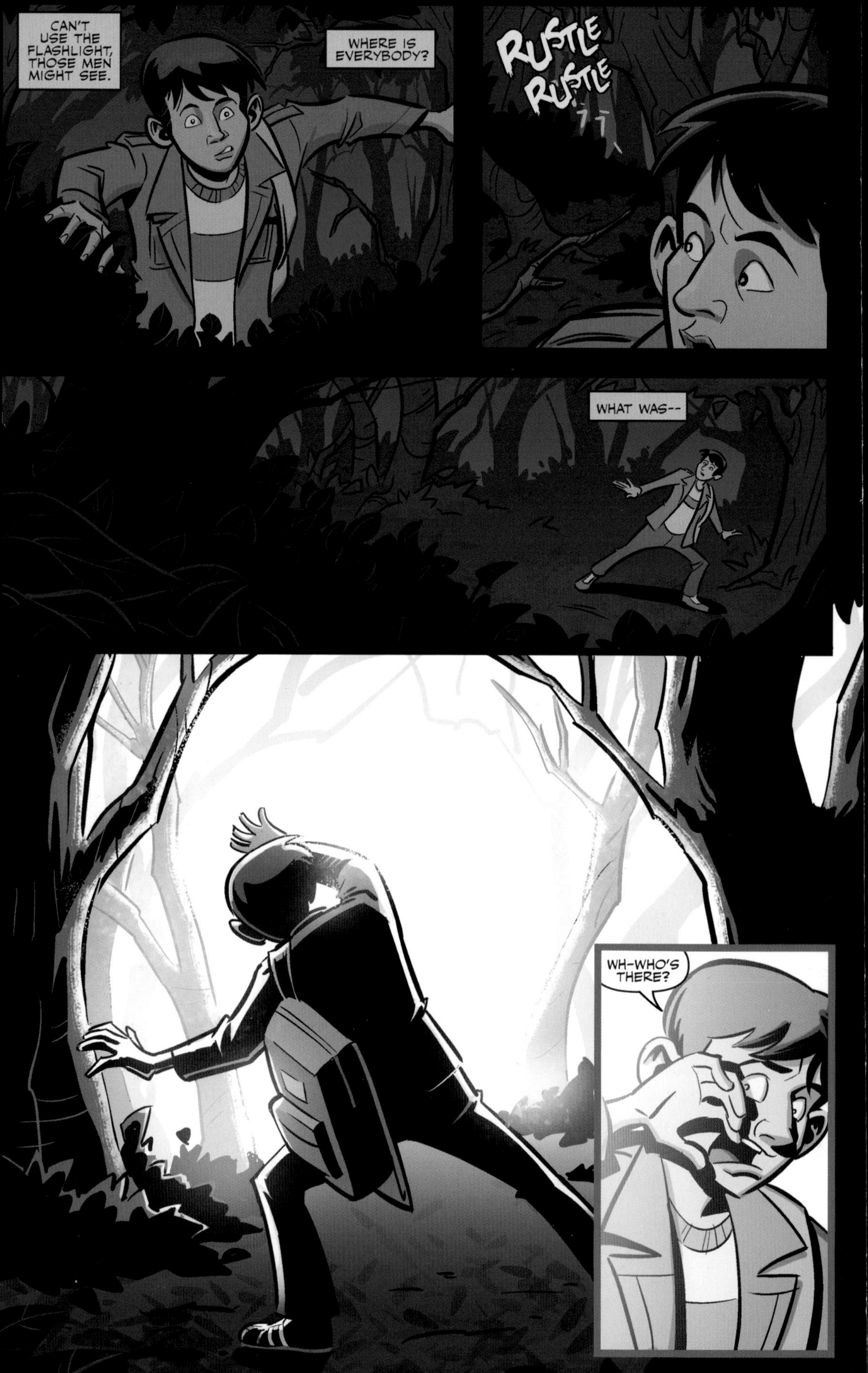
CAN'T USE THE FLASHLIGHT, THOSE MEN MIGHT SEE.
WHERE IS EVERYBODY?
RUSTLE
RUSTLE
WHAT WAS--
WH-WHO'S THERE?

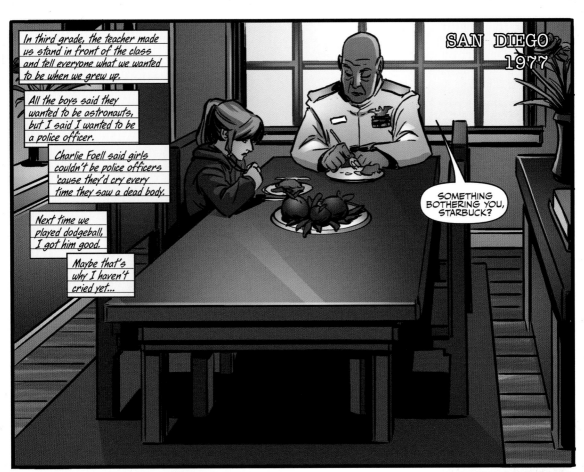

In third grade, the teacher made us stand in front of the class and tell everyone what we wanted to be when we grew up.

All the boys said they wanted to be astronauts, but I said I wanted to be a police officer.

Charlie Foell said girls couldn't be police officers 'cause they'd cry every time they saw a dead body.

Next time we played dodgeball, I got him good.

Maybe that's why I haven't cried yet...

SOMETHING BOTHERING YOU, STARBUCK?

...I don't want jerks like Charlie to think they're right.

YOUR MOTHER TOLD ME ABOUT YOUR SUNDAY SCHOOL TEACHER.

I KNOW YOU TWO WERE CLOSE.

SORRY TO HEAR ABOUT...

YOU KNOW...

WHAT HAPPENED.

THEY SHOT HIM.

HE WAS UNLOADING HIS CAR AND SOMEONE JUST CAME UP AND SHOT HIM.

RIGHT THERE IN HIS OWN DRIVEWAY.

AND THE POLICE DON'T EVEN CARE.

NOW, DANA...

I'M SURE THAT ISN'T THE CASE. THE POLICE WILL GET TO THE BOTTOM OF IT.

BUT I *HEARD* THEM AT MR. WILSON'S HOUSE...

NOT SURE I LIKE YOU GOING OVER THERE, STARBUCK. A CRIME SCENE IS NO PLACE FOR A YOUNG GIRL.

I NEEDED TO SEE.

WE'LL REVISIT THIS CONVERSATION AT A LATER DATE. RIGHT NOW THEY NEED ME BACK TO THE OFFICE.

I BET OLD AHAB NEVER HAD TO DEAL WITH BUDGET REPORTS.

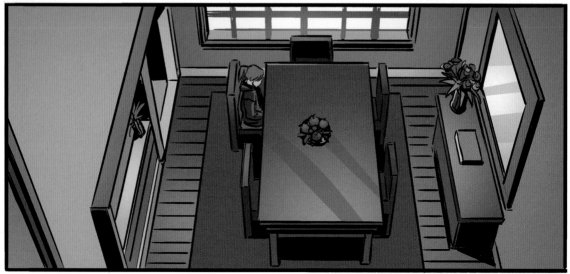

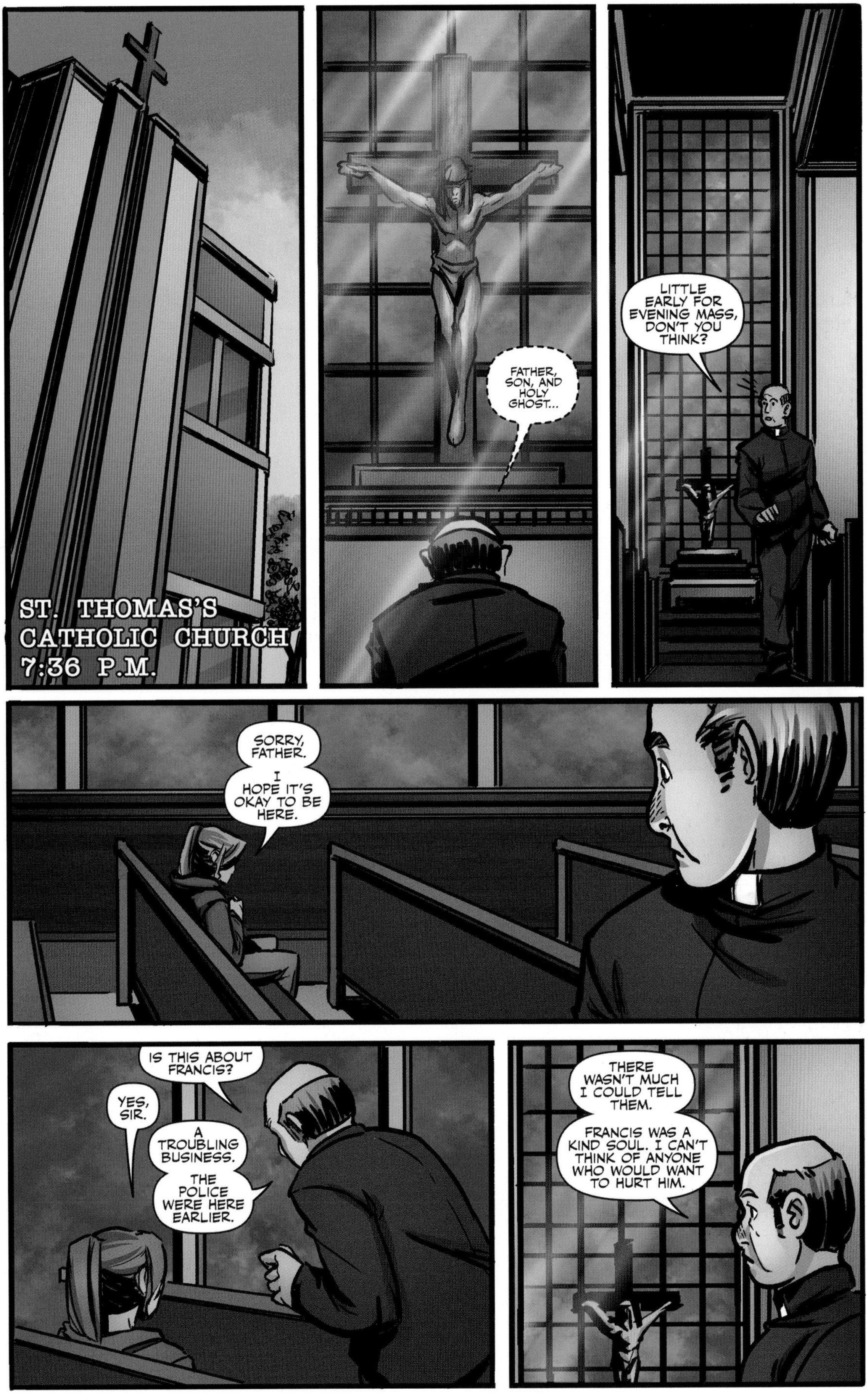
ST. THOMAS'S CATHOLIC CHURCH 7:36 P.M.
FATHER, SON, AND HOLY GHOST...
LITTLE EARLY FOR EVENING MASS, DON'T YOU THINK?
SORRY, FATHER.
I HOPE IT'S OKAY TO BE HERE.
IS THIS ABOUT FRANCIS?
YES, SIR.
A TROUBLING BUSINESS.
THE POLICE WERE HERE EARLIER.
THERE WASN'T MUCH I COULD TELL THEM.
FRANCIS WAS A KIND SOUL. I CAN'T THINK OF ANYONE WHO WOULD WANT TO HURT HIM.

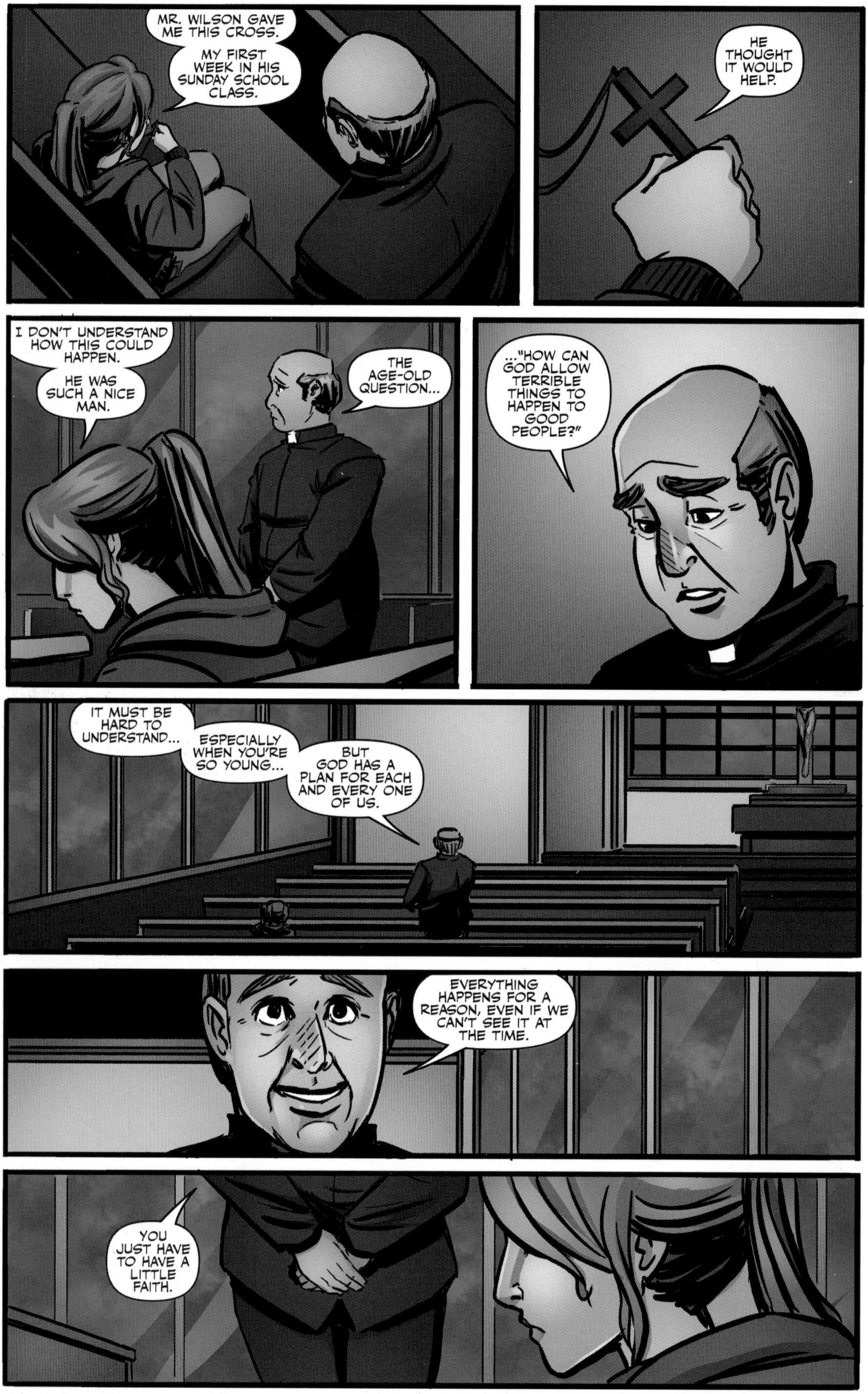
MR. WILSON GAVE ME THIS CROSS.
MY FIRST WEEK IN HIS SUNDAY SCHOOL CLASS.
HE THOUGHT IT WOULD HELP.
I DON'T UNDERSTAND HOW THIS COULD HAPPEN.
HE WAS SUCH A NICE MAN.
THE AGE-OLD QUESTION...
..."HOW CAN GOD ALLOW TERRIBLE THINGS TO HAPPEN TO GOOD PEOPLE?"
IT MUST BE HARD TO UNDERSTAND...
ESPECIALLY WHEN YOU'RE SO YOUNG...
BUT GOD HAS A PLAN FOR EACH AND EVERY ONE OF US.
EVERYTHING HAPPENS FOR A REASON, EVEN IF WE CAN'T SEE IT AT THE TIME.
YOU JUST HAVE TO HAVE A LITTLE FAITH.

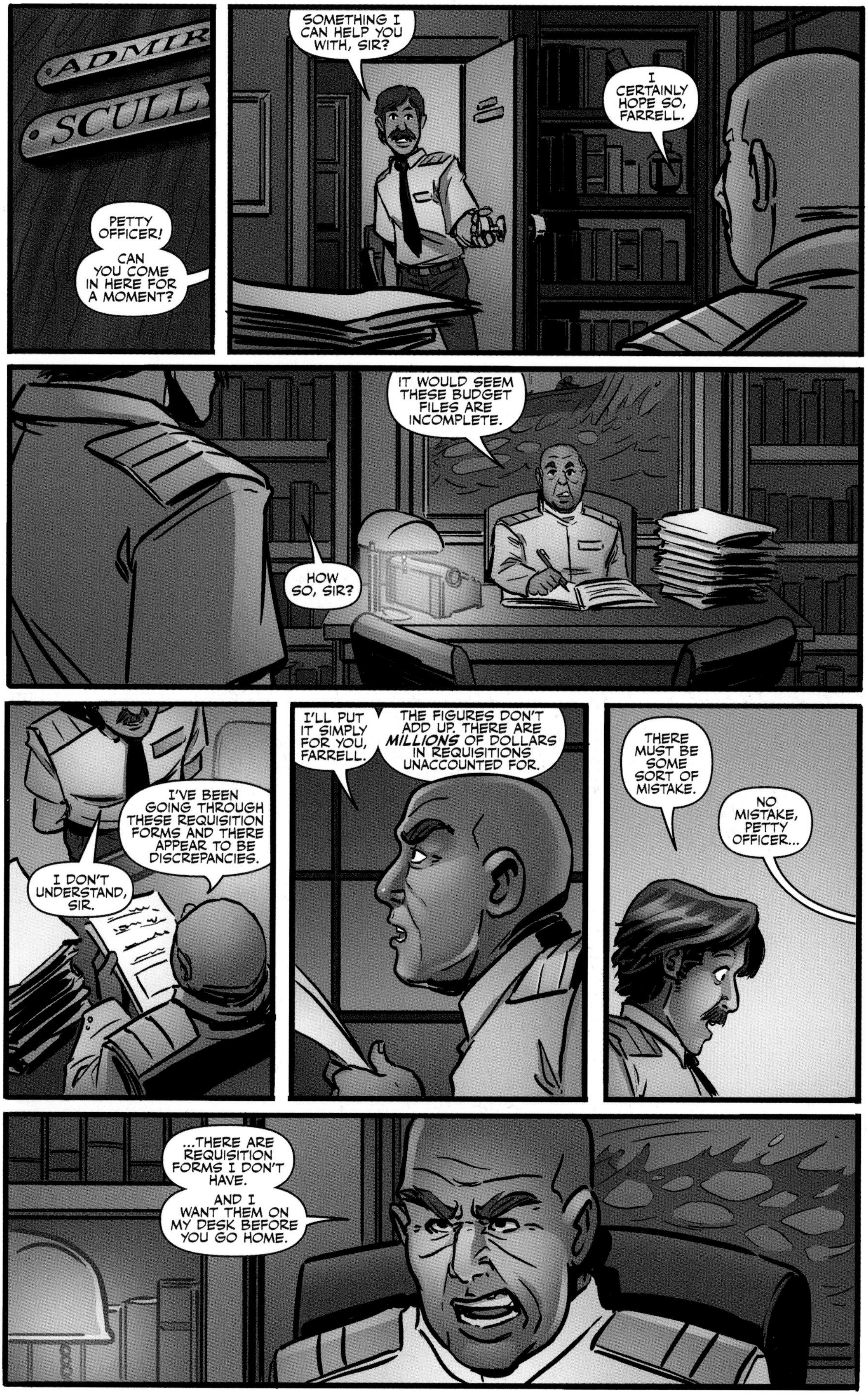
ADMIR
SCULL
PETTY OFFICER!
CAN YOU COME IN HERE FOR A MOMENT?
SOMETHING I CAN HELP YOU WITH, SIR?
I CERTAINLY HOPE SO, FARRELL.
IT WOULD SEEM THESE BUDGET FILES ARE INCOMPLETE.
HOW SO, SIR?
I'VE BEEN GOING THROUGH THESE REQUISITION FORMS AND THERE APPEAR TO BE DISCREPANCIES.
I DON'T UNDERSTAND, SIR.
I'LL PUT IT SIMPLY FOR YOU, FARRELL.
THE FIGURES DON'T ADD UP. THERE ARE *MILLIONS* OF DOLLARS IN REQUISITIONS UNACCOUNTED FOR.
THERE MUST BE SOME SORT OF MISTAKE.
NO MISTAKE, PETTY OFFICER...
...THERE ARE REQUISITION FORMS I DON'T HAVE.
AND I WANT THEM ON MY DESK BEFORE YOU GO HOME.

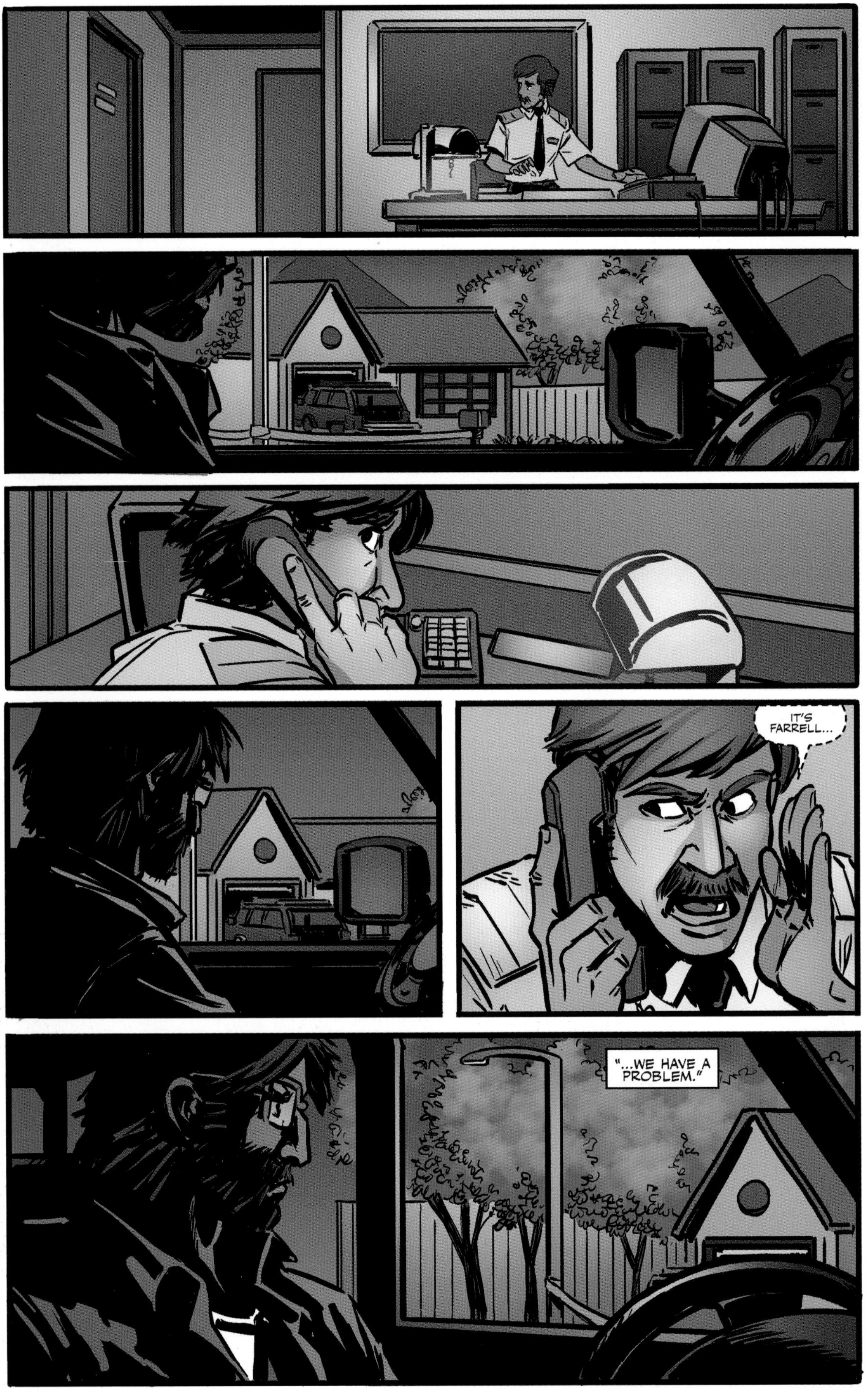
IT'S FARRELL...
"...WE HAVE A PROBLEM."

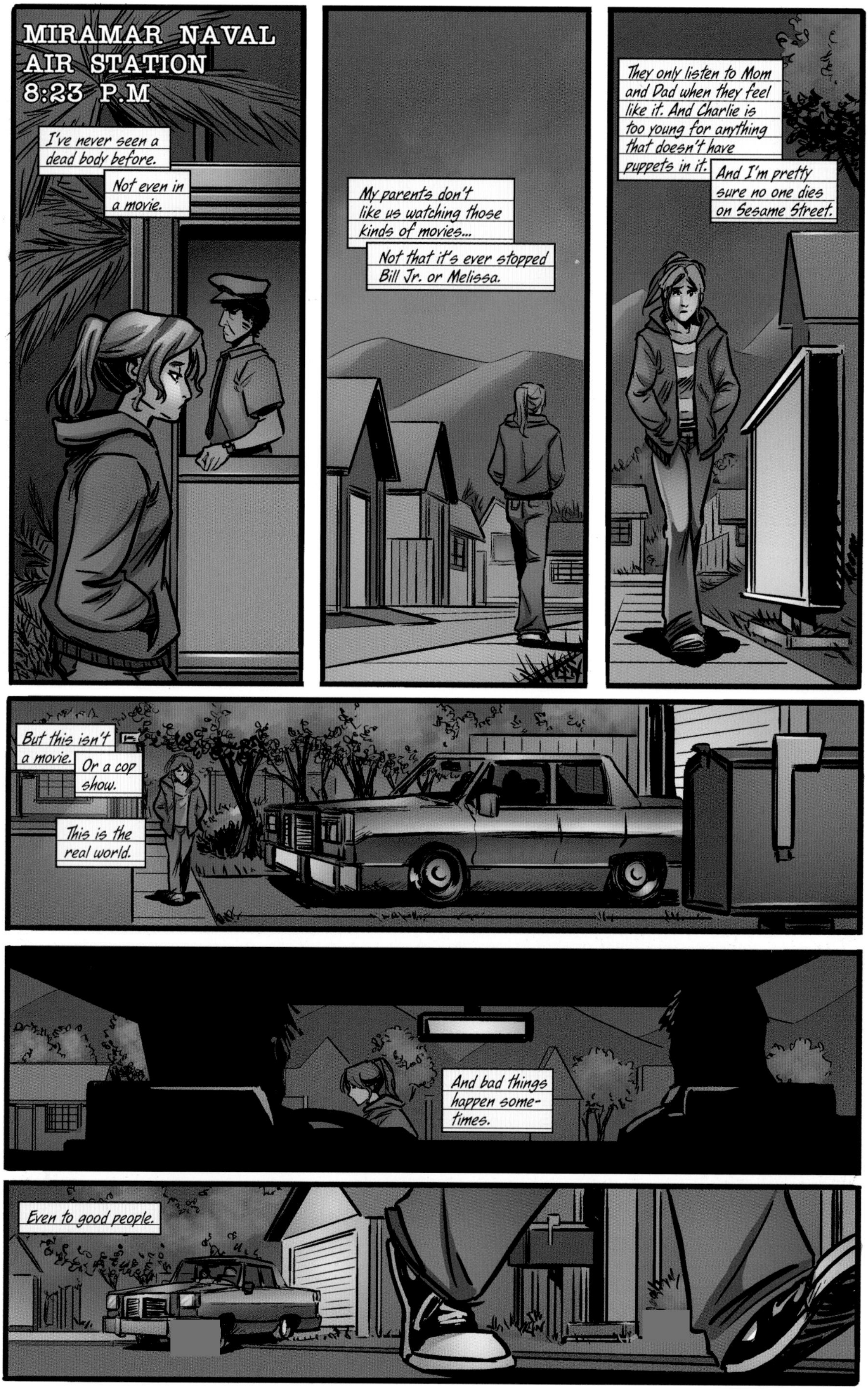
MIRAMAR NAVAL AIR STATION 8:23 P.M
I've never seen a dead body before.
Not even in a movie.
My parents don't like us watching those kinds of movies...
Not that it's ever stopped Bill Jr. or Melissa.
They only listen to Mom and Dad when they feel like it. And Charlie is too young for anything that doesn't have puppets in it.
And I'm pretty sure no one dies on Sesame Street.
But this isn't a movie.
Or a cop show.
This is the real world.
And bad things happen some-times.
Even to good people.

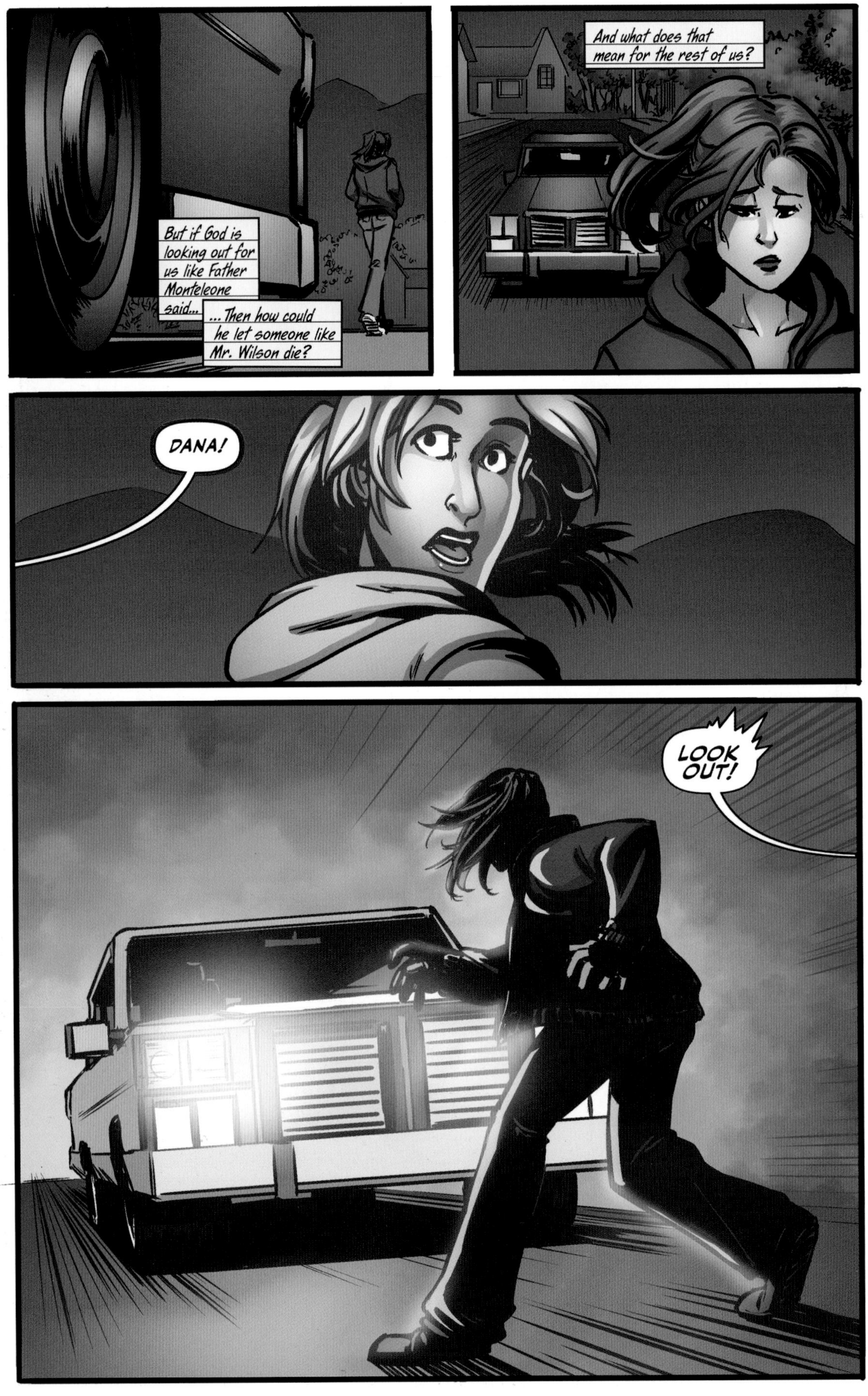

But if God is looking out for us like Father Monteleone said...
...Then how could he let someone like Mr. Wilson die?
And what does that mean for the rest of us?
DANA!
LOOK OUT!

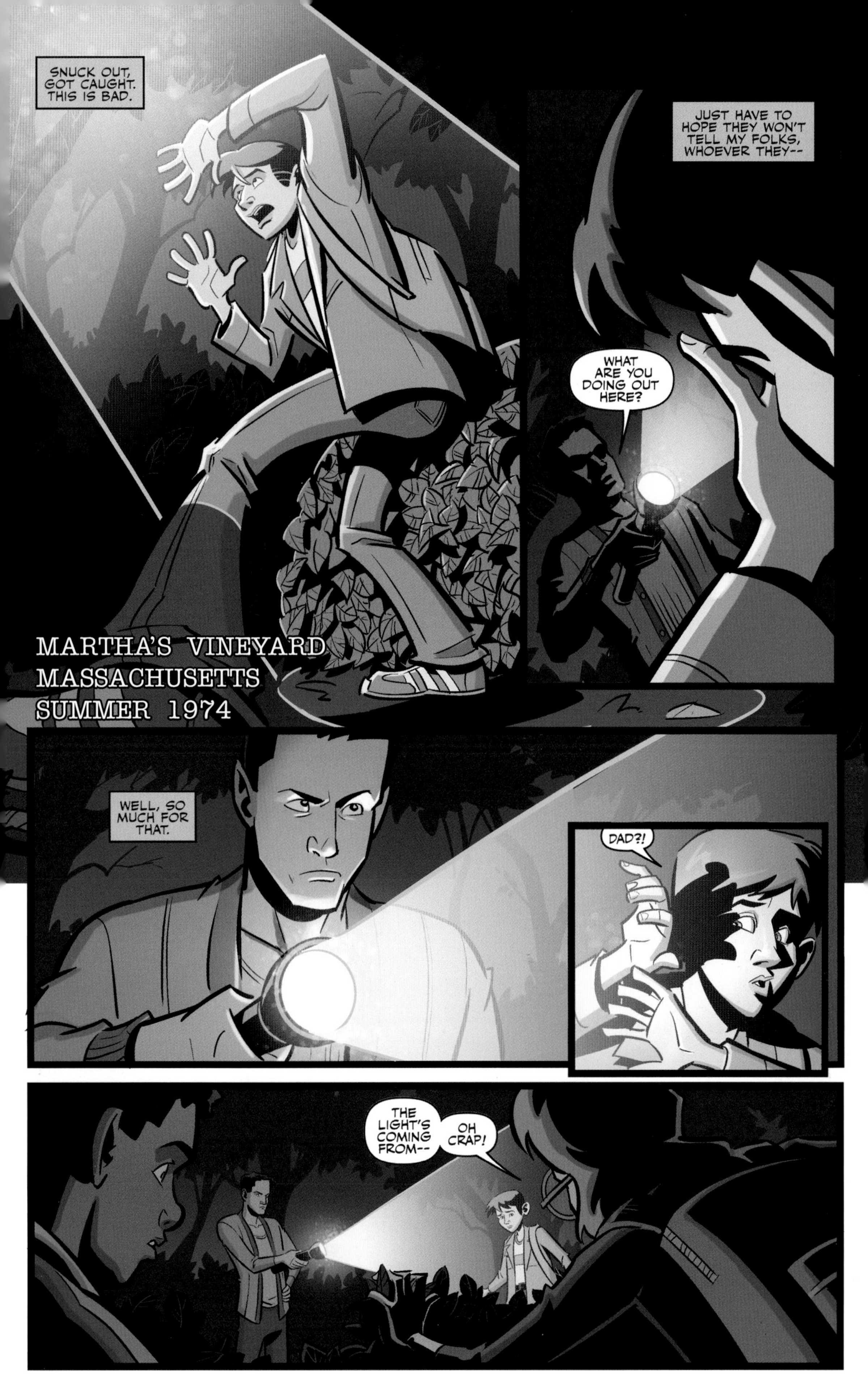
SNUCK OUT, GOT CAUGHT. THIS IS BAD.
JUST HAVE TO HOPE THEY WON'T TELL MY FOLKS, WHOEVER THEY--
WHAT ARE YOU DOING OUT HERE?
MARTHA'S VINEYARD
MASSACHUSETTS
SUMMER 1974
WELL, SO MUCH FOR THAT.
DAD?!
THE LIGHT'S COMING FROM--
OH CRAP!

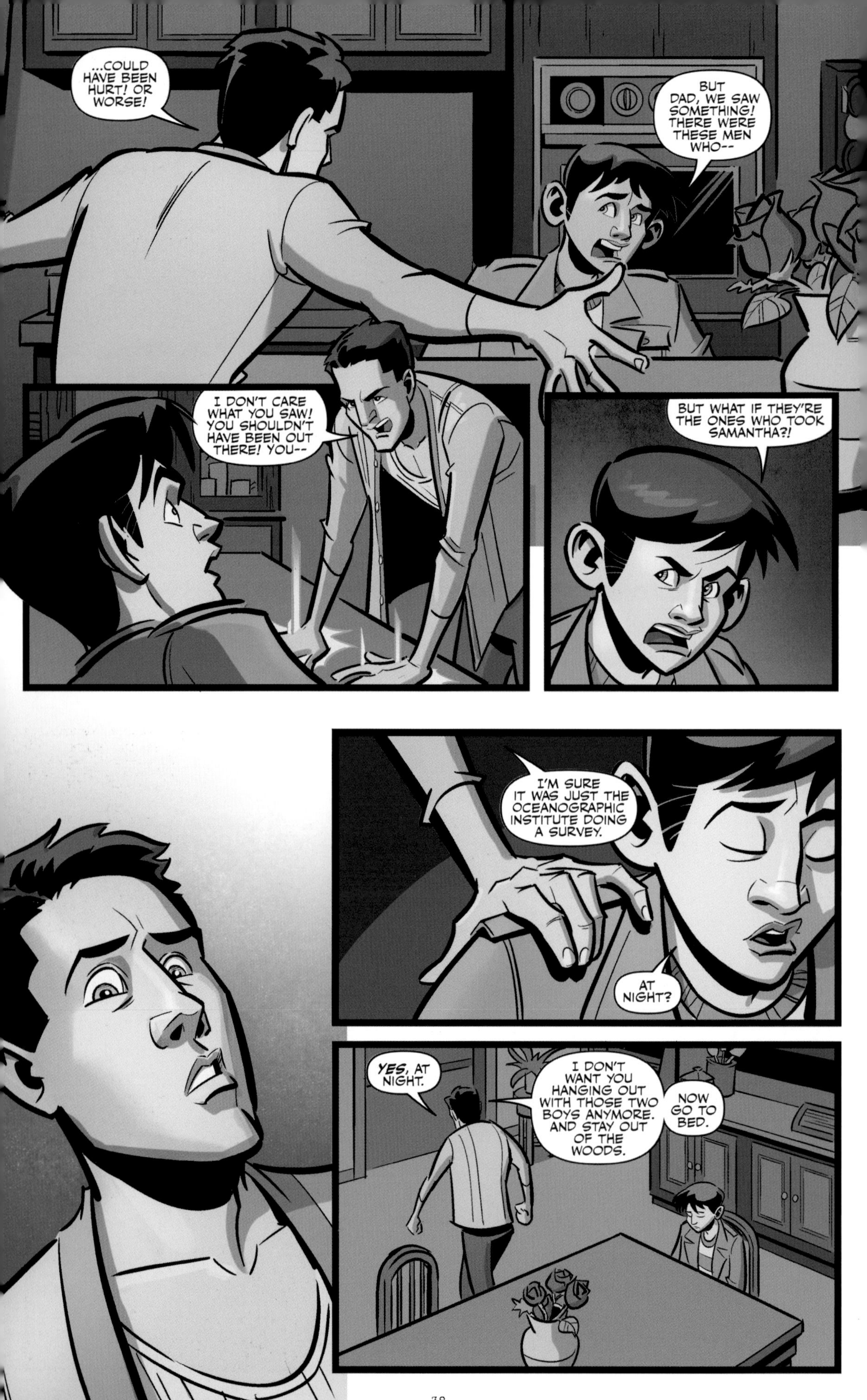
...COULD HAVE BEEN HURT! OR WORSE!
BUT DAD, WE SAW SOMETHING! THERE WERE THESE MEN WHO--
I DON'T CARE WHAT YOU SAW! YOU SHOULDN'T HAVE BEEN OUT THERE! YOU--
BUT WHAT IF THEY'RE THE ONES WHO TOOK SAMANTHA?!
I'M SURE IT WAS JUST THE OCEANOGRAPHIC INSTITUTE DOING A SURVEY.
AT NIGHT?
YES, AT NIGHT.
I DON'T WANT YOU HANGING OUT WITH THOSE TWO BOYS ANYMORE. AND STAY OUT OF THE WOODS.
NOW GO TO BED.

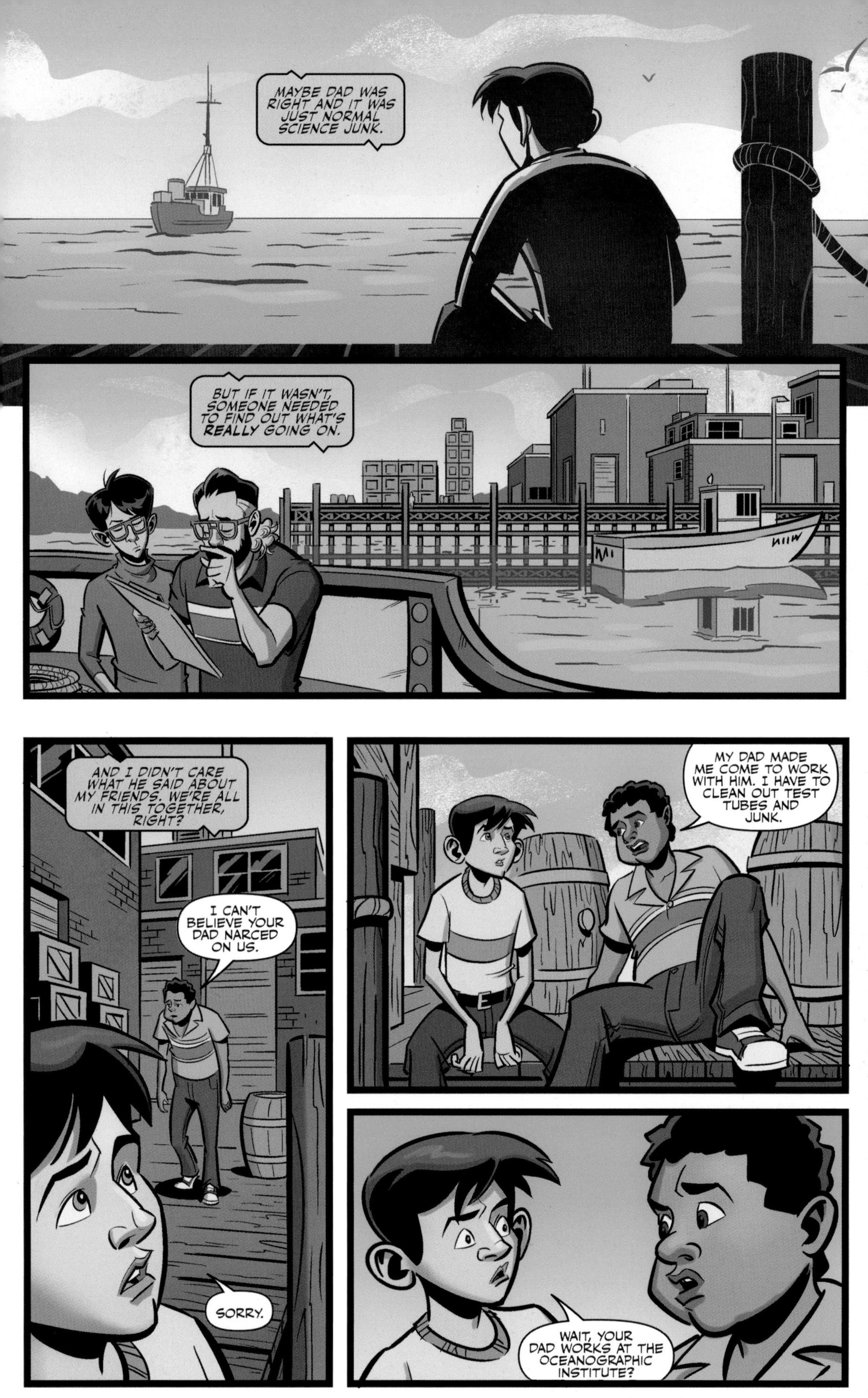
MAYBE DAD WAS RIGHT AND IT WAS JUST NORMAL SCIENCE JUNK.
BUT IF IT WASN'T, SOMEONE NEEDED TO FIND OUT WHAT'S REALLY GOING ON.
AND I DIDN'T CARE WHAT HE SAID ABOUT MY FRIENDS. WE'RE ALL IN THIS TOGETHER, RIGHT?
I CAN'T BELIEVE YOUR DAD NARCED ON US.
SORRY.
MY DAD MADE ME COME TO WORK WITH HIM. I HAVE TO CLEAN OUT TEST TUBES AND JUNK.
WAIT, YOUR DAD WORKS AT THE OCEANOGRAPHIC INSTITUTE?

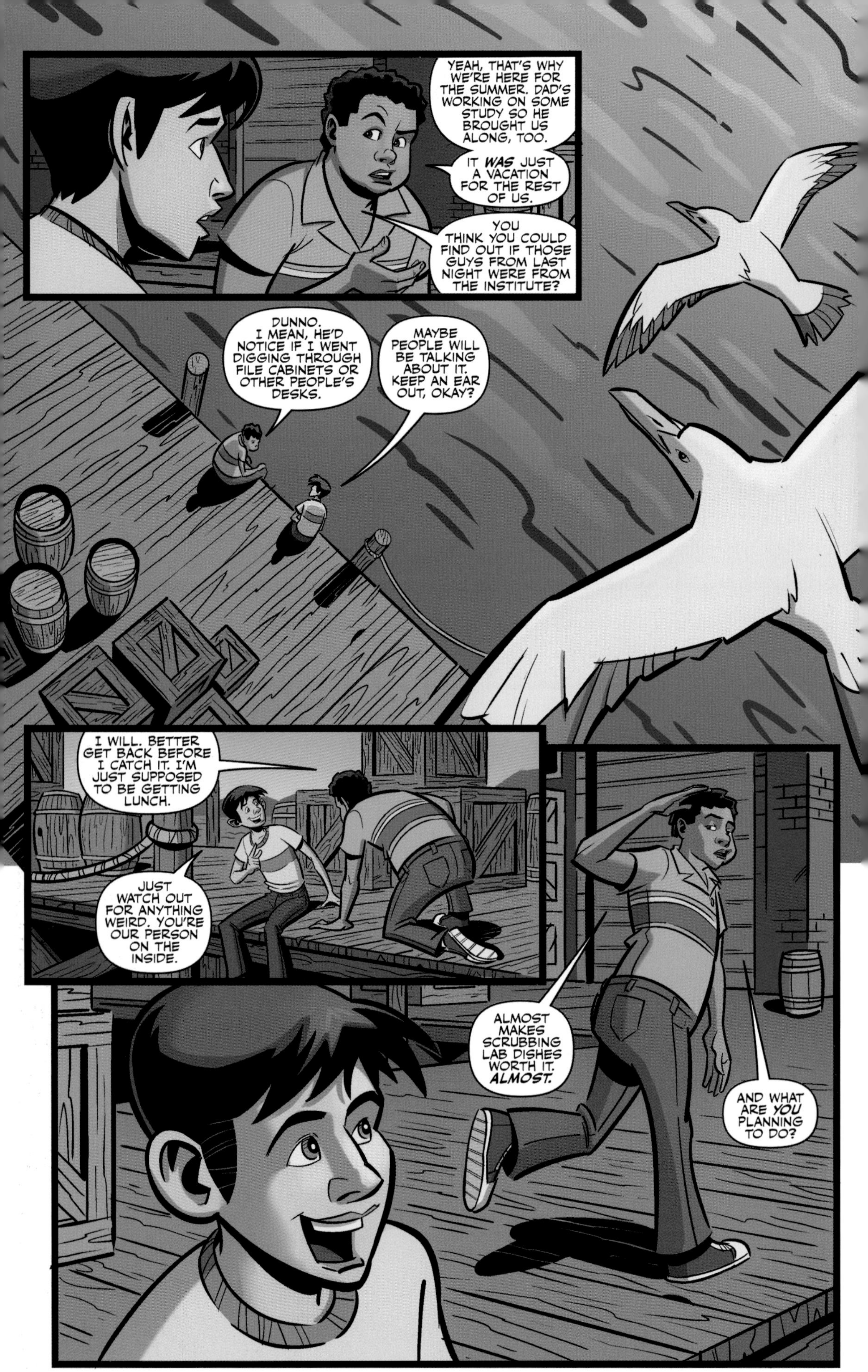
YEAH, THAT'S WHY WE'RE HERE FOR THE SUMMER. DAD'S WORKING ON SOME STUDY SO HE BROUGHT US ALONG, TOO.
IT *WAS* JUST A VACATION FOR THE REST OF US.
YOU THINK YOU COULD FIND OUT IF THOSE GUYS FROM LAST NIGHT WERE FROM THE INSTITUTE?
DUNNO. I MEAN, HE'D NOTICE IF I WENT DIGGING THROUGH FILE CABINETS OR OTHER PEOPLE'S DESKS.
MAYBE PEOPLE WILL BE TALKING ABOUT IT. KEEP AN EAR OUT, OKAY?
I WILL. BETTER GET BACK BEFORE I CATCH IT. I'M JUST SUPPOSED TO BE GETTING LUNCH.
JUST WATCH OUT FOR ANYTHING WEIRD. YOU'RE OUR PERSON ON THE INSIDE.
ALMOST MAKES SCRUBBING LAB DISHES WORTH IT. *ALMOST.*
AND WHAT ARE *YOU* PLANNING TO DO?

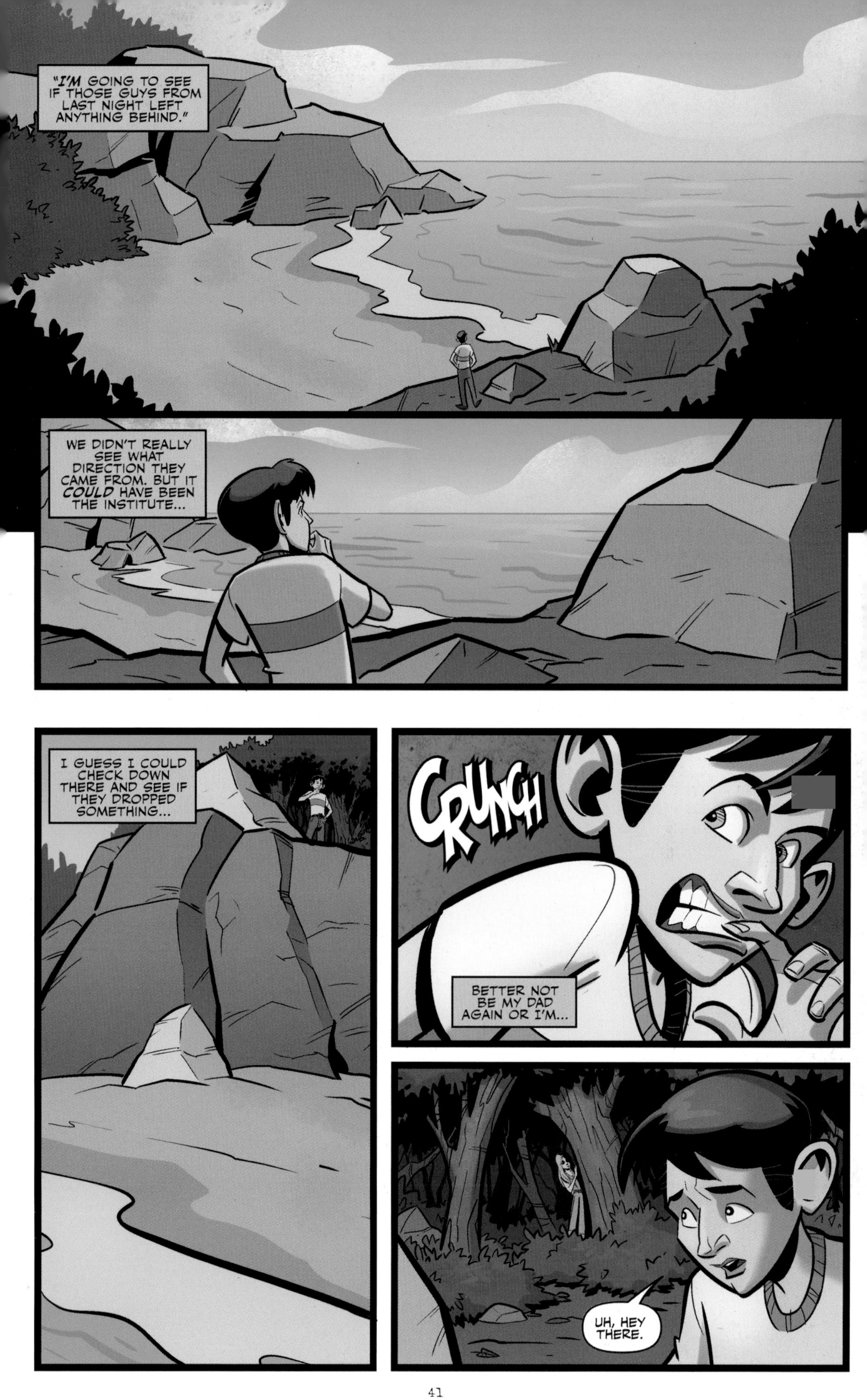
"I'M GOING TO SEE IF THOSE GUYS FROM LAST NIGHT LEFT ANYTHING BEHIND."
WE DIDN'T REALLY SEE WHAT DIRECTION THEY CAME FROM. BUT IT COULD HAVE BEEN THE INSTITUTE...
I GUESS I COULD CHECK DOWN THERE AND SEE IF THEY DROPPED SOMETHING...
CRUNCH
BETTER NOT BE MY DAD AGAIN OR I'M...
UH, HEY THERE.

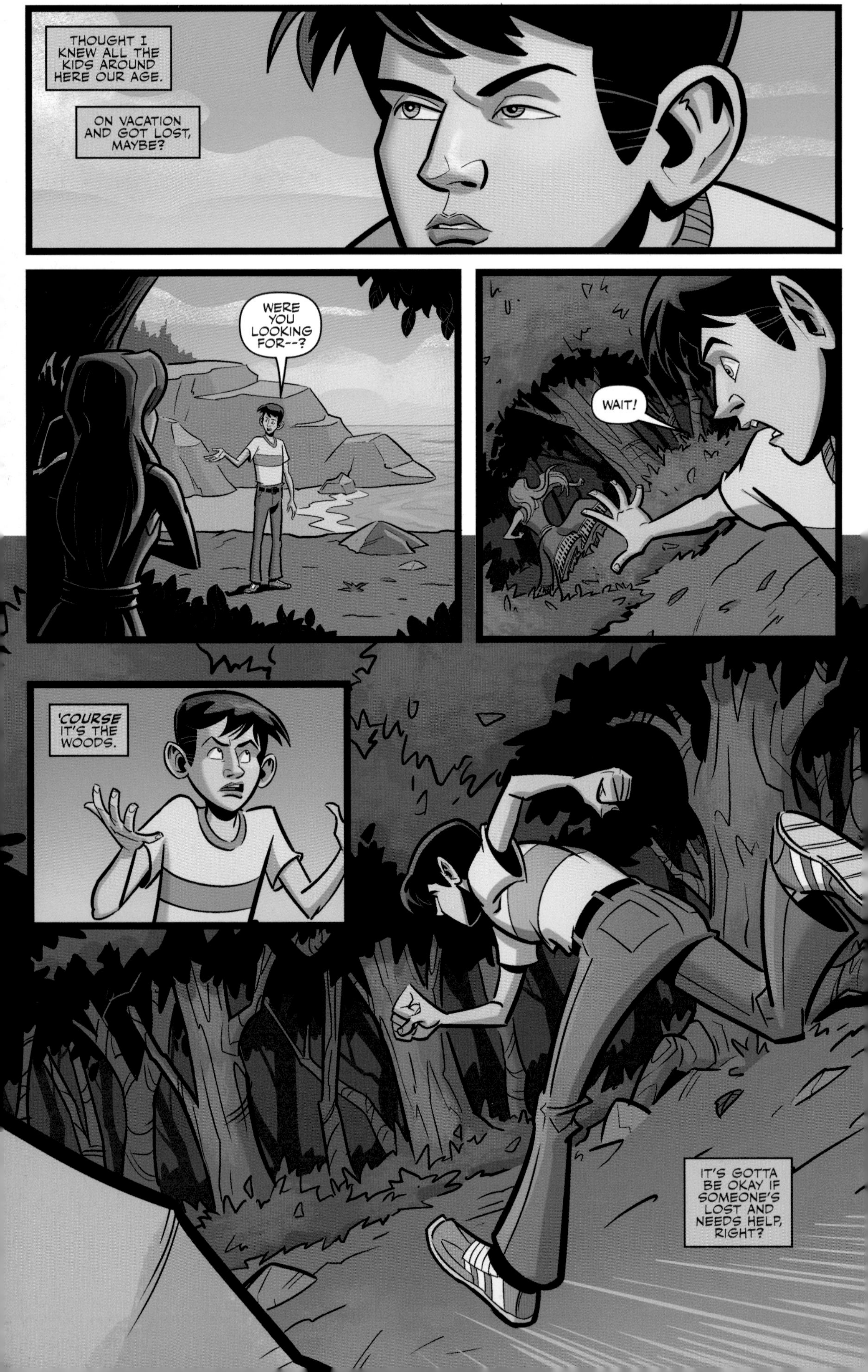
THOUGHT I KNEW ALL THE KIDS AROUND HERE OUR AGE.
ON VACATION AND GOT LOST, MAYBE?
WERE YOU LOOKING FOR--?
WAIT!
'COURSE IT'S THE WOODS.
IT'S GOTTA BE OKAY IF SOMEONE'S LOST AND NEEDS HELP, RIGHT?

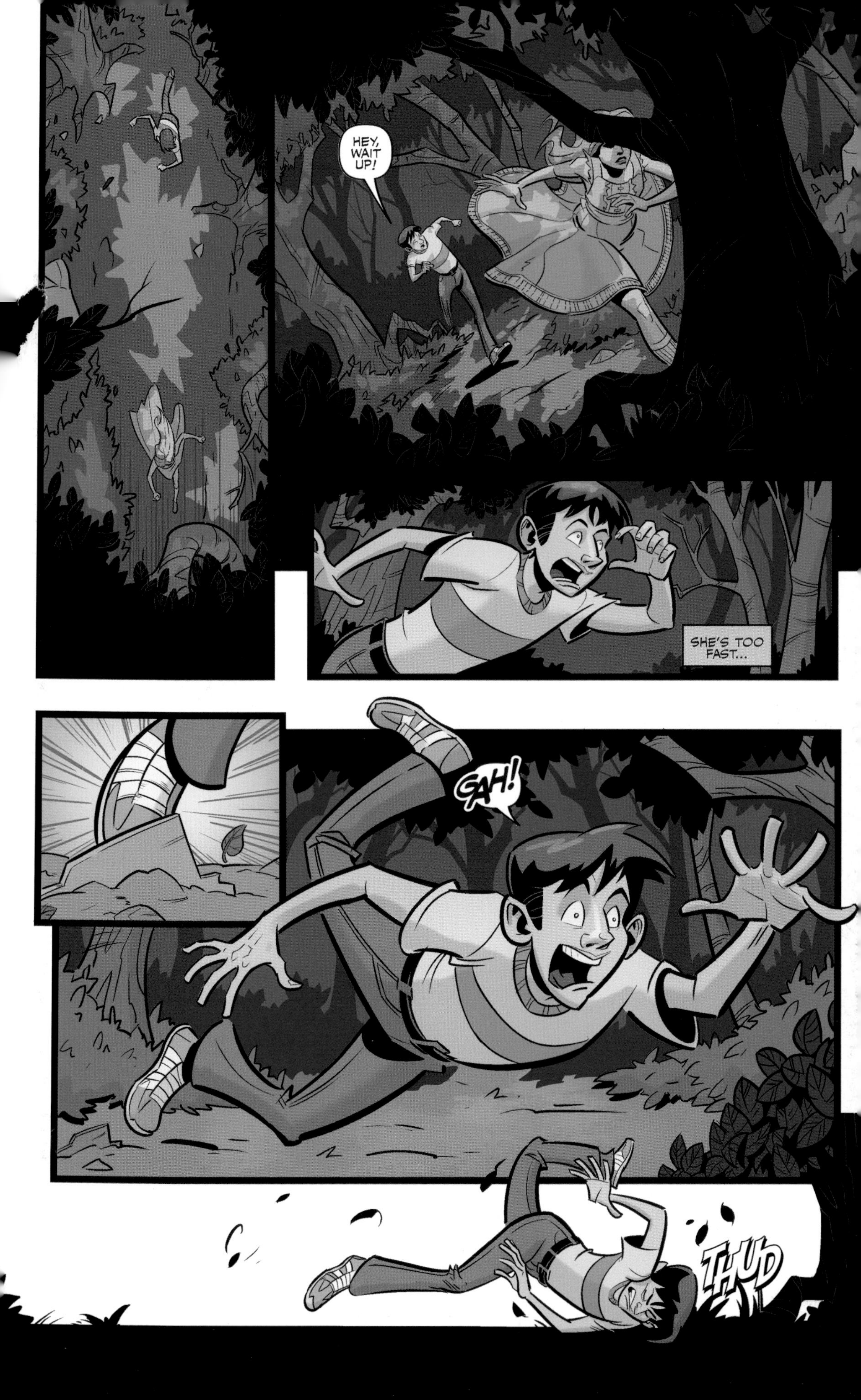
HEY, WAIT UP!
SHE'S TOO FAST...
GAH!
THUD

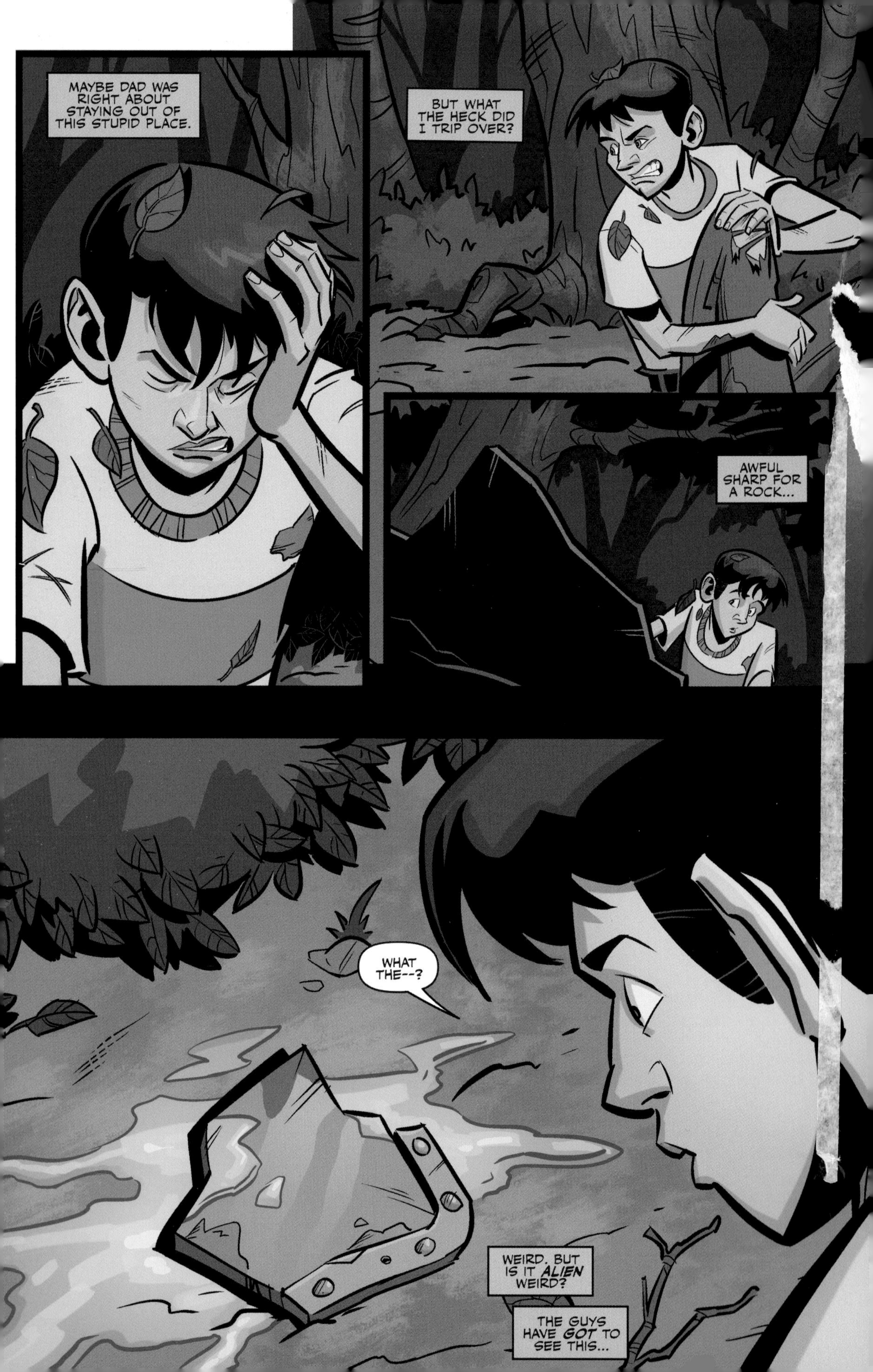
MAYBE DAD WAS RIGHT ABOUT STAYING OUT OF THIS STUPID PLACE.
BUT WHAT THE HECK DID I TRIP OVER?
AWFUL SHARP FOR A ROCK...
WHAT THE--?
WEIRD. BUT IS IT *ALIEN* WEIRD?
THE GUYS HAVE *GOT* TO SEE THIS...

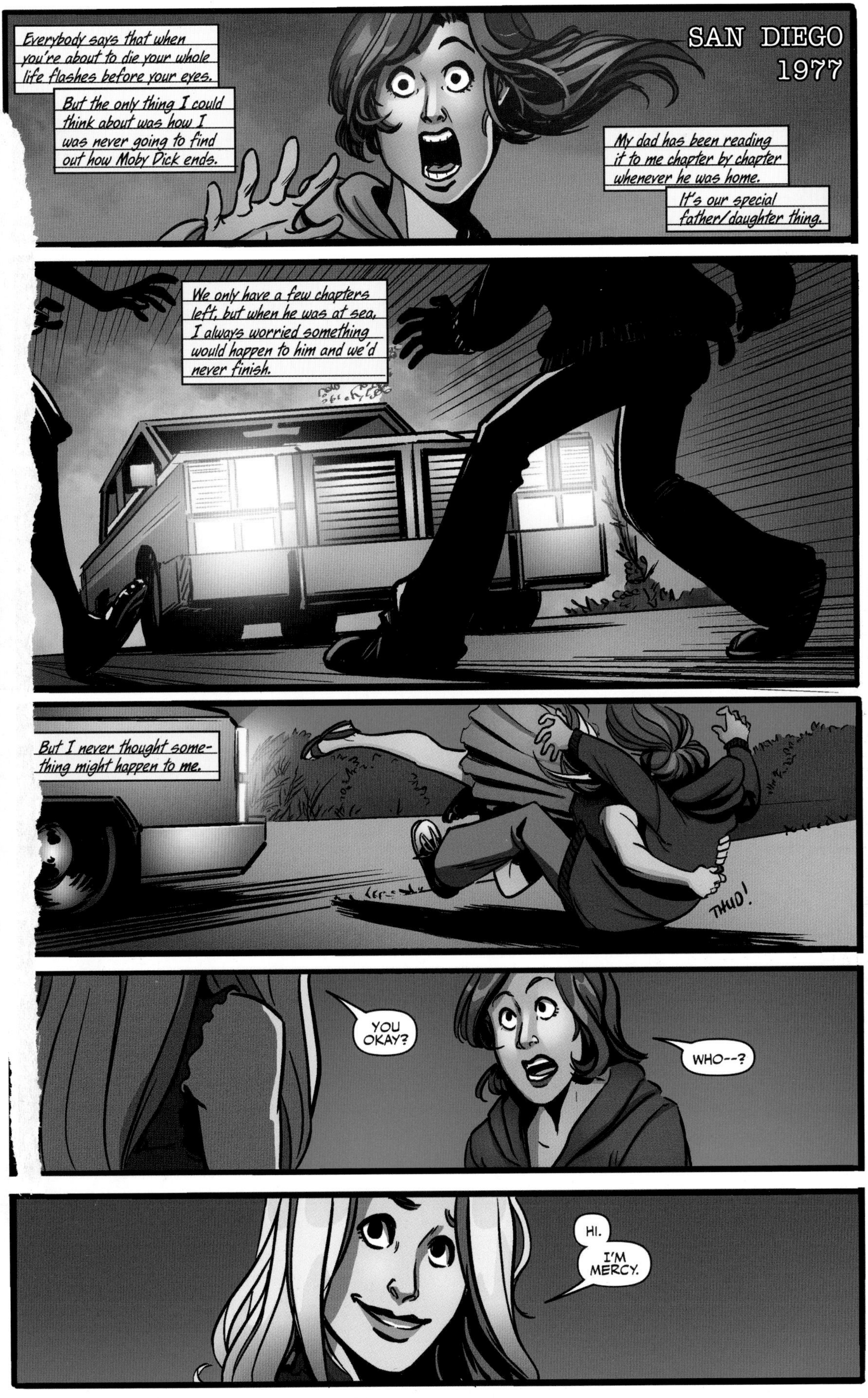

SAN DIEGO 1977
Everybody says that when you're about to die your whole life flashes before your eyes.
But the only thing I could think about was how I was never going to find out how Moby Dick ends.
My dad has been reading it to me chapter by chapter whenever he was home.
It's our special father/daughter thing.
We only have a few chapters left, but when he was at sea, I always worried something would happen to him and we'd never finish.
But I never thought something might happen to me.
THUD!
YOU OKAY?
WHO--?
HI.
I'M MERCY.

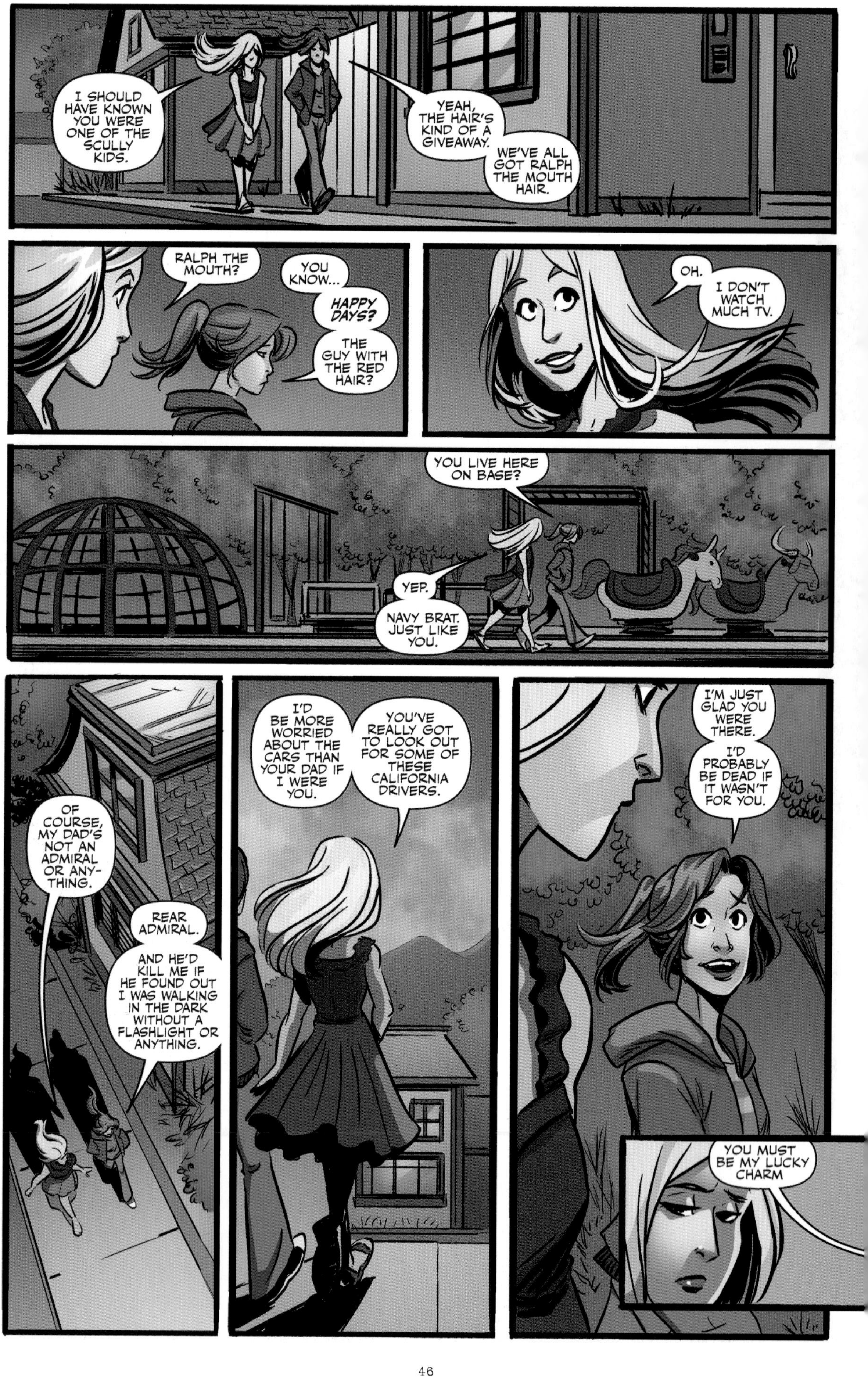
I SHOULD HAVE KNOWN YOU WERE ONE OF THE SCULLY KIDS.
YEAH, THE HAIR'S KIND OF A GIVEAWAY.
WE'VE ALL GOT RALPH THE MOUTH HAIR.
RALPH THE MOUTH?
YOU KNOW...
HAPPY DAYS?
THE GUY WITH THE RED HAIR?
OH.
I DON'T WATCH MUCH TV.
YOU LIVE HERE ON BASE?
YEP.
NAVY BRAT. JUST LIKE YOU.
OF COURSE, MY DAD'S NOT AN ADMIRAL OR ANY-THING.
REAR ADMIRAL.
AND HE'D KILL ME IF HE FOUND OUT I WAS WALKING IN THE DARK WITHOUT A FLASHLIGHT OR ANYTHING.
I'D BE MORE WORRIED ABOUT THE CARS THAN YOUR DAD IF I WERE YOU.
YOU'VE REALLY GOT TO LOOK OUT FOR SOME OF THESE CALIFORNIA DRIVERS.
I'M JUST GLAD YOU WERE THERE.
I'D PROBABLY BE DEAD IF IT WASN'T FOR YOU.
YOU MUST BE MY LUCKY CHARM

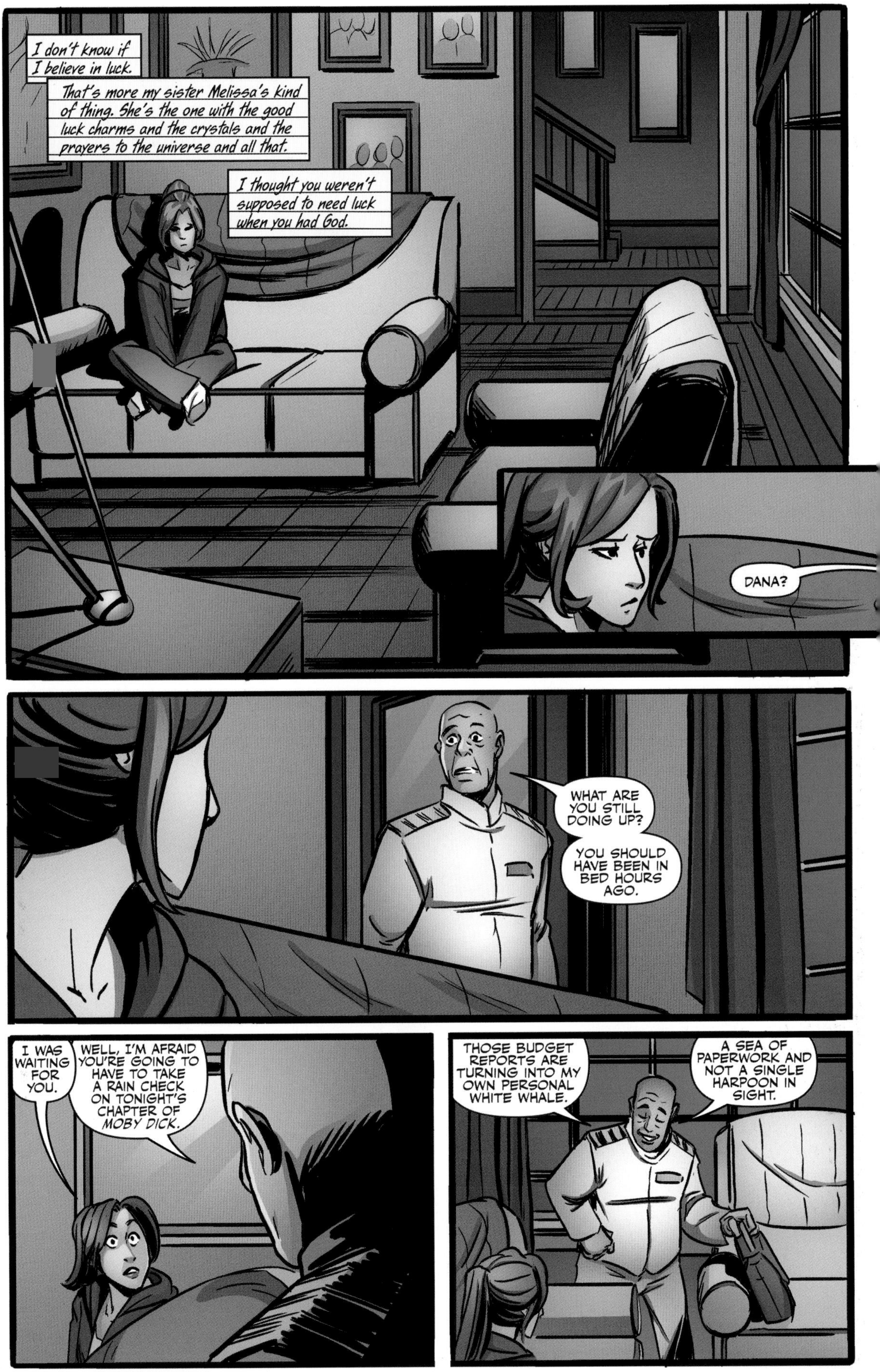

I don't know if I believe in luck.
That's more my sister Melissa's kind of thing. She's the one with the good luck charms and the crystals and the prayers to the universe and all that.
I thought you weren't supposed to need luck when you had God.
DANA?
WHAT ARE YOU STILL DOING UP?
YOU SHOULD HAVE BEEN IN BED HOURS AGO.
I WAS WAITING FOR YOU.
WELL, I'M AFRAID YOU'RE GOING TO HAVE TO TAKE A RAIN CHECK ON TONIGHT'S CHAPTER OF MOBY DICK.
THOSE BUDGET REPORTS ARE TURNING INTO MY OWN PERSONAL WHITE WHALE.
A SEA OF PAPERWORK AND NOT A SINGLE HARPOON IN SIGHT.

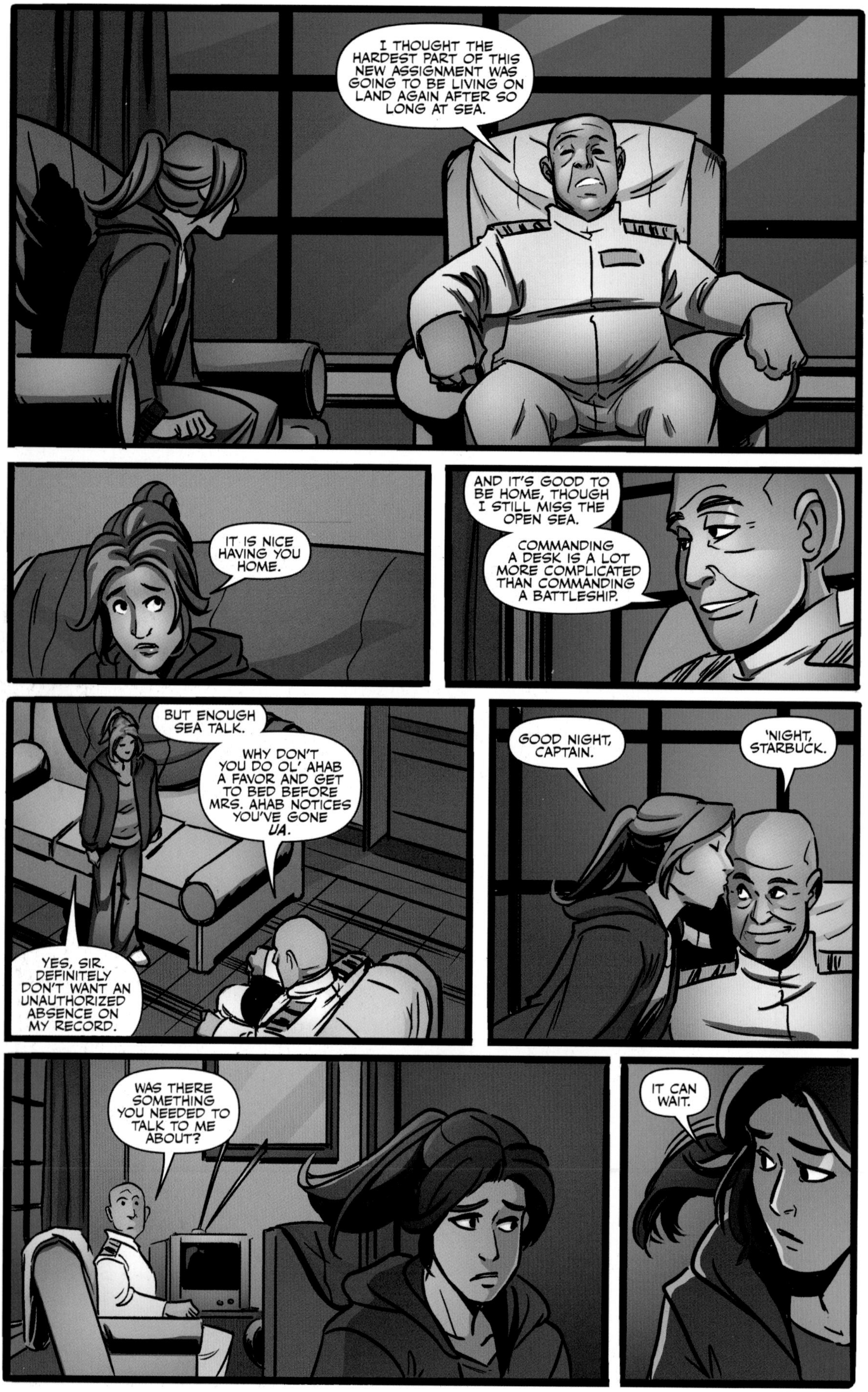
I THOUGHT THE HARDEST PART OF THIS NEW ASSIGNMENT WAS GOING TO BE LIVING ON LAND AGAIN AFTER SO LONG AT SEA.
IT IS NICE HAVING YOU HOME.
AND IT'S GOOD TO BE HOME, THOUGH I STILL MISS THE OPEN SEA.
COMMANDING A DESK IS A LOT MORE COMPLICATED THAN COMMANDING A BATTLESHIP.
BUT ENOUGH SEA TALK.
WHY DON'T YOU DO OL' AHAB A FAVOR AND GET TO BED BEFORE MRS. AHAB NOTICES YOU'VE GONE *UA*.
YES, SIR. DEFINITELY DON'T WANT AN UNAUTHORIZED ABSENCE ON MY RECORD.
GOOD NIGHT, CAPTAIN.
'NIGHT, STARBUCK.
WAS THERE SOMETHING YOU NEEDED TO TALK TO ME ABOUT?
IT CAN WAIT.

Talking to your dad is hard enough...

...But when your dad's a Navy admiral it's kind of impossible.

Having a hard time with your math homework must seem pretty stupid to a guy who's commanded a Navy destroyer.

Though almost getting run over is a lot more serious than your first pimple.

First, Mr. Wilson dies, and then I almost die.

I don't know what to think...

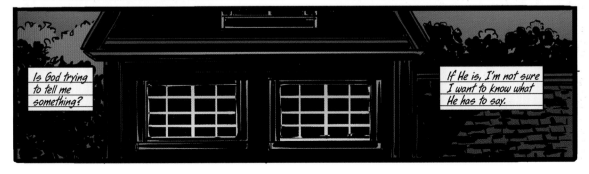

Is God trying to tell me something?

If He is, I'm not sure I want to know what He has to say.

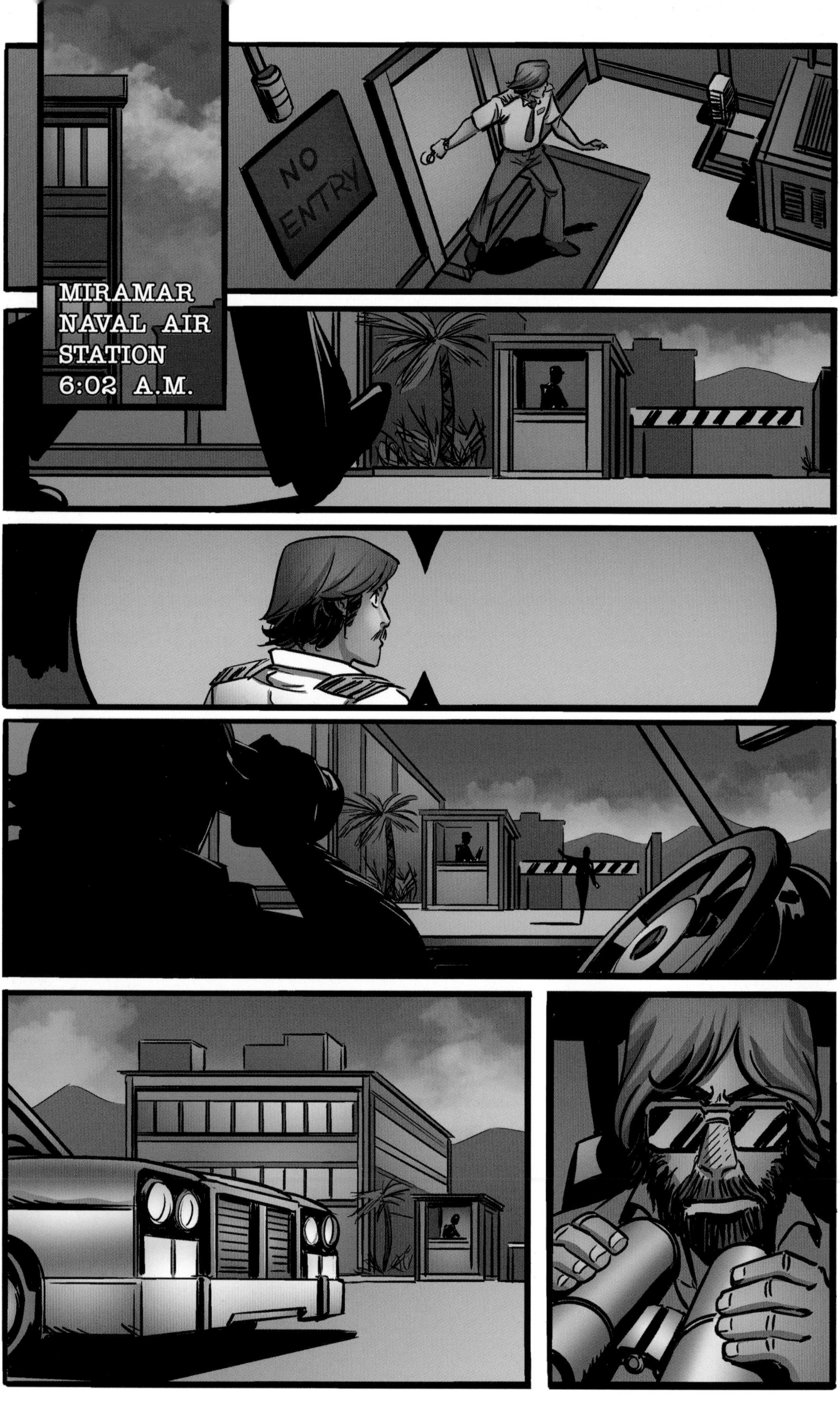

NO ENTRY
MIRAMAR NAVAL AIR STATION 6:02 A.M.

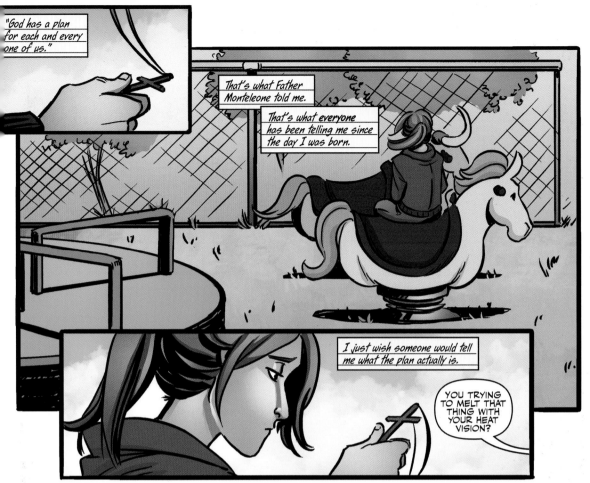

"God has a plan for each and every one of us."

That's what Father Monteleone told me.

That's what everyone has been telling me since the day I was born.

I just wish someone would tell me what the plan actually is.

YOU TRYING TO MELT THAT THING WITH YOUR HEAT VISION?

HEY.

I DIDN'T SEE YOU THERE.

YOU'RE STARING AT THAT CROSS LIKE IT MIGHT EXPLODE.

MY SUNDAY SCHOOL TEACHER GAVE THIS TO ME.

HE DIED.

OH.

SORRY.

IT'S OKAY.

BUT I REALLY LIKED HIM.

AND NOW HE'S GONE.

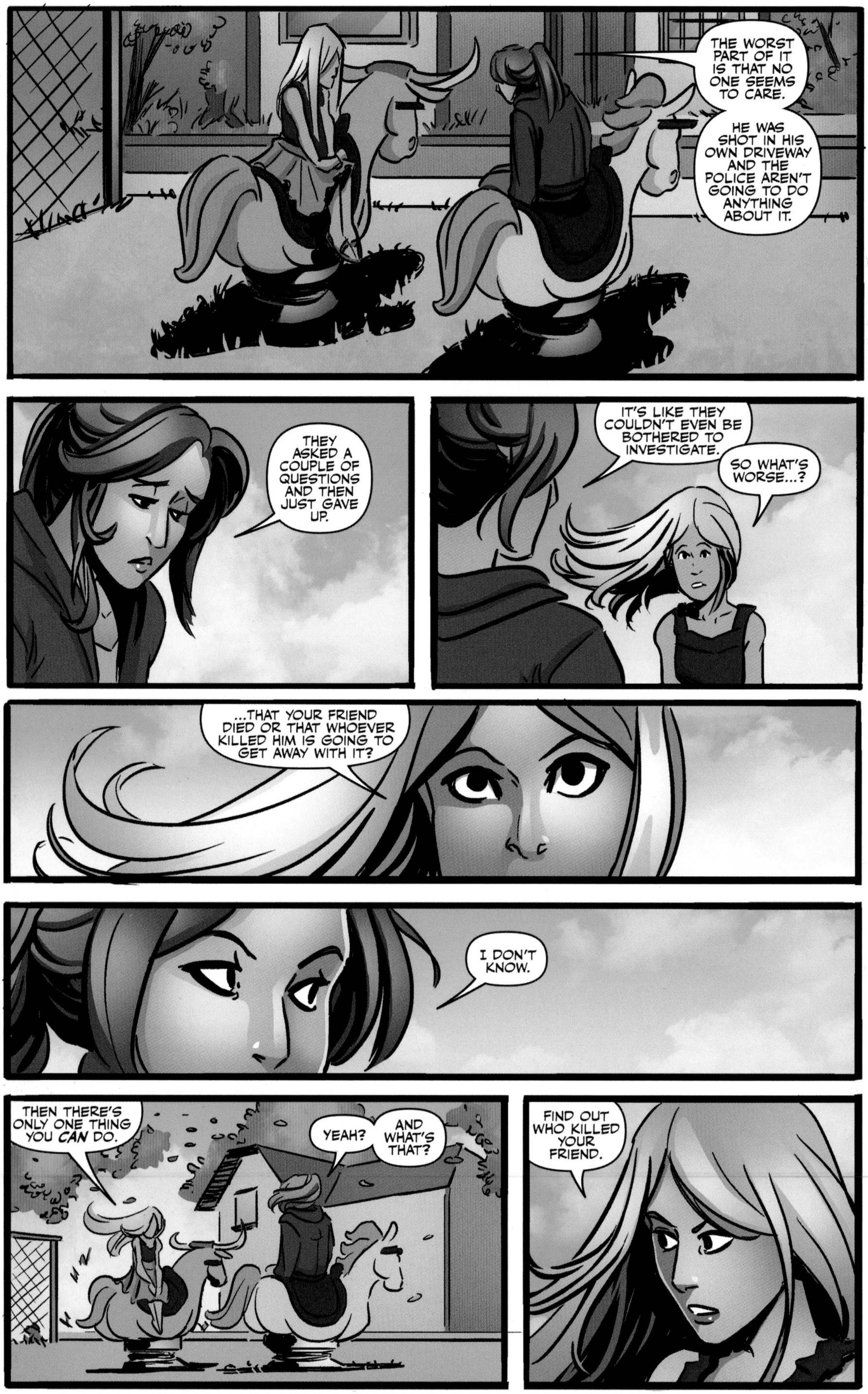
THE WORST PART OF IT IS THAT NO ONE SEEMS TO CARE.
HE WAS SHOT IN HIS OWN DRIVEWAY AND THE POLICE AREN'T GOING TO DO ANYTHING ABOUT IT.
THEY ASKED A COUPLE OF QUESTIONS AND THEN JUST GAVE UP.
IT'S LIKE THEY COULDN'T EVEN BE BOTHERED TO INVESTIGATE.
SO WHAT'S WORSE...?
...THAT YOUR FRIEND DIED OR THAT WHOEVER KILLED HIM IS GOING TO GET AWAY WITH IT?
I DON'T KNOW.
THEN THERE'S ONLY ONE THING YOU *CAN* DO.
YEAH?
AND WHAT'S THAT?
FIND OUT WHO KILLED YOUR FRIEND.

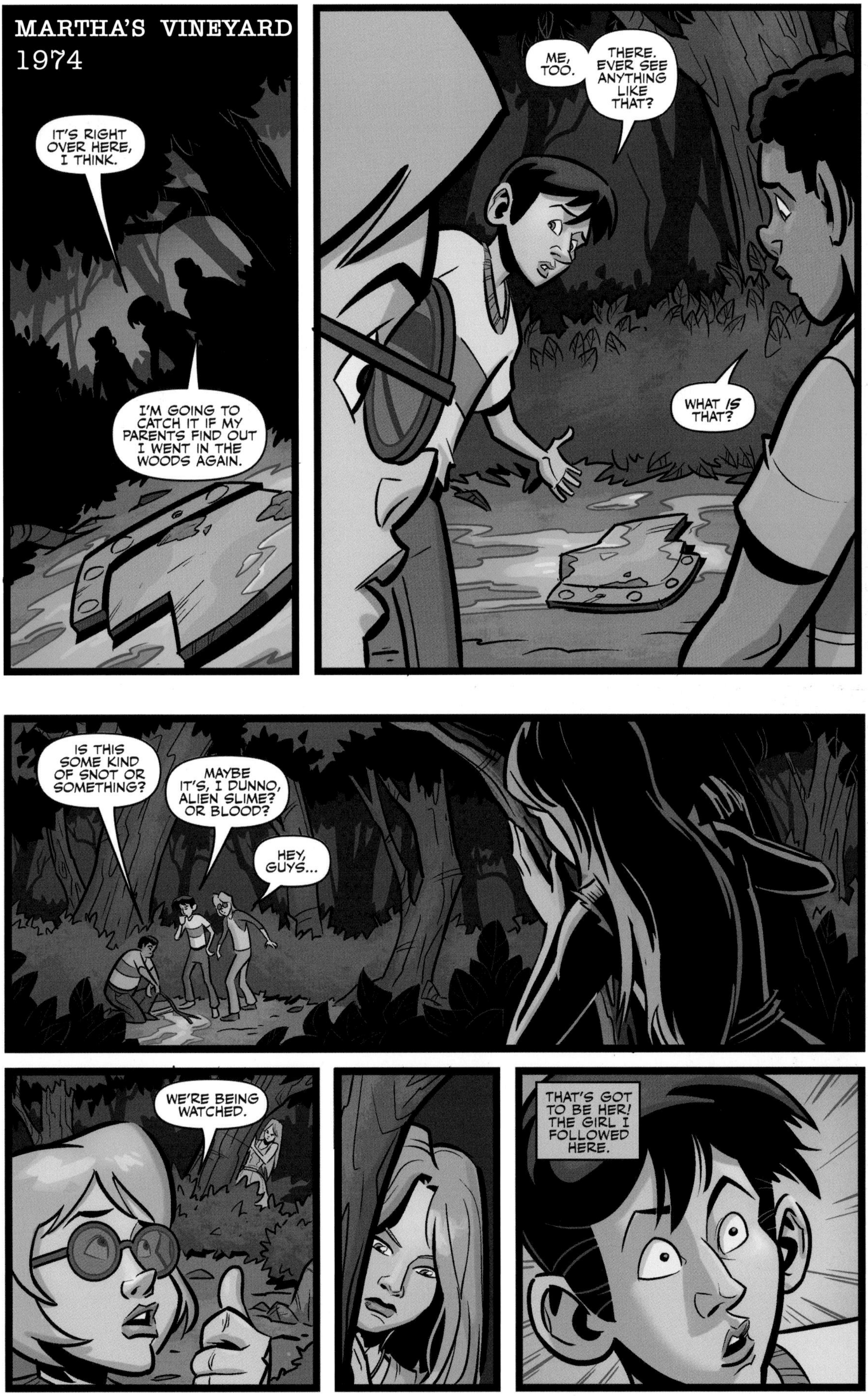
MARTHA'S VINEYARD
1974
IT'S RIGHT OVER HERE, I THINK.
I'M GOING TO CATCH IT IF MY PARENTS FIND OUT I WENT IN THE WOODS AGAIN.
THERE. EVER SEE ANYTHING LIKE THAT?
ME, TOO.
WHAT *IS* THAT?
IS THIS SOME KIND OF SNOT OR SOMETHING?
MAYBE IT'S, I DUNNO, ALIEN SLIME? OR BLOOD?
HEY, GUYS...
WE'RE BEING WATCHED.
THAT'S GOT TO BE HER! THE GIRL I FOLLOWED HERE.

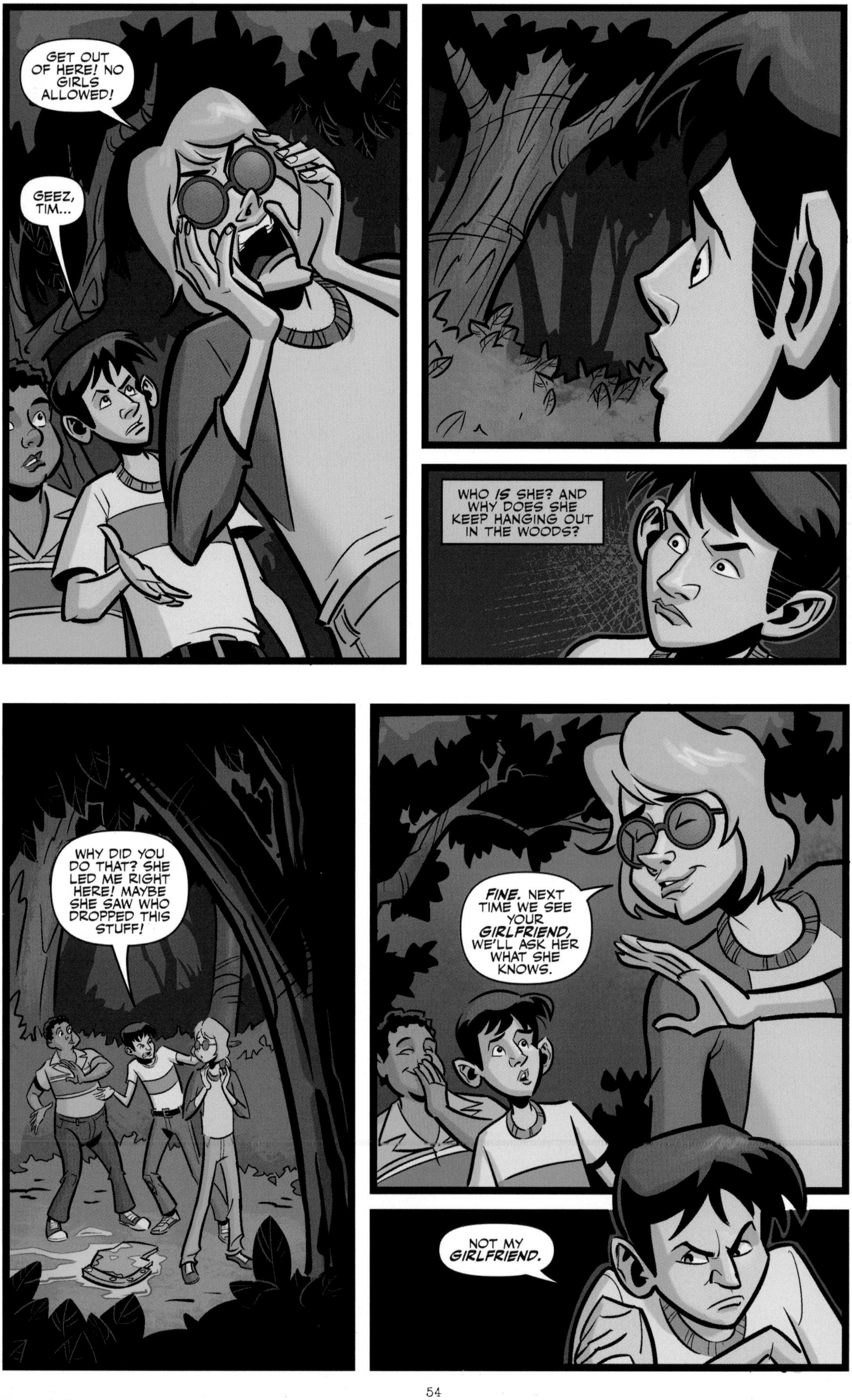
GET OUT OF HERE! NO GIRLS ALLOWED!
GEEZ, TIM...
WHO *IS* SHE? AND WHY DOES SHE KEEP HANGING OUT IN THE WOODS?
WHY DID YOU DO THAT? SHE LED ME RIGHT HERE! MAYBE SHE SAW WHO DROPPED THIS STUFF!
FINE. NEXT TIME WE SEE YOUR *GIRLFRIEND,* WE'LL ASK HER WHAT SHE KNOWS.
NOT MY *GIRLFRIEND.*

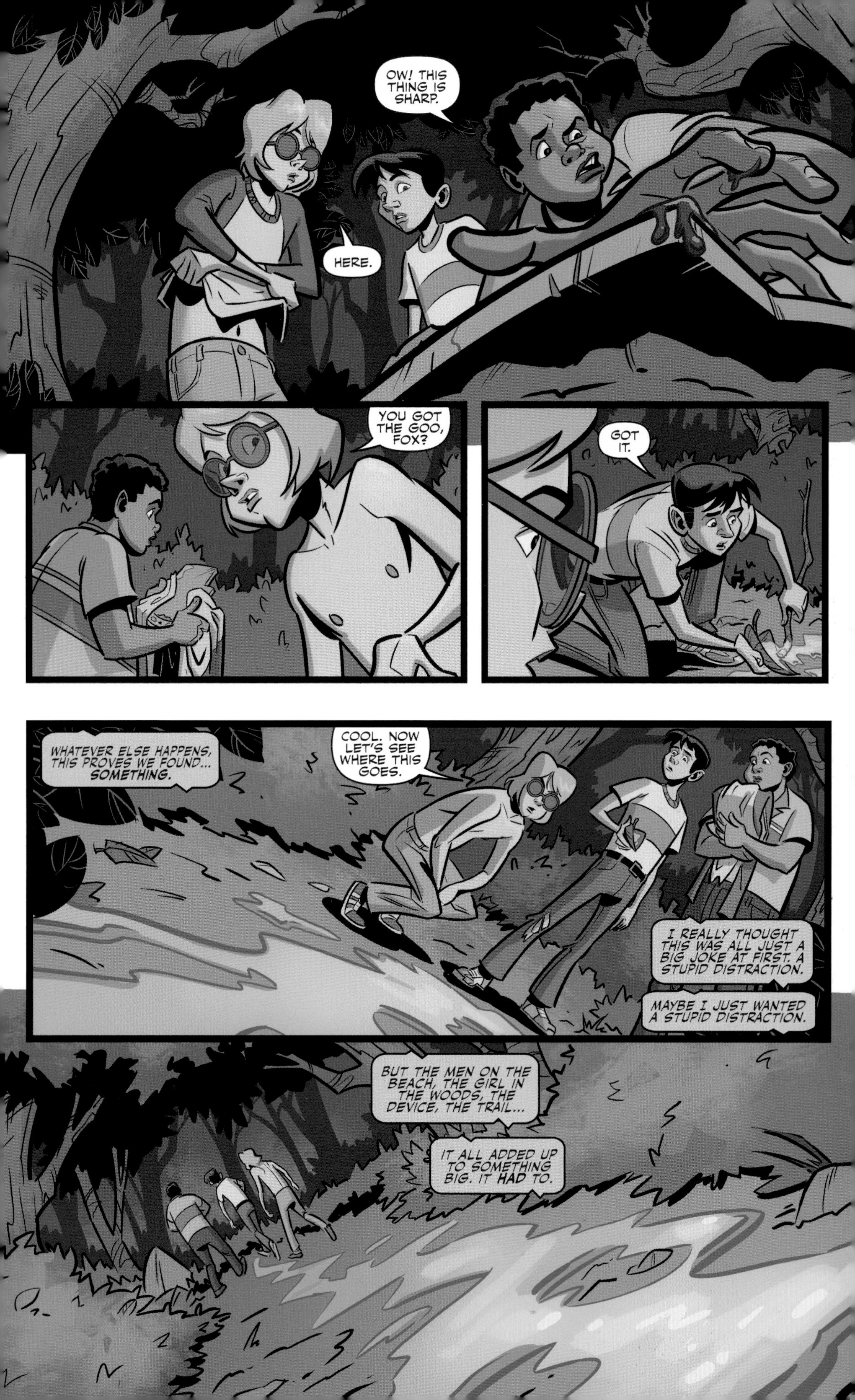

OW! THIS THING IS SHARP.
HERE.
YOU GOT THE GOO, FOX?
GOT IT.
WHATEVER ELSE HAPPENS, THIS PROVES WE FOUND... **SOMETHING.**
COOL. NOW LET'S SEE WHERE THIS GOES.
I REALLY THOUGHT THIS WAS ALL JUST A BIG JOKE AT FIRST. A STUPID DISTRACTION.
MAYBE I JUST WANTED A STUPID DISTRACTION.
BUT THE MEN ON THE BEACH, THE GIRL IN THE WOODS, THE DEVICE, THE TRAIL...
IT ALL ADDED UP TO SOMETHING BIG. IT **HAD** TO.

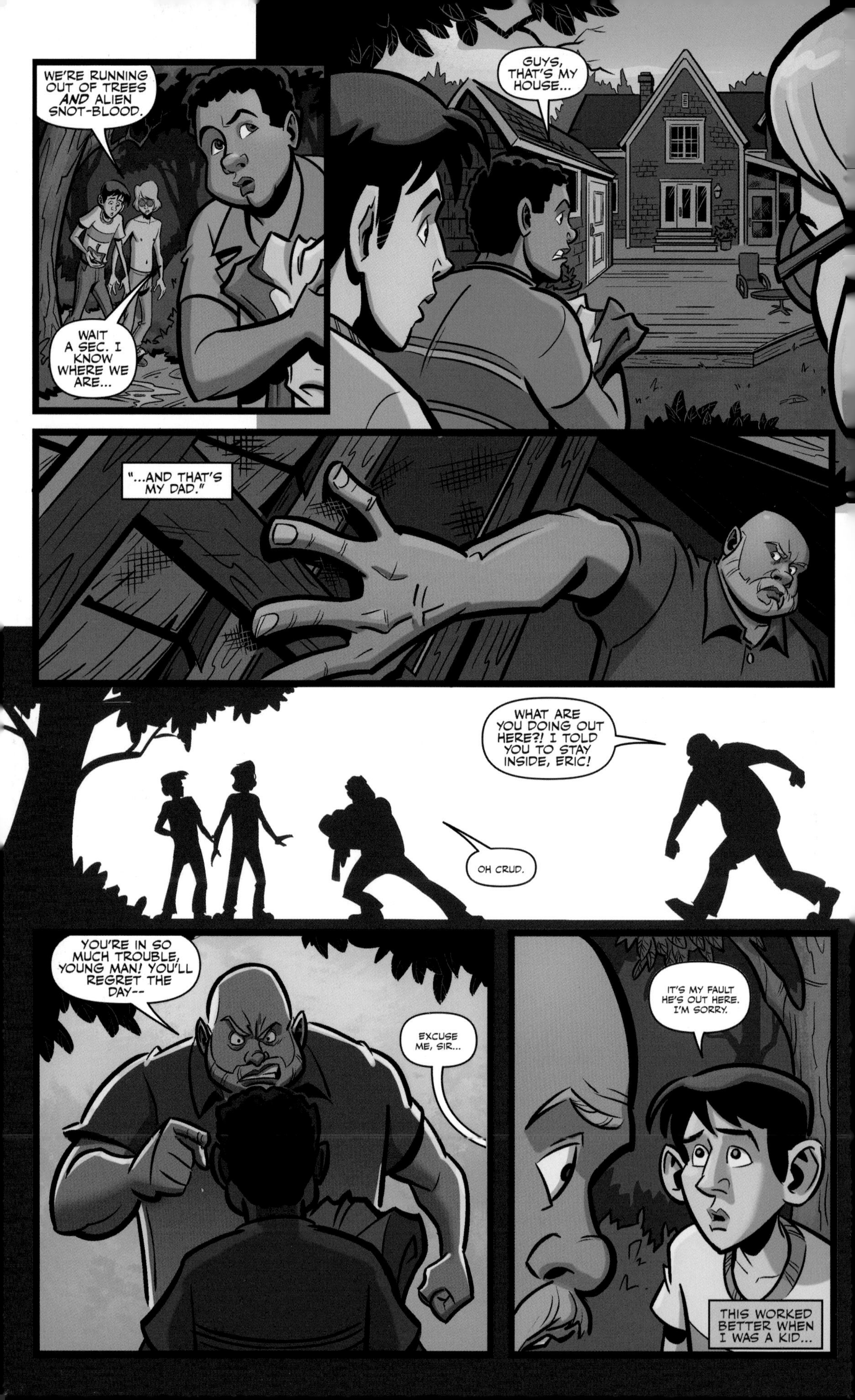
WE'RE RUNNING OUT OF TREES AND ALIEN SNOT-BLOOD.
WAIT A SEC. I KNOW WHERE WE ARE...
GUYS, THAT'S MY HOUSE...
"...AND THAT'S MY DAD."
WHAT ARE YOU DOING OUT HERE?! I TOLD YOU TO STAY INSIDE, ERIC!
OH CRUD.
YOU'RE IN SO MUCH TROUBLE, YOUNG MAN! YOU'LL REGRET THE DAY--
EXCUSE ME, SIR...
IT'S MY FAULT HE'S OUT HERE. I'M SORRY.
THIS WORKED BETTER WHEN I WAS A KID...

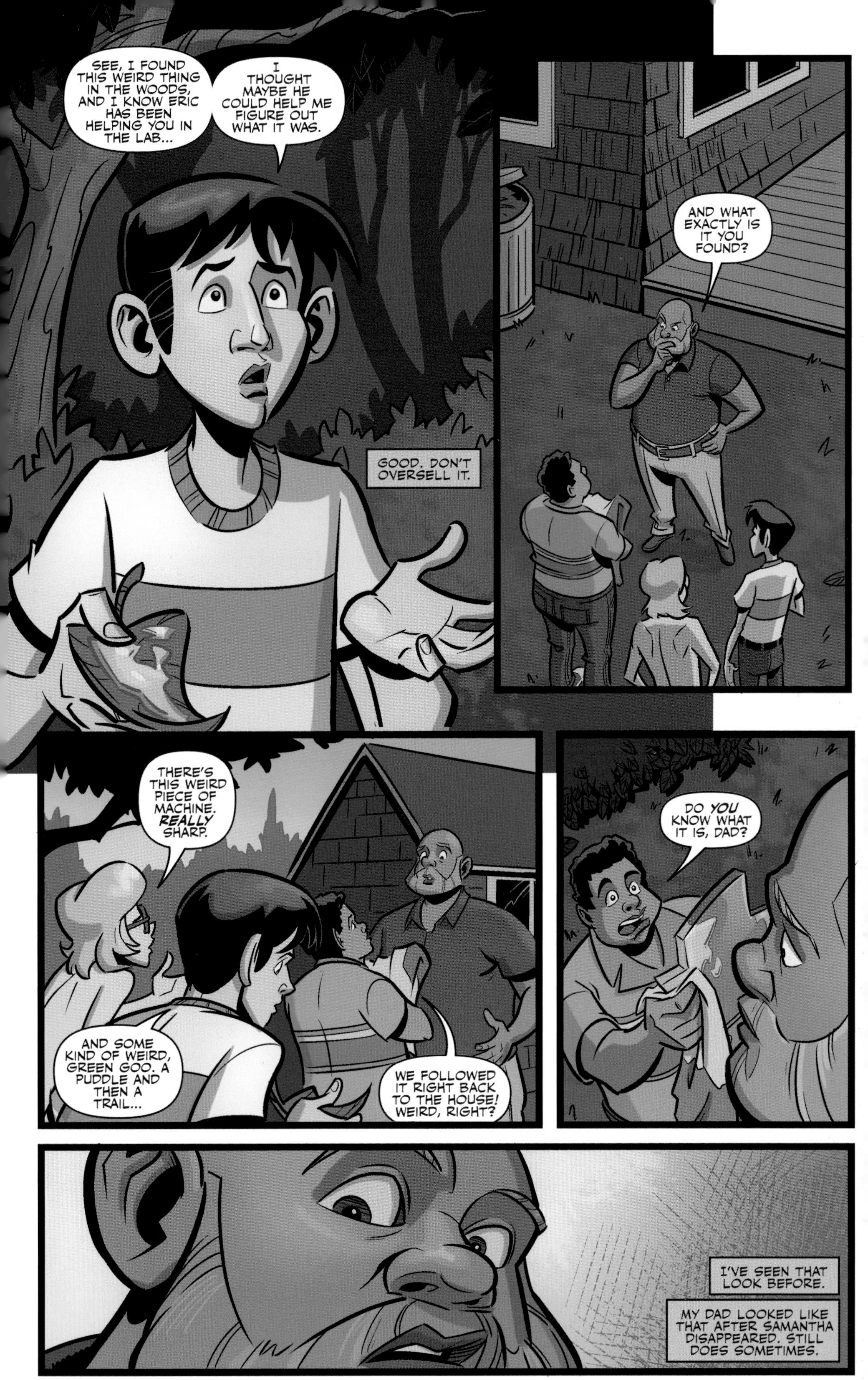
SEE, I FOUND THIS WEIRD THING IN THE WOODS, AND I KNOW ERIC HAS BEEN HELPING YOU IN THE LAB...
I THOUGHT MAYBE HE COULD HELP ME FIGURE OUT WHAT IT WAS.
GOOD. DON'T OVERSELL IT.
AND WHAT EXACTLY IS IT YOU FOUND?
THERE'S THIS WEIRD PIECE OF MACHINE. *REALLY* SHARP.
AND SOME KIND OF WEIRD, GREEN GOO. A PUDDLE AND THEN A TRAIL...
WE FOLLOWED IT RIGHT BACK TO THE HOUSE! WEIRD, RIGHT?
DO *YOU* KNOW WHAT IT IS, DAD?
I'VE SEEN THAT LOOK BEFORE.
MY DAD LOOKED LIKE THAT AFTER SAMANTHA DISAPPEARED. STILL DOES SOMETIMES.

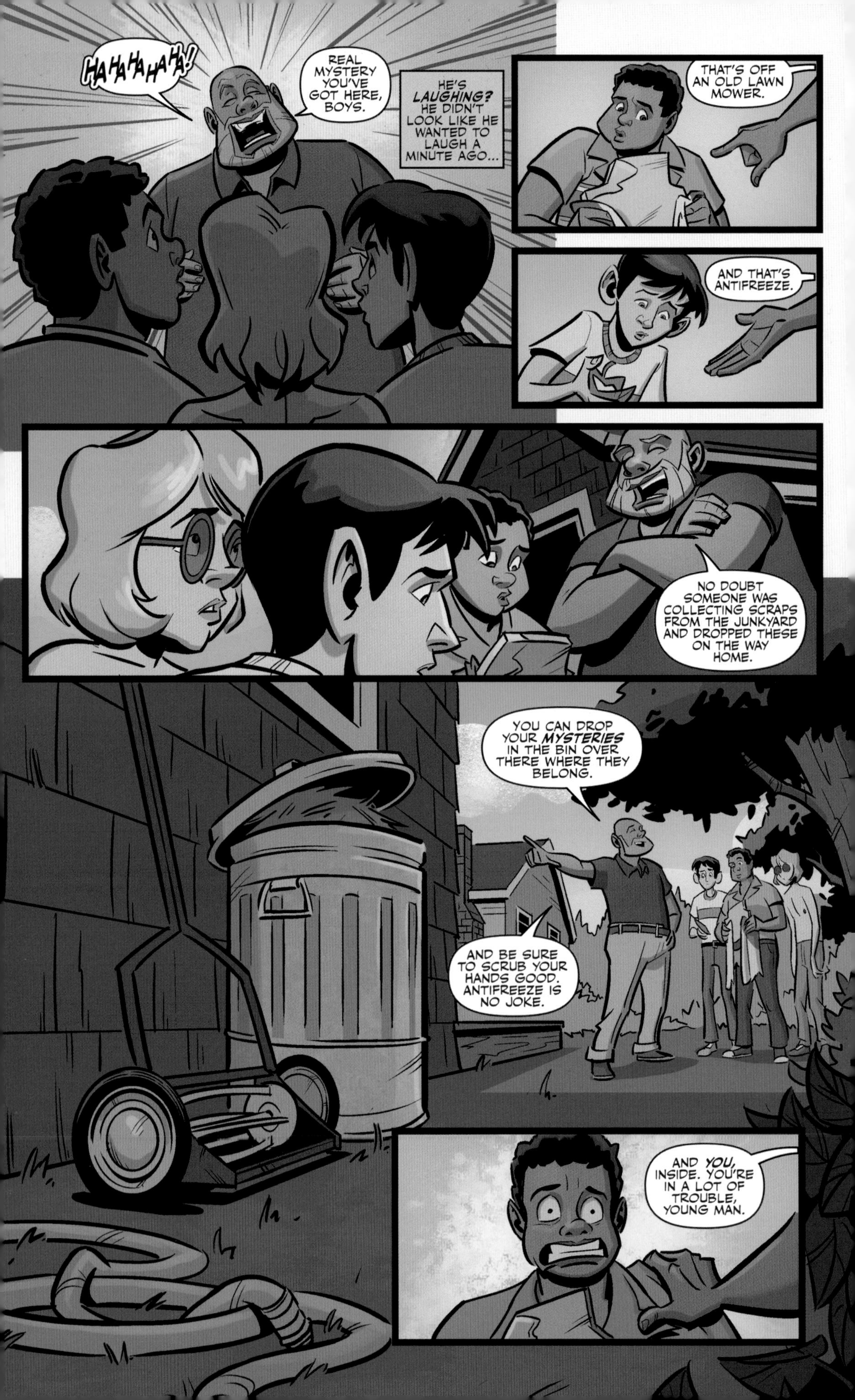
HAHAHAHAHA!
REAL MYSTERY YOU'VE GOT HERE, BOYS.
HE'S LAUGHING? HE DIDN'T LOOK LIKE HE WANTED TO LAUGH A MINUTE AGO...
THAT'S OFF AN OLD LAWN MOWER.
AND THAT'S ANTIFREEZE.
NO DOUBT SOMEONE WAS COLLECTING SCRAPS FROM THE JUNKYARD AND DROPPED THESE ON THE WAY HOME.
YOU CAN DROP YOUR MYSTERIES IN THE BIN OVER THERE WHERE THEY BELONG.
AND BE SURE TO SCRUB YOUR HANDS GOOD. ANTIFREEZE IS NO JOKE.
AND YOU, INSIDE. YOU'RE IN A LOT OF TROUBLE, YOUNG MAN.

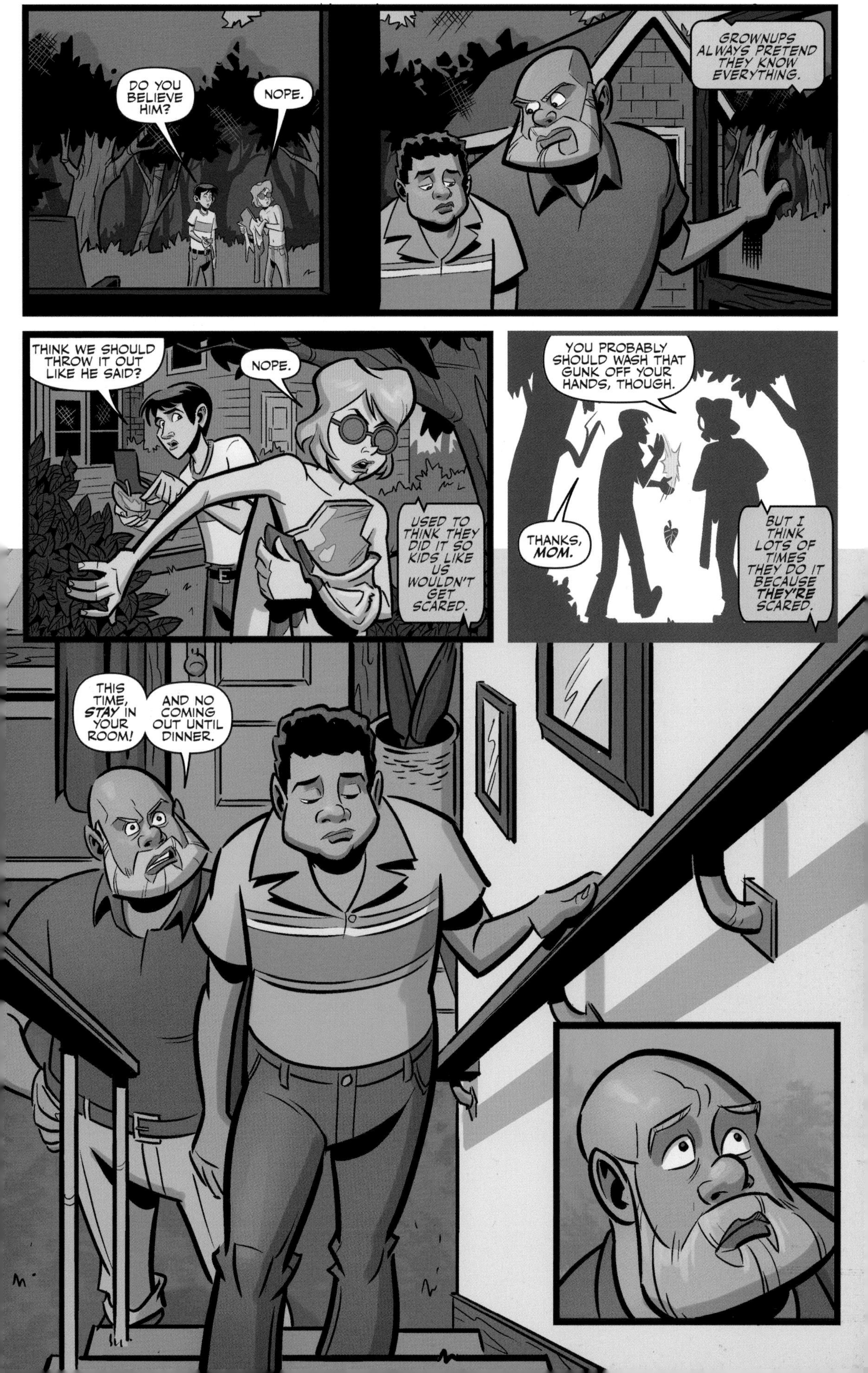
DO YOU BELIEVE HIM?
NOPE.
GROWNUPS ALWAYS PRETEND THEY KNOW EVERYTHING.
THINK WE SHOULD THROW IT OUT LIKE HE SAID?
NOPE.
USED TO THINK THEY DID IT SO KIDS LIKE US WOULDN'T GET SCARED.
YOU PROBABLY SHOULD WASH THAT GUNK OFF YOUR HANDS, THOUGH.
THANKS, MOM.
BUT I THINK LOTS OF TIMES THEY DO IT BECAUSE THEY'RE SCARED.
THIS TIME, STAY IN YOUR ROOM!
AND NO COMING OUT UNTIL DINNER.

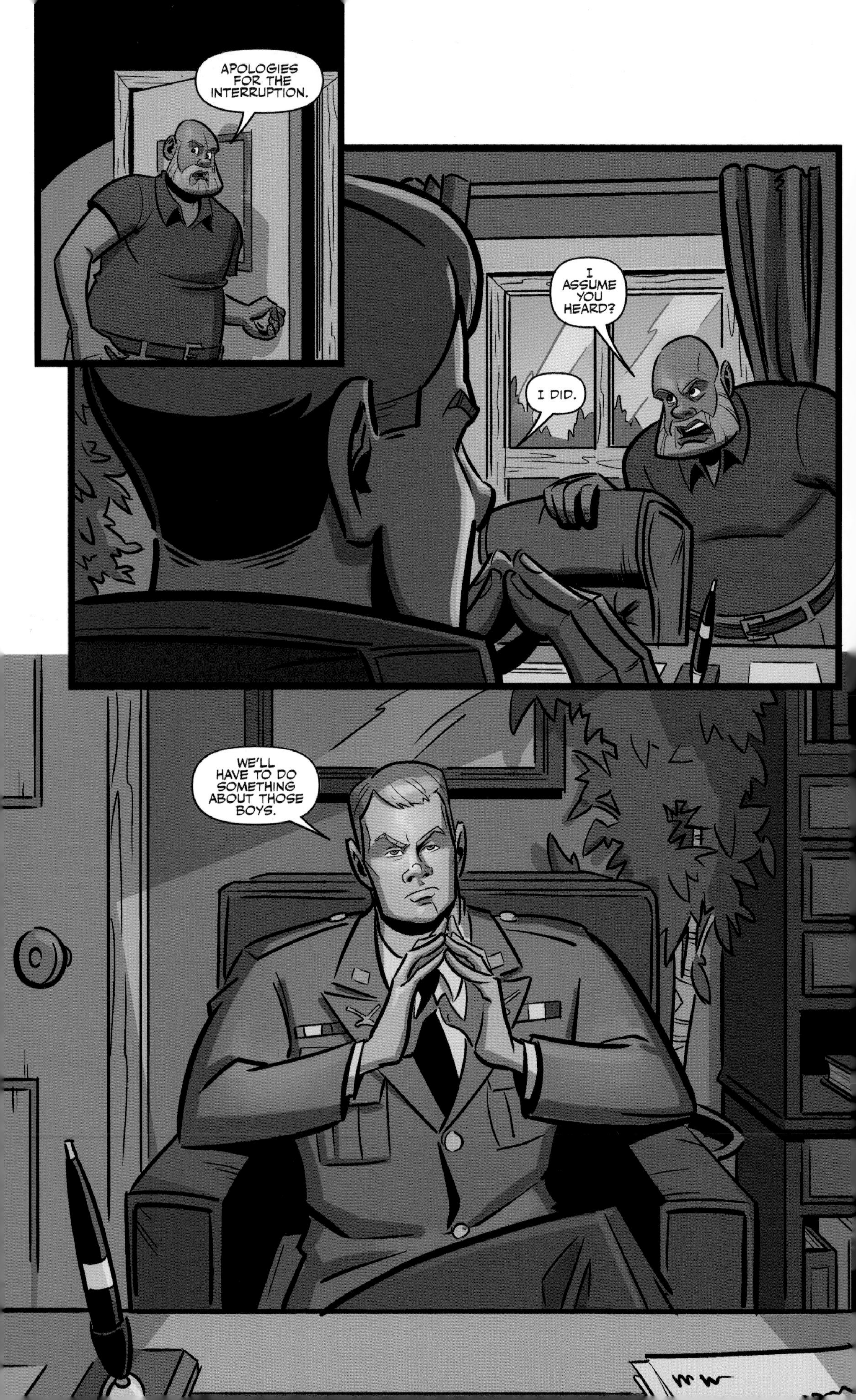
APOLOGIES FOR THE INTERRUPTION.
I ASSUME YOU HEARD?
I DID.
WE'LL HAVE TO DO SOMETHING ABOUT THOSE BOYS.

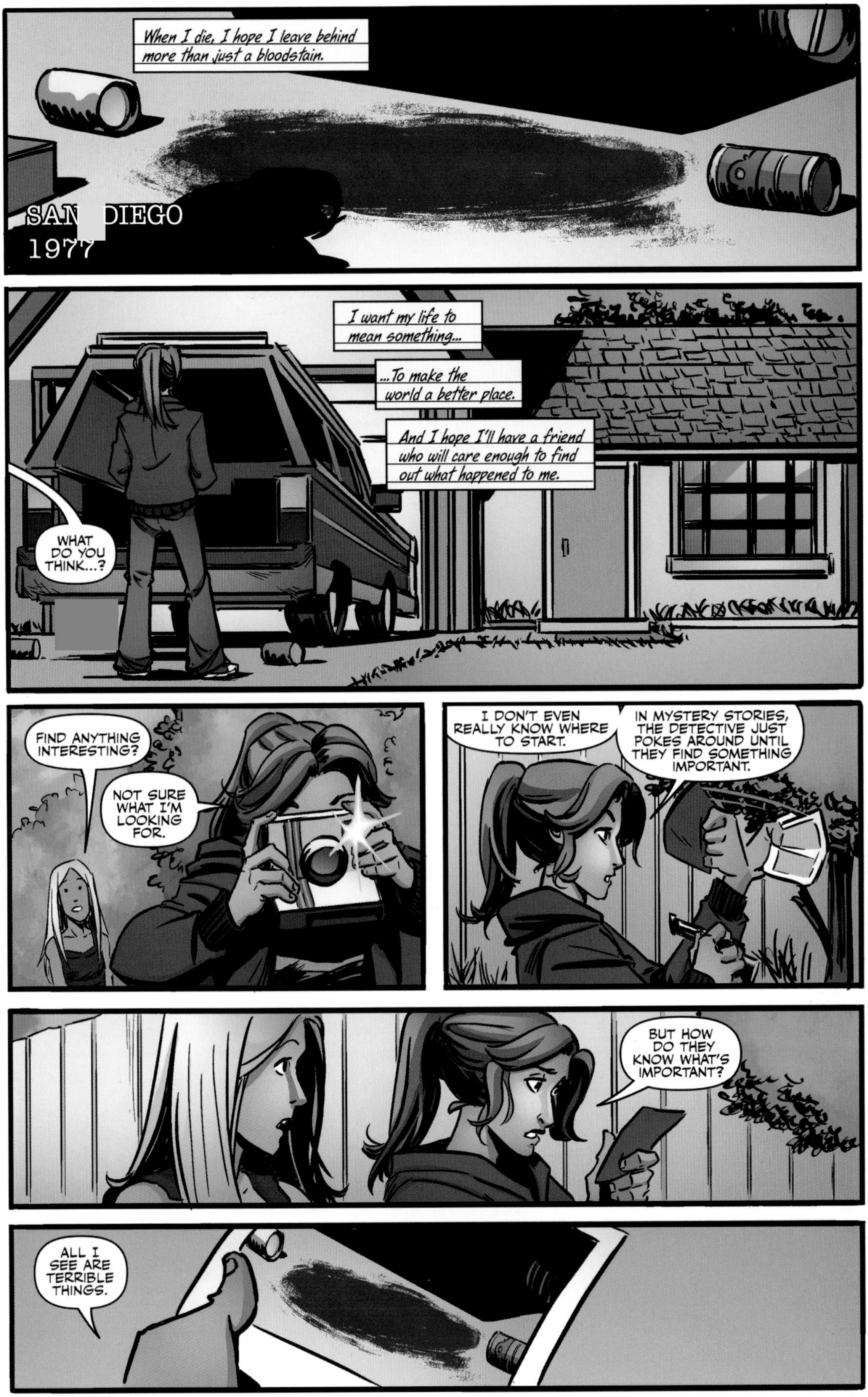
When I die, I hope I leave behind more than just a bloodstain.
SAN DIEGO
1977
I want my life to mean something...
...To make the world a better place.
And I hope I'll have a friend who will care enough to find out what happened to me.
WHAT DO YOU THINK...?
FIND ANYTHING INTERESTING?
NOT SURE WHAT I'M LOOKING FOR.
I DON'T EVEN REALLY KNOW WHERE TO START.
IN MYSTERY STORIES, THE DETECTIVE JUST POKES AROUND UNTIL THEY FIND SOMETHING IMPORTANT.
BUT HOW DO THEY KNOW WHAT'S IMPORTANT?
ALL I SEE ARE TERRIBLE THINGS.

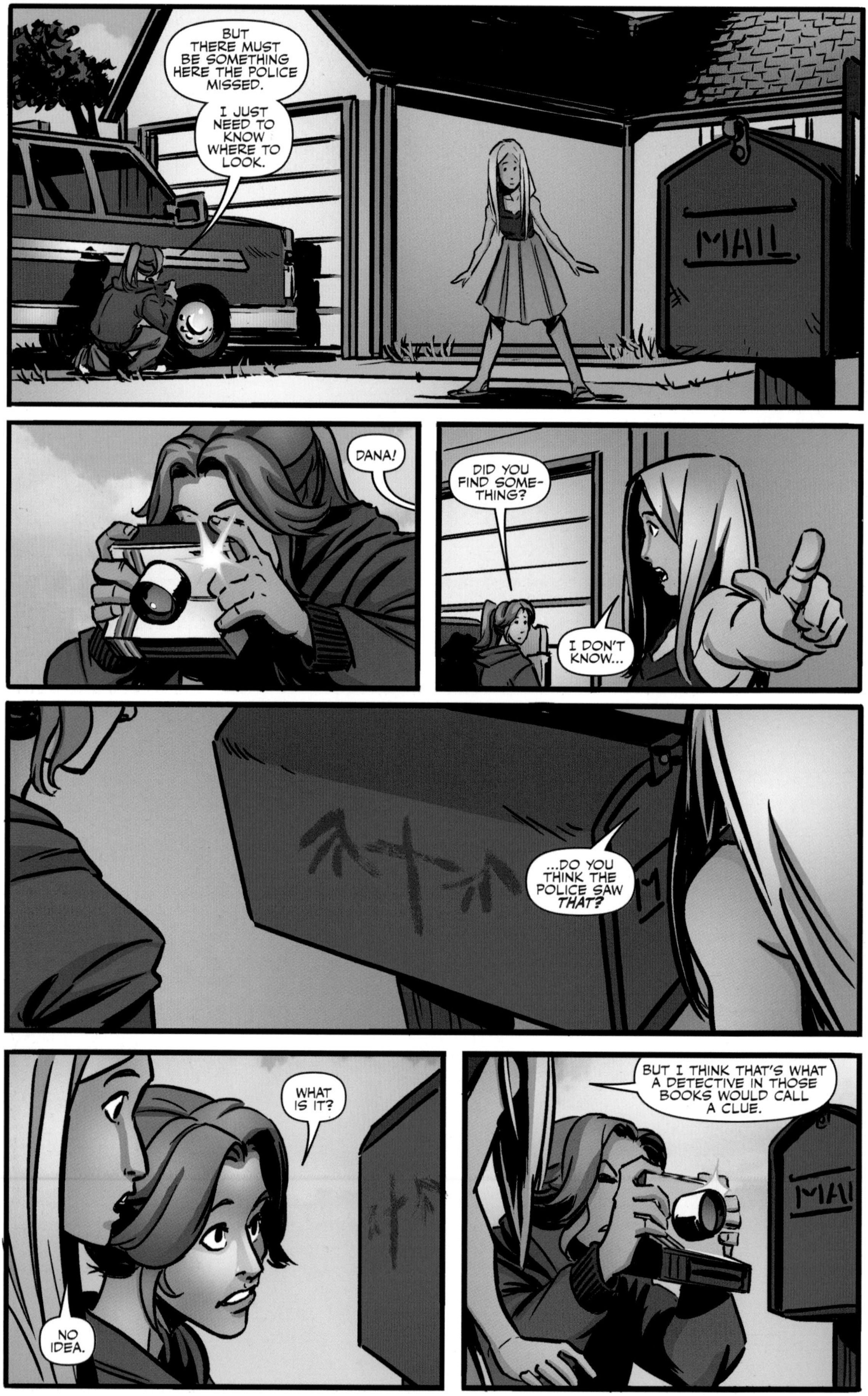
BUT THERE MUST BE SOMETHING HERE THE POLICE MISSED.
I JUST NEED TO KNOW WHERE TO LOOK.
MAIL
DANA!
DID YOU FIND SOME-THING?
I DON'T KNOW...
...DO YOU THINK THE POLICE SAW *THAT?*
WHAT IS IT?
NO IDEA.
BUT I THINK THAT'S WHAT A DETECTIVE IN THOSE BOOKS WOULD CALL A CLUE.

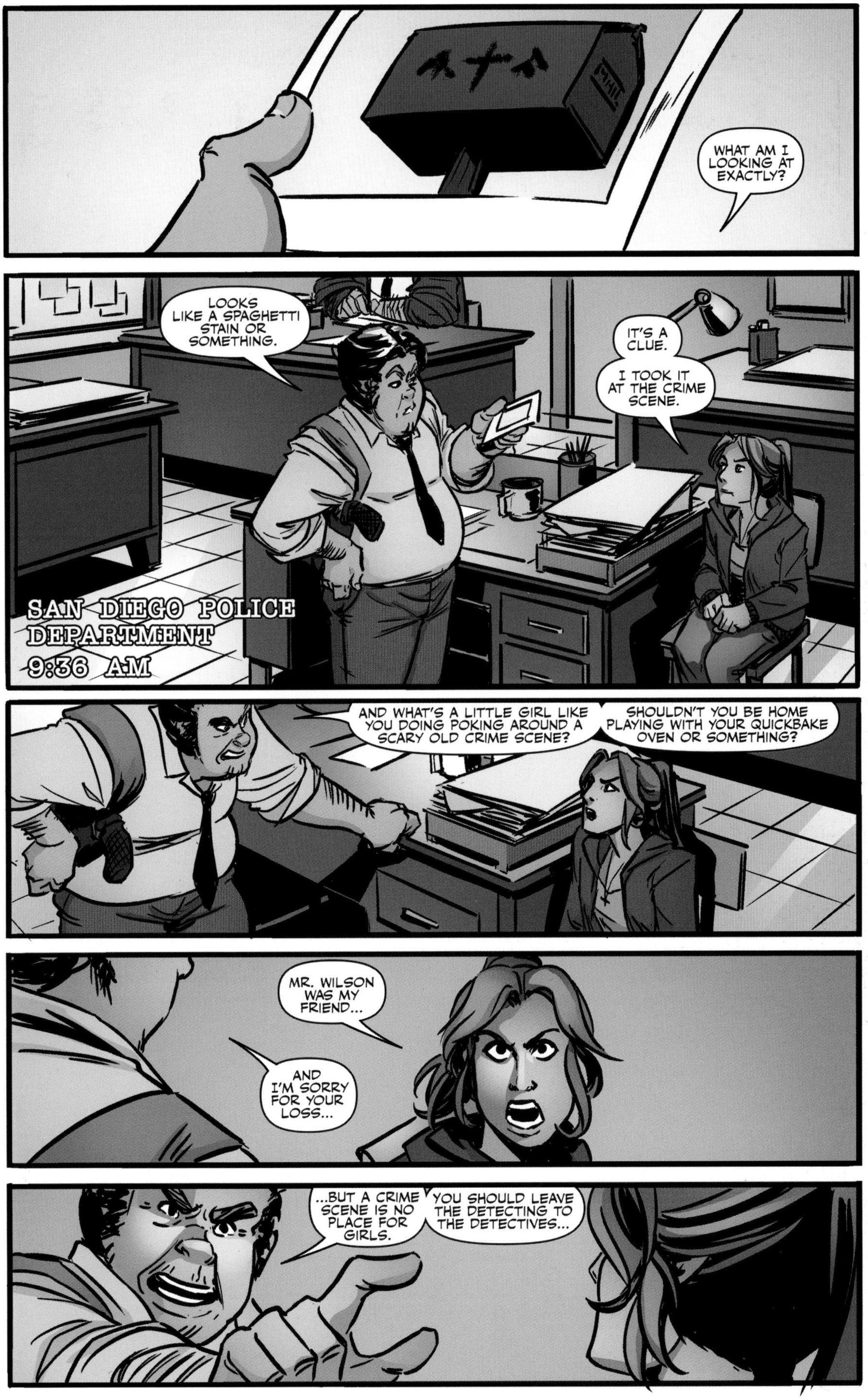
WHAT AM I LOOKING AT EXACTLY?
LOOKS LIKE A SPAGHETTI STAIN OR SOMETHING.
IT'S A CLUE.
I TOOK IT AT THE CRIME SCENE.
SAN DIEGO POLICE DEPARTMENT 9:36 AM
AND WHAT'S A LITTLE GIRL LIKE YOU DOING POKING AROUND A SCARY OLD CRIME SCENE?
SHOULDN'T YOU BE HOME PLAYING WITH YOUR QUICKBAKE OVEN OR SOMETHING?
MR. WILSON WAS MY FRIEND...
AND I'M SORRY FOR YOUR LOSS...
...BUT A CRIME SCENE IS NO PLACE FOR GIRLS.
YOU SHOULD LEAVE THE DETECTING TO THE DETECTIVES...

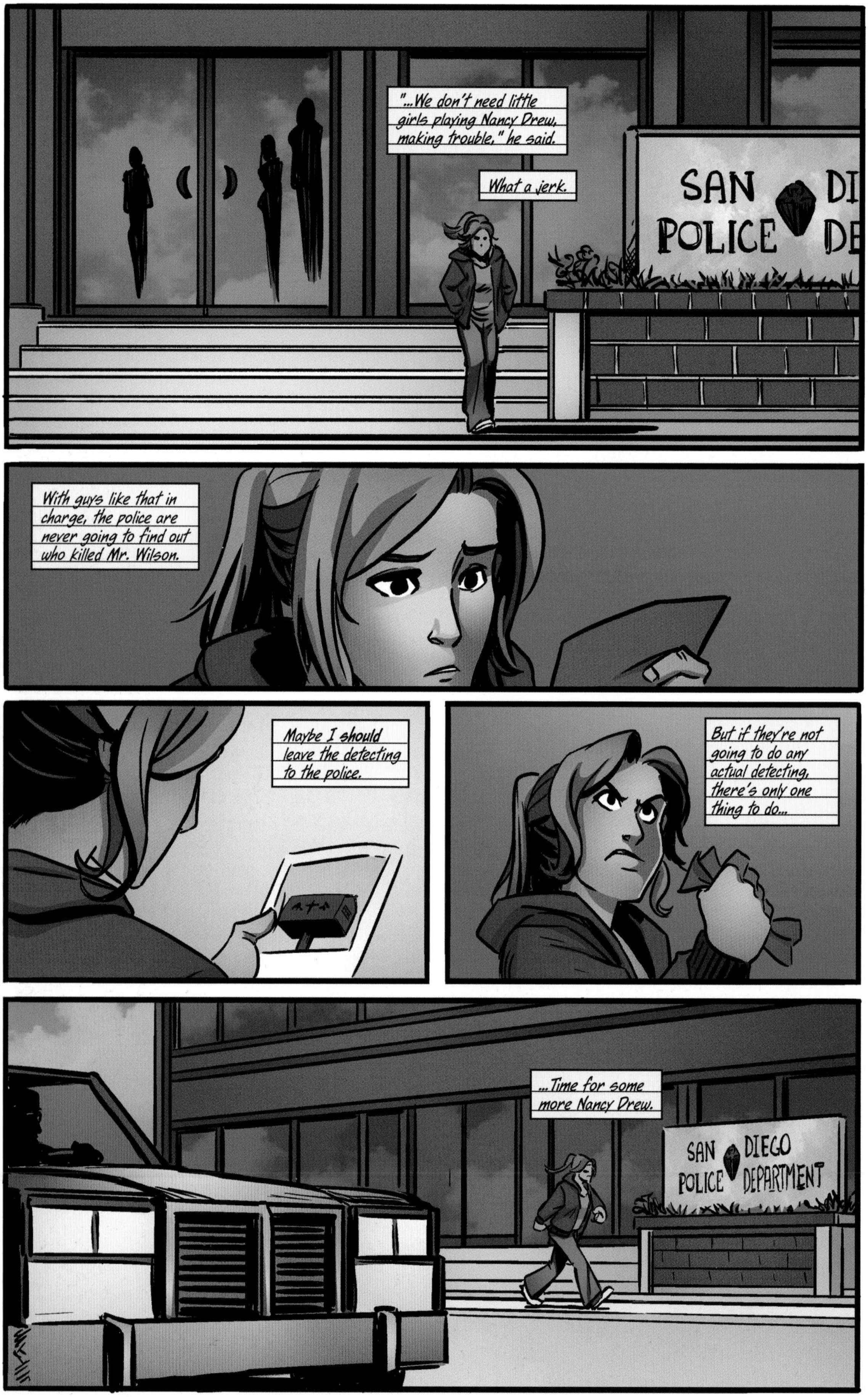
"...We don't need little girls playing Nancy Drew, making trouble," he said.
What a jerk.
SAN POLICE
With guys like that in charge, the police are never going to find out who killed Mr. Wilson.
Maybe I should leave the detecting to the police.
But if they're not going to do any actual detecting, there's only one thing to do...
...Time for some more Nancy Drew.
SAN DIEGO POLICE DEPARTMENT

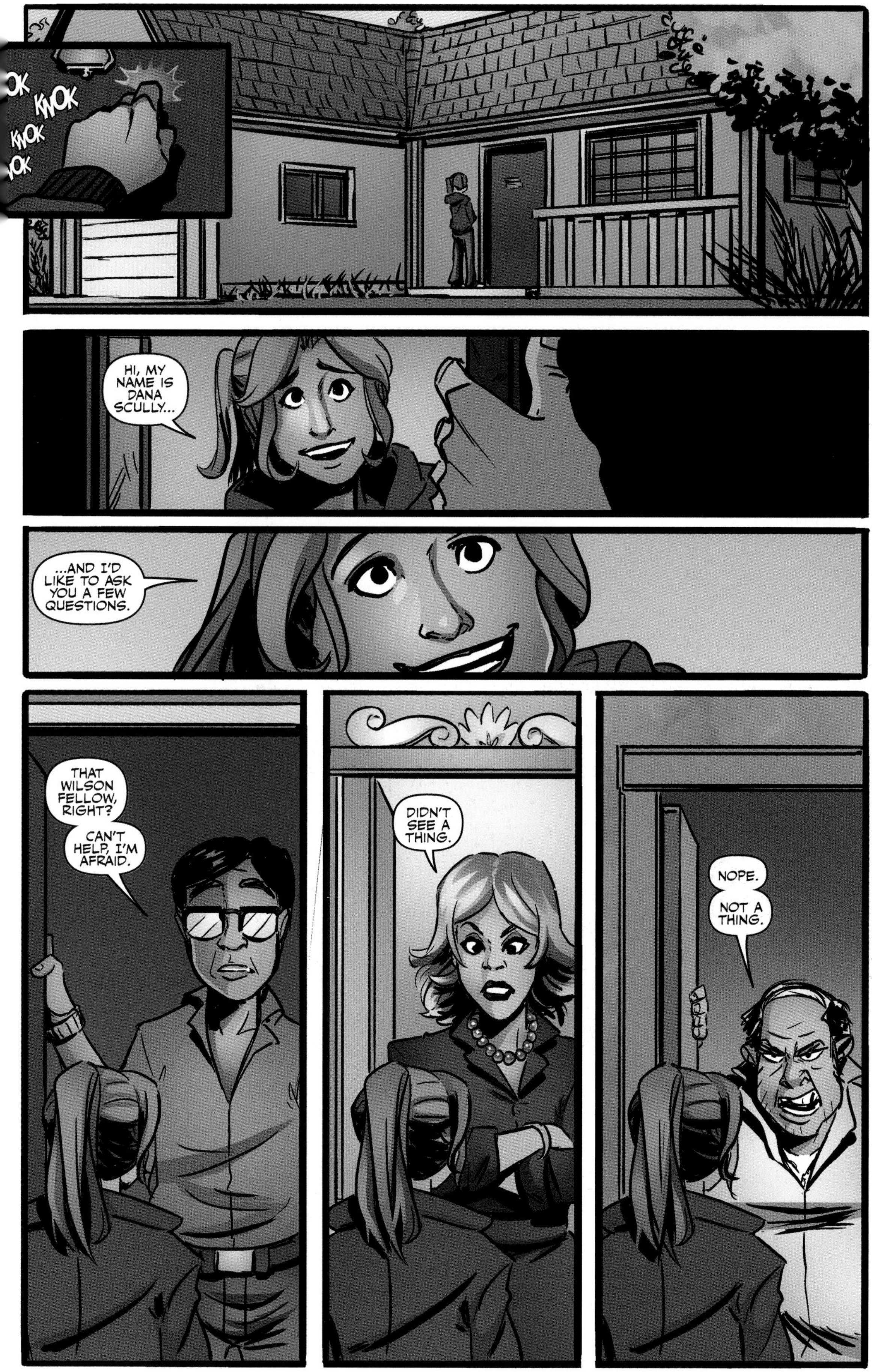
KNOK
KNOK
KNOK
KNOK
HI, MY NAME IS DANA SCULLY...
...AND I'D LIKE TO ASK YOU A FEW QUESTIONS.
THAT WILSON FELLOW, RIGHT?
CAN'T HELP, I'M AFRAID.
DIDN'T SEE A THING.
NOPE.
NOT A THING.

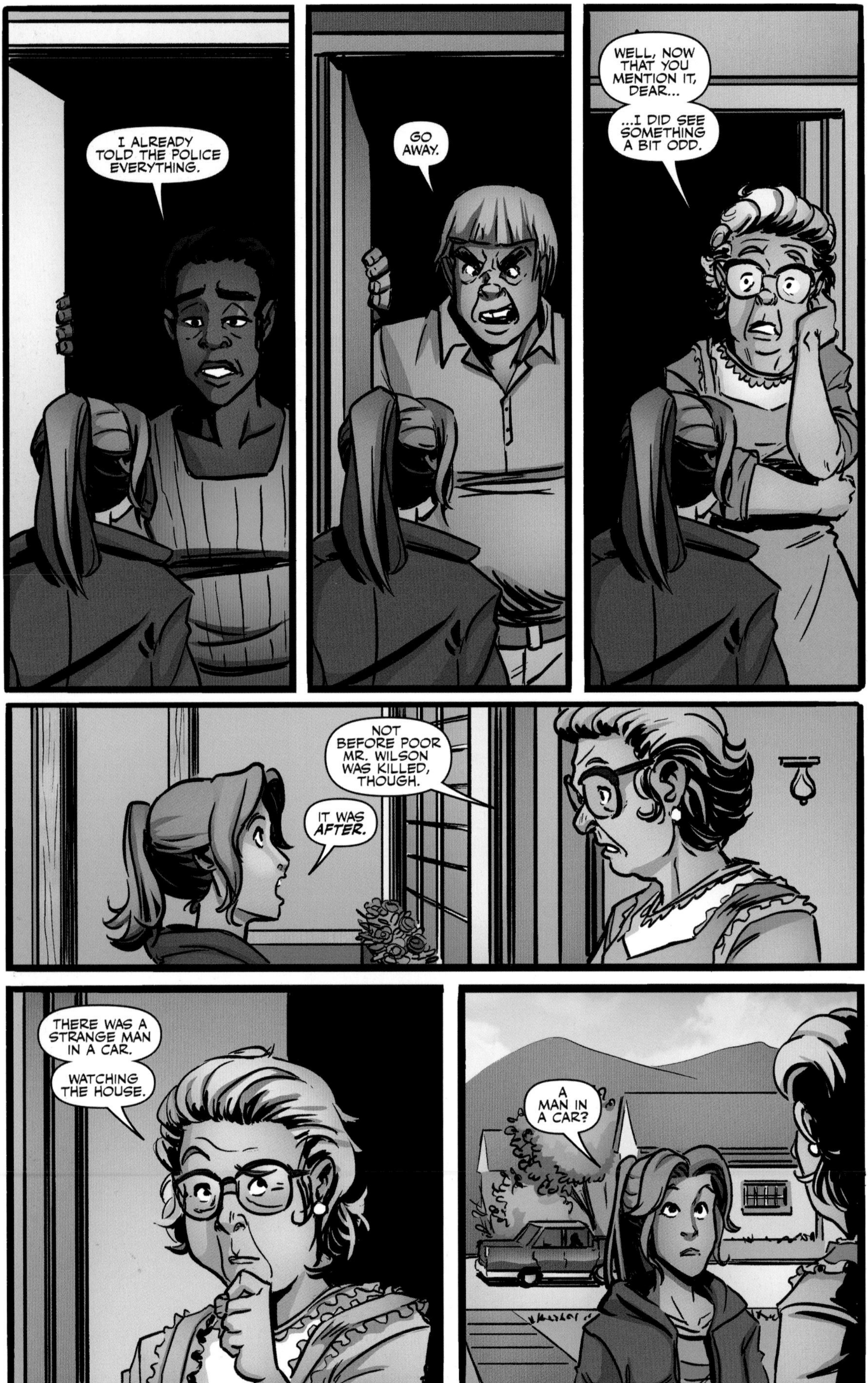
I ALREADY TOLD THE POLICE EVERYTHING.
GO AWAY.
WELL, NOW THAT YOU MENTION IT, DEAR...
...I DID SEE SOMETHING A BIT ODD.
NOT BEFORE POOR MR. WILSON WAS KILLED, THOUGH.
IT WAS *AFTER.*
THERE WAS A STRANGE MAN IN A CAR.
WATCHING THE HOUSE.
A MAN IN A CAR?

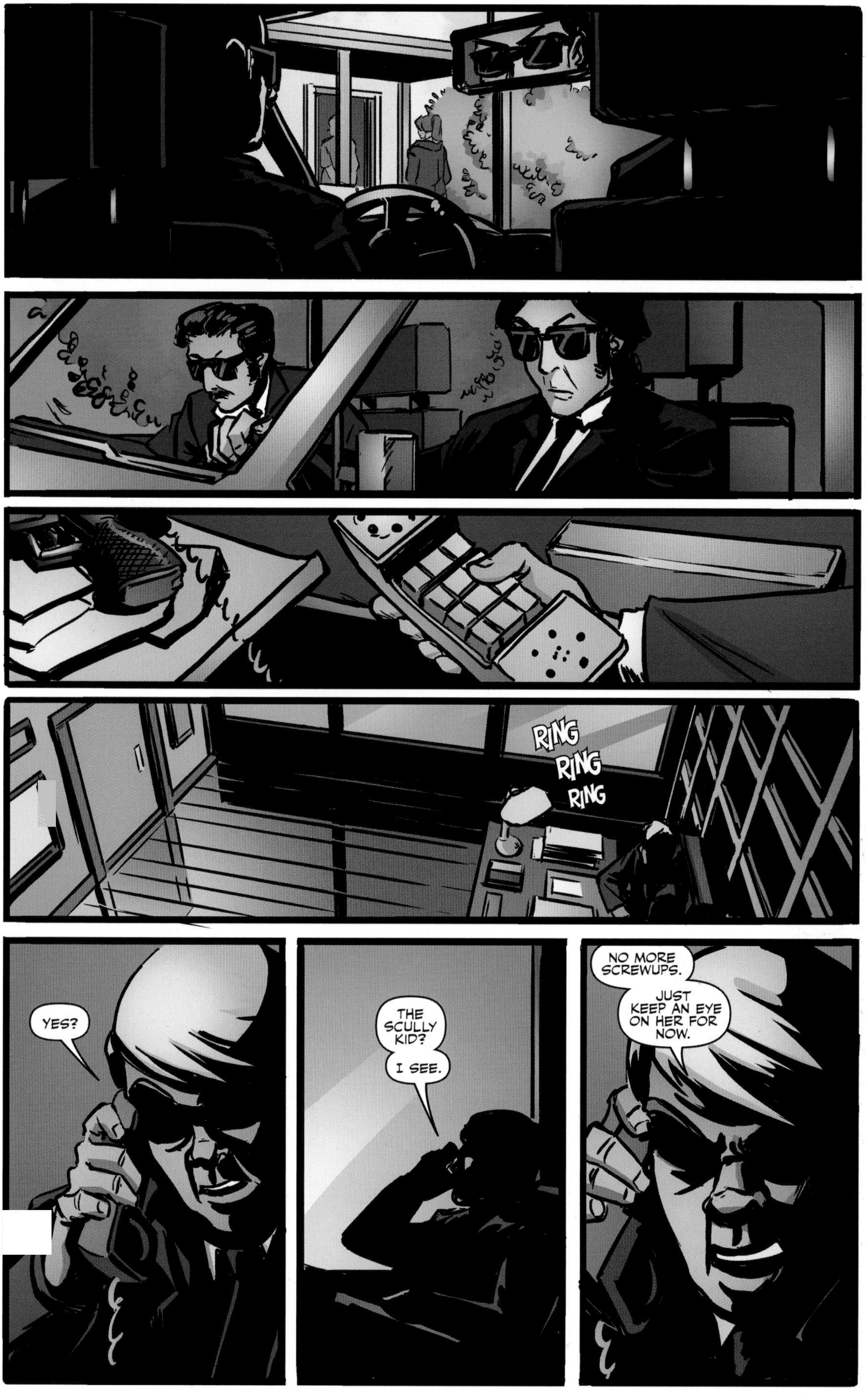
RING
RING
RING
YES?
THE SCULLY KID?
I SEE.
NO MORE SCREWUPS.
JUST KEEP AN EYE ON HER FOR NOW.

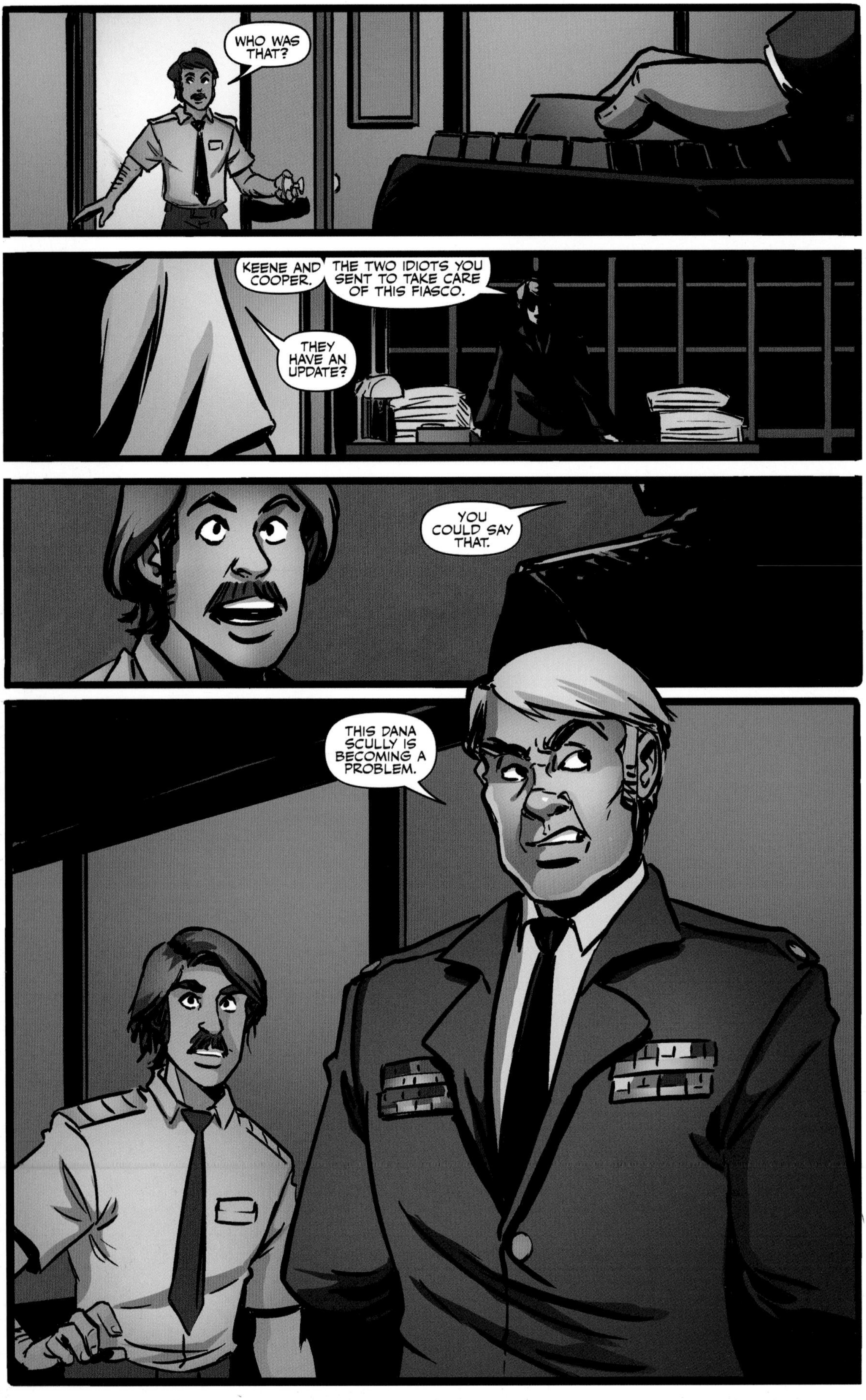
WHO WAS THAT?
KEENE AND COOPER.
THE TWO IDIOTS YOU SENT TO TAKE CARE OF THIS FIASCO.
THEY HAVE AN UPDATE?
YOU COULD SAY THAT.
THIS DANA SCULLY IS BECOMING A PROBLEM.

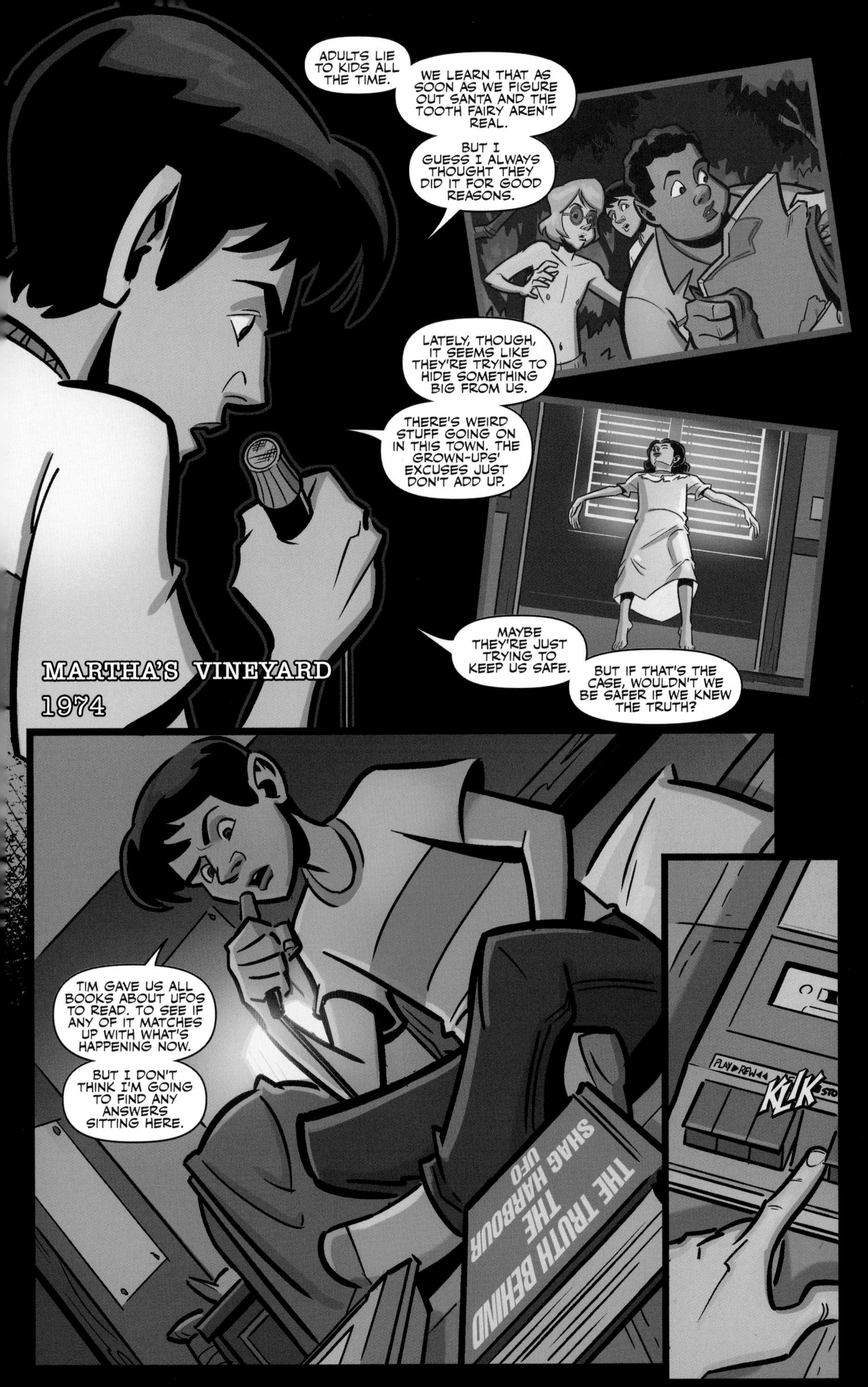
ADULTS LIE TO KIDS ALL THE TIME.
WE LEARN THAT AS SOON AS WE FIGURE OUT SANTA AND THE TOOTH FAIRY AREN'T REAL.
BUT I GUESS I ALWAYS THOUGHT THEY DID IT FOR GOOD REASONS.
LATELY, THOUGH, IT SEEMS LIKE THEY'RE TRYING TO HIDE SOMETHING BIG FROM US.
THERE'S WEIRD STUFF GOING ON IN THIS TOWN. THE GROWN-UPS' EXCUSES JUST DON'T ADD UP.
MAYBE THEY'RE JUST TRYING TO KEEP US SAFE.
BUT IF THAT'S THE CASE, WOULDN'T WE BE SAFER IF WE KNEW THE TRUTH?
MARTHA'S VINEYARD
1974
TIM GAVE US ALL BOOKS ABOUT UFOS TO READ. TO SEE IF ANY OF IT MATCHES UP WITH WHAT'S HAPPENING NOW.
BUT I DON'T THINK I'M GOING TO FIND ANY ANSWERS SITTING HERE.
THE TRUTH BEHIND THE SHAG HARBOUR UFO
PLAY ▸ REW ◂◂
KLIK

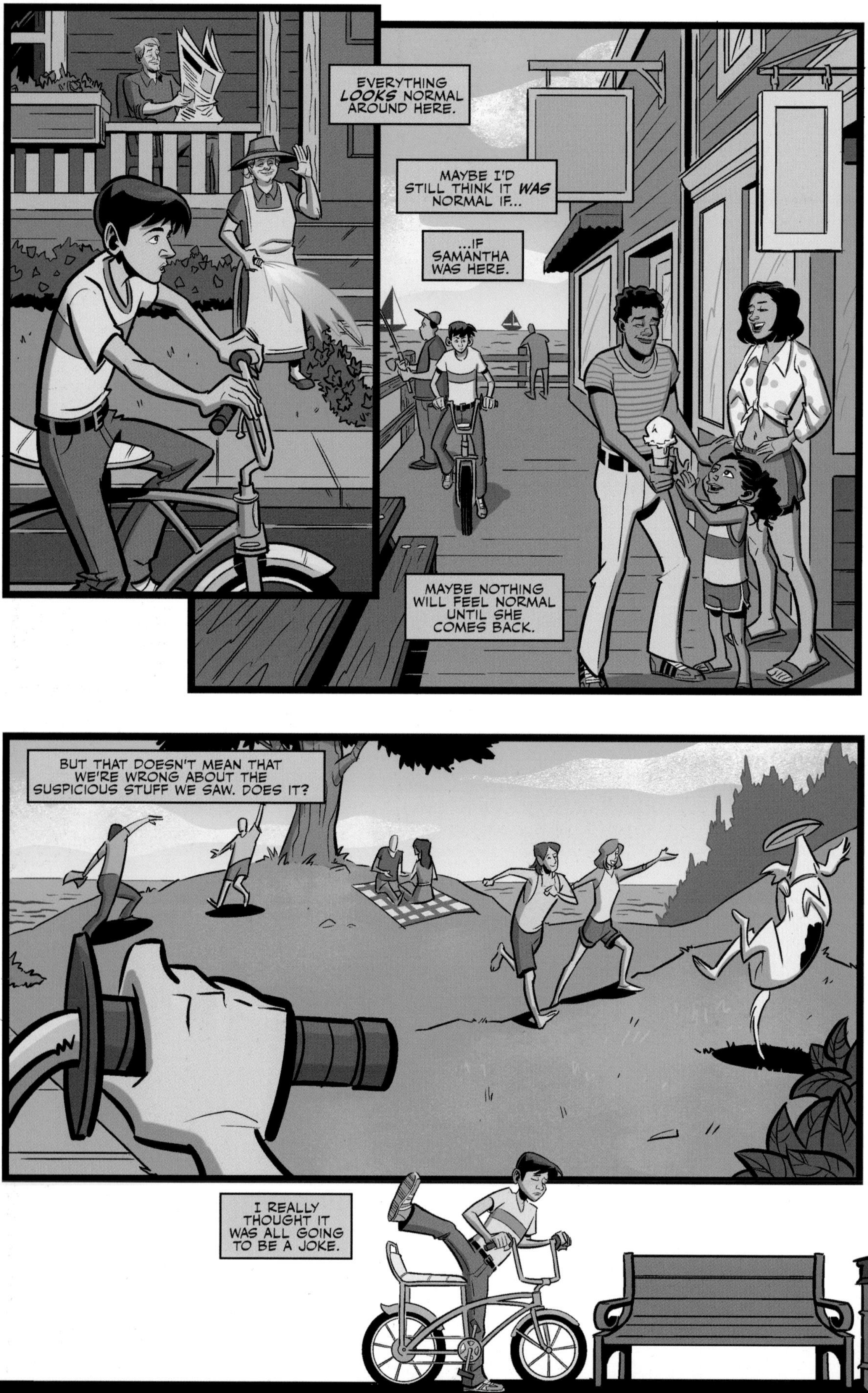
EVERYTHING LOOKS NORMAL AROUND HERE.
MAYBE I'D STILL THINK IT WAS NORMAL IF...
...IF SAMANTHA WAS HERE.
MAYBE NOTHING WILL FEEL NORMAL UNTIL SHE COMES BACK.
BUT THAT DOESN'T MEAN THAT WE'RE WRONG ABOUT THE SUSPICIOUS STUFF WE SAW. DOES IT?
I REALLY THOUGHT IT WAS ALL GOING TO BE A JOKE.

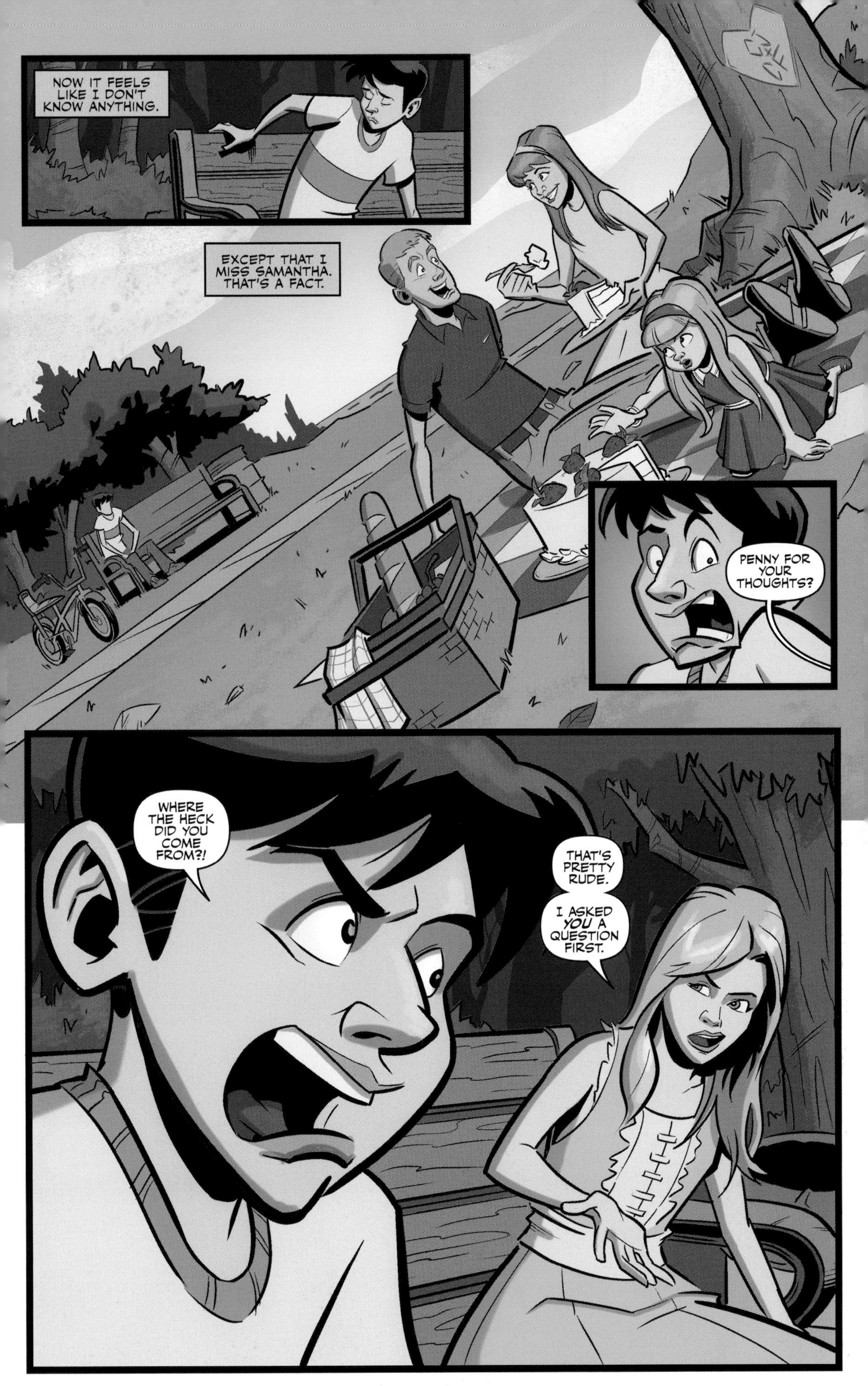
NOW IT FEELS LIKE I DON'T KNOW ANYTHING.
EXCEPT THAT I MISS SAMANTHA. THAT'S A FACT.
PENNY FOR YOUR THOUGHTS?
WHERE THE HECK DID YOU COME FROM?!
THAT'S PRETTY RUDE.
I ASKED *YOU* A QUESTION FIRST.

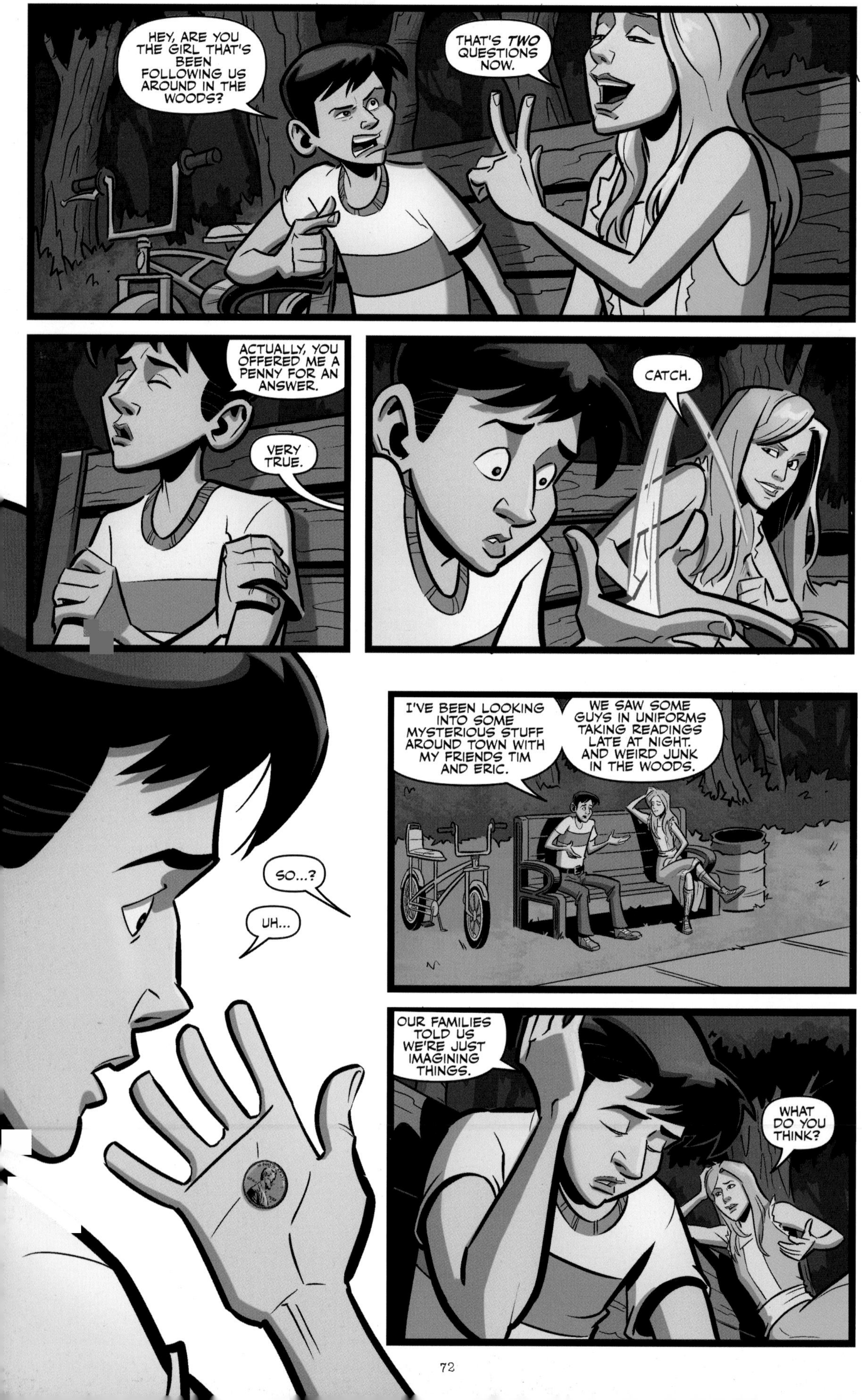
HEY, ARE YOU THE GIRL THAT'S BEEN FOLLOWING US AROUND IN THE WOODS?
THAT'S *TWO* QUESTIONS NOW.
ACTUALLY, YOU OFFERED ME A PENNY FOR AN ANSWER.
VERY TRUE.
CATCH.
SO...?
UH...
I'VE BEEN LOOKING INTO SOME MYSTERIOUS STUFF AROUND TOWN WITH MY FRIENDS TIM AND ERIC.
WE SAW SOME GUYS IN UNIFORMS TAKING READINGS LATE AT NIGHT. AND WEIRD JUNK IN THE WOODS.
OUR FAMILIES TOLD US WE'RE JUST IMAGINING THINGS.
WHAT DO YOU THINK?

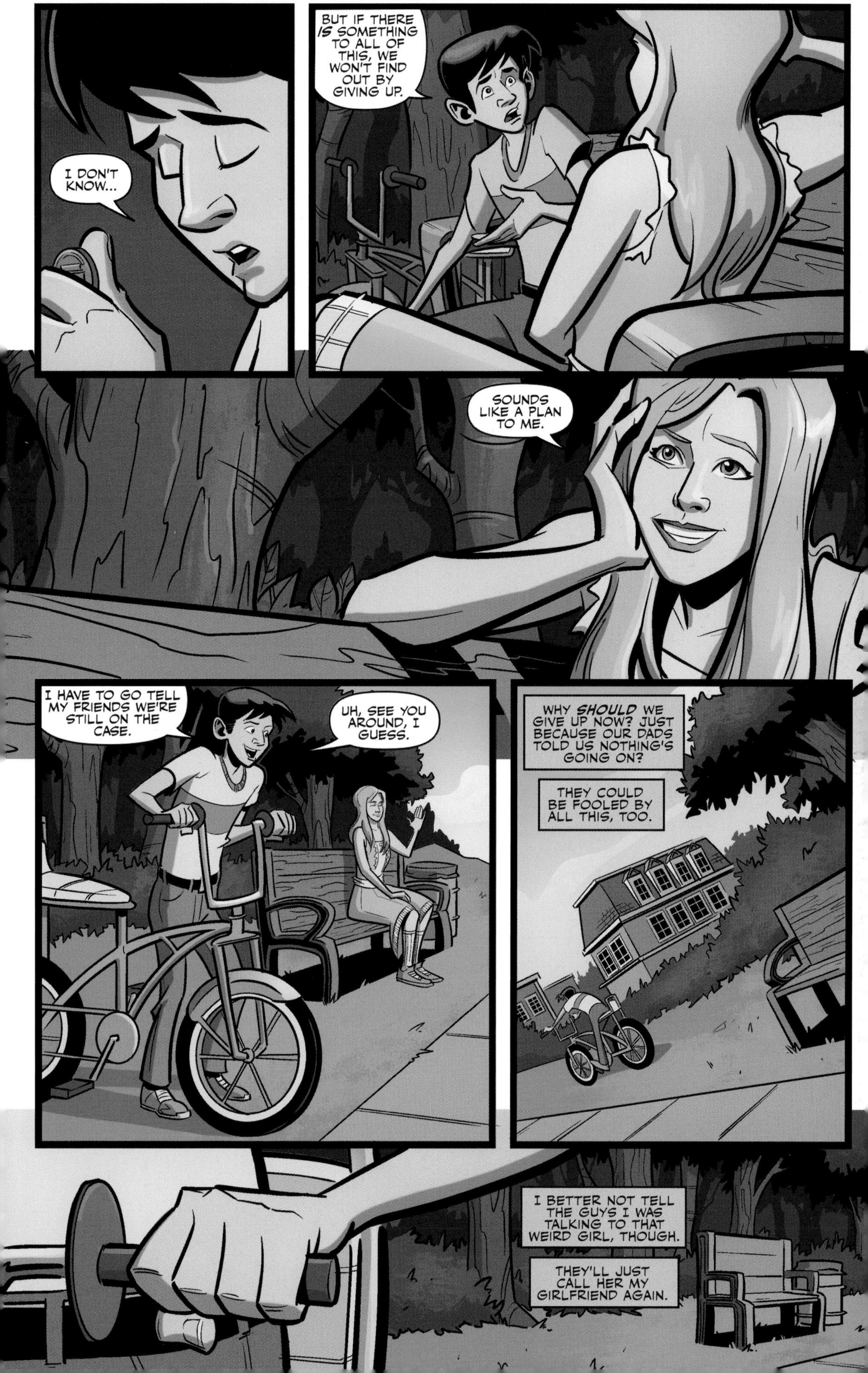

I DON'T KNOW...
BUT IF THERE *IS* SOMETHING TO ALL OF THIS, WE WON'T FIND OUT BY GIVING UP.
SOUNDS LIKE A PLAN TO ME.
I HAVE TO GO TELL MY FRIENDS WE'RE STILL ON THE CASE.
UH, SEE YOU AROUND, I GUESS.
WHY *SHOULD* WE GIVE UP NOW? JUST BECAUSE OUR DADS TOLD US NOTHING'S GOING ON?
THEY COULD BE FOOLED BY ALL THIS, TOO.
I BETTER NOT TELL THE GUYS I WAS TALKING TO THAT WEIRD GIRL, THOUGH.
THEY'LL JUST CALL HER MY GIRLFRIEND AGAIN.

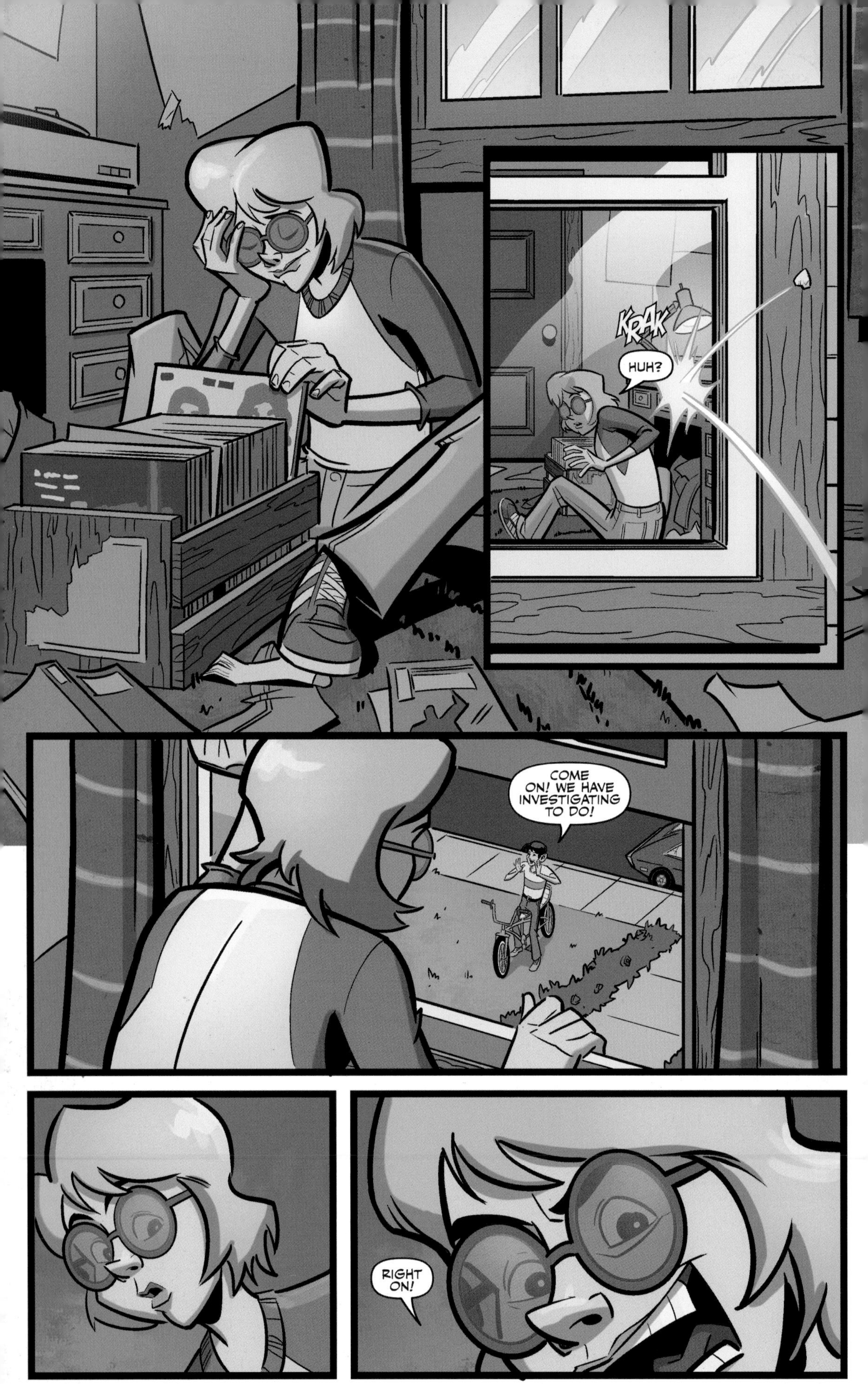
KRAK
HUH?
COME ON! WE HAVE INVESTIGATING TO DO!
RIGHT ON!

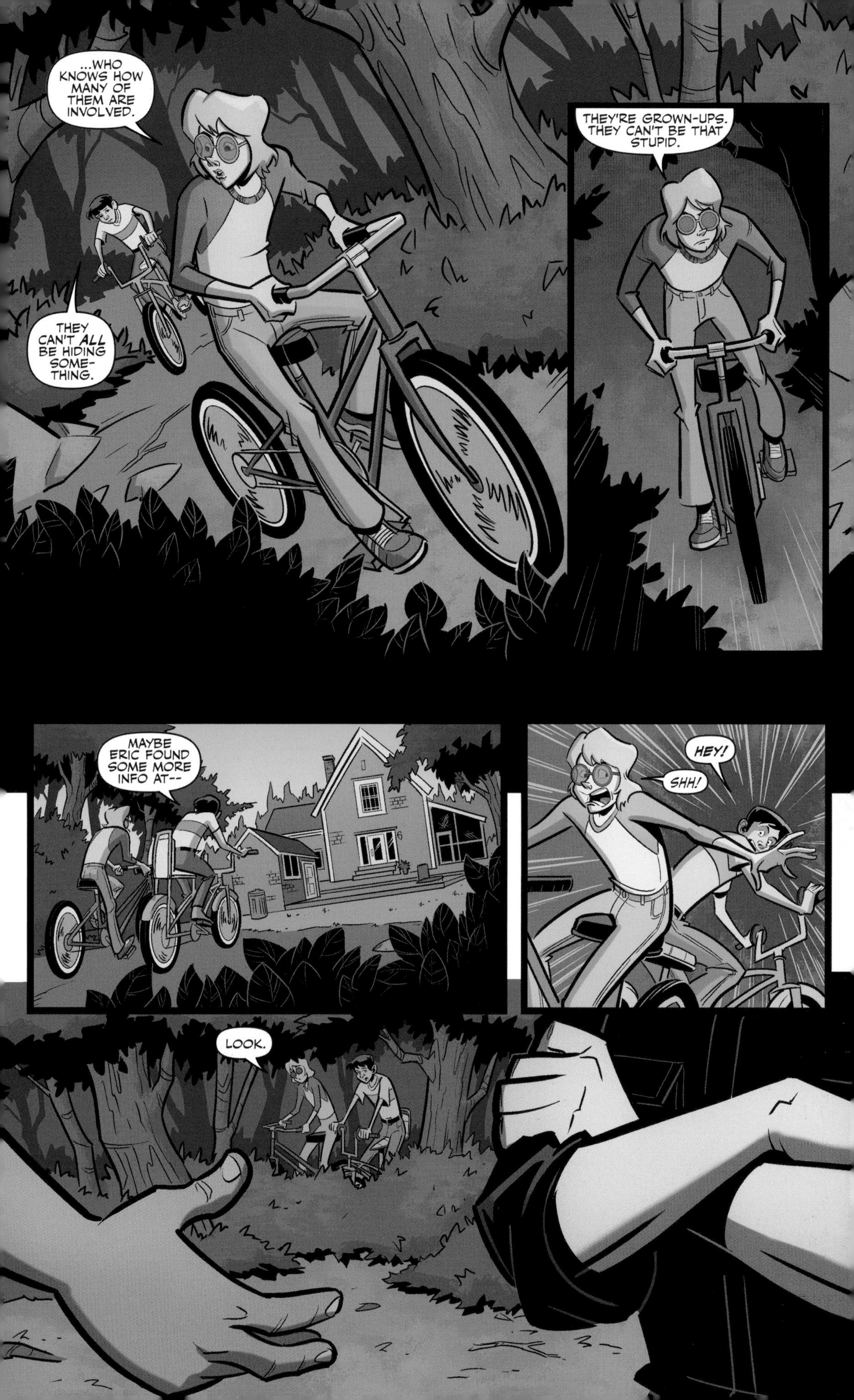
...WHO KNOWS HOW MANY OF THEM ARE INVOLVED.
THEY CAN'T ALL BE HIDING SOME-THING.
THEY'RE GROWN-UPS. THEY CAN'T BE THAT STUPID.
MAYBE ERIC FOUND SOME MORE INFO AT--
HEY!
SHH!
LOOK.

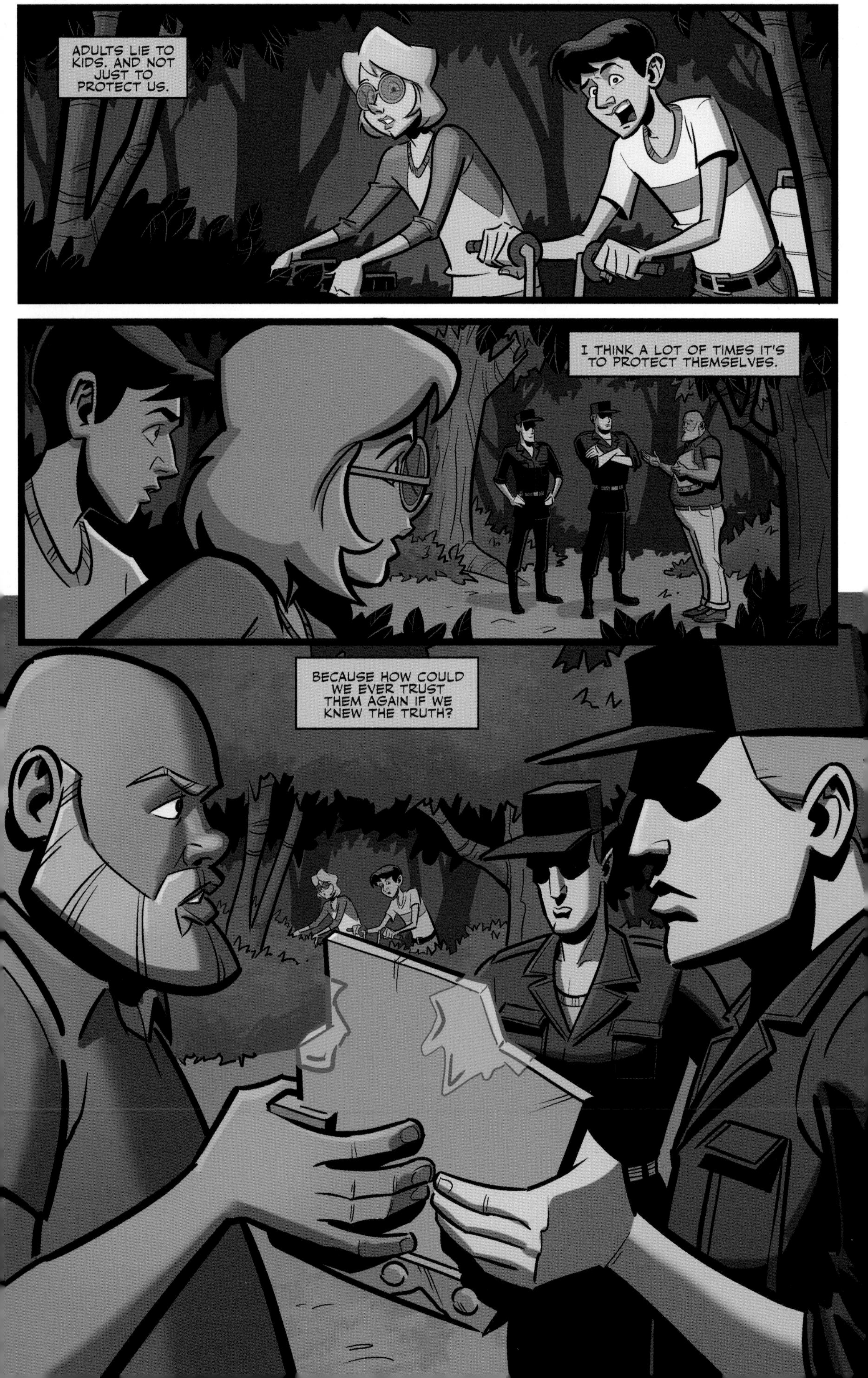

ADULTS LIE TO KIDS. AND NOT JUST TO PROTECT US.
I THINK A LOT OF TIMES IT'S TO PROTECT THEMSELVES.
BECAUSE HOW COULD WE EVER TRUST THEM AGAIN IF WE KNEW THE TRUTH?

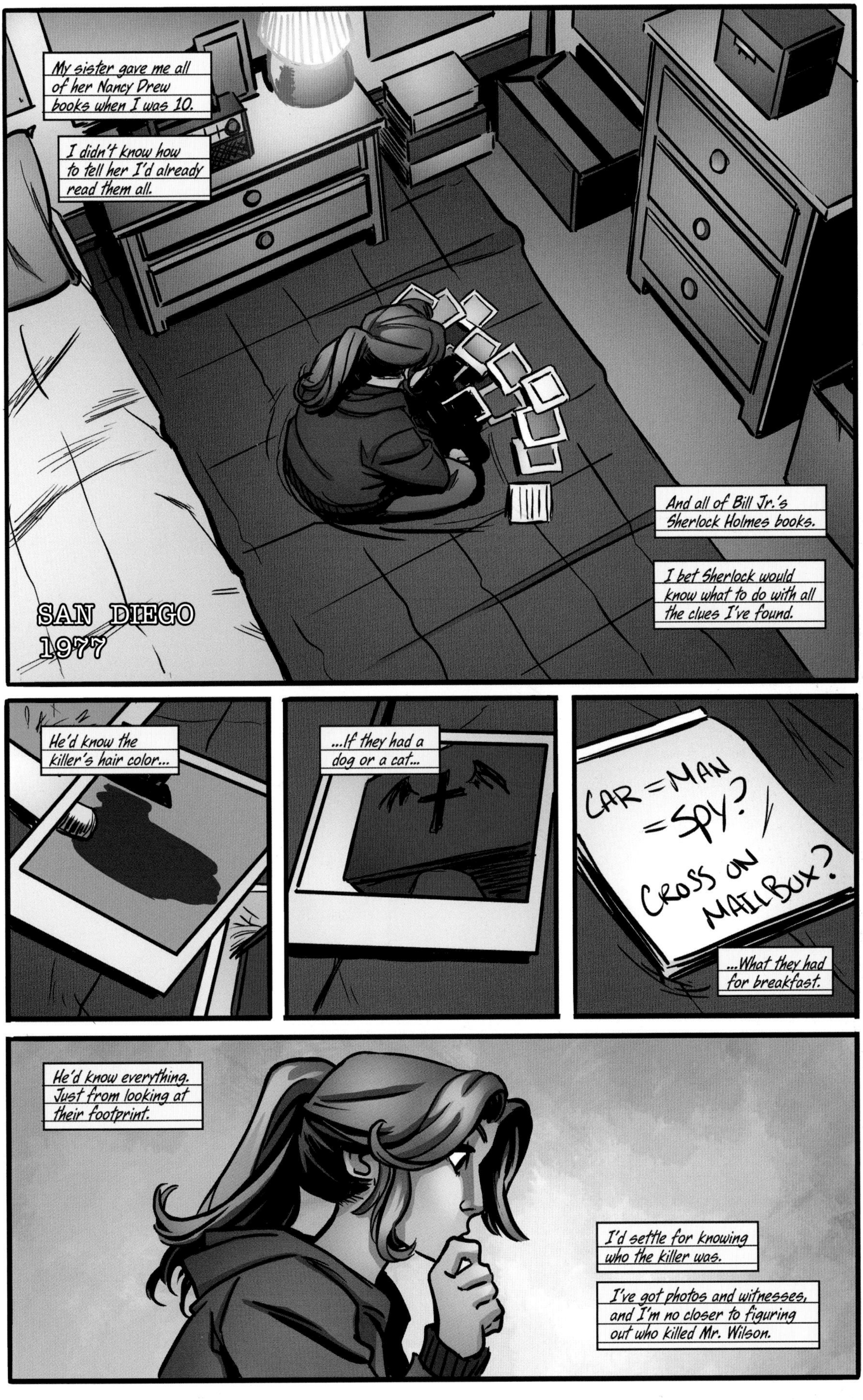
My sister gave me all of her Nancy Drew books when I was 10.
I didn't know how to tell her I'd already read them all.
SAN DIEGO 1977
And all of Bill Jr.'s Sherlock Holmes books.
I bet Sherlock would know what to do with all the clues I've found.
He'd know the killer's hair color...
...If they had a dog or a cat...
CAR = MAN = SPY? CROSS ON MAILBOX?
...What they had for breakfast.
He'd know everything. Just from looking at their footprint.
I'd settle for knowing who the killer was.
I've got photos and witnesses, and I'm no closer to figuring out who killed Mr. Wilson.

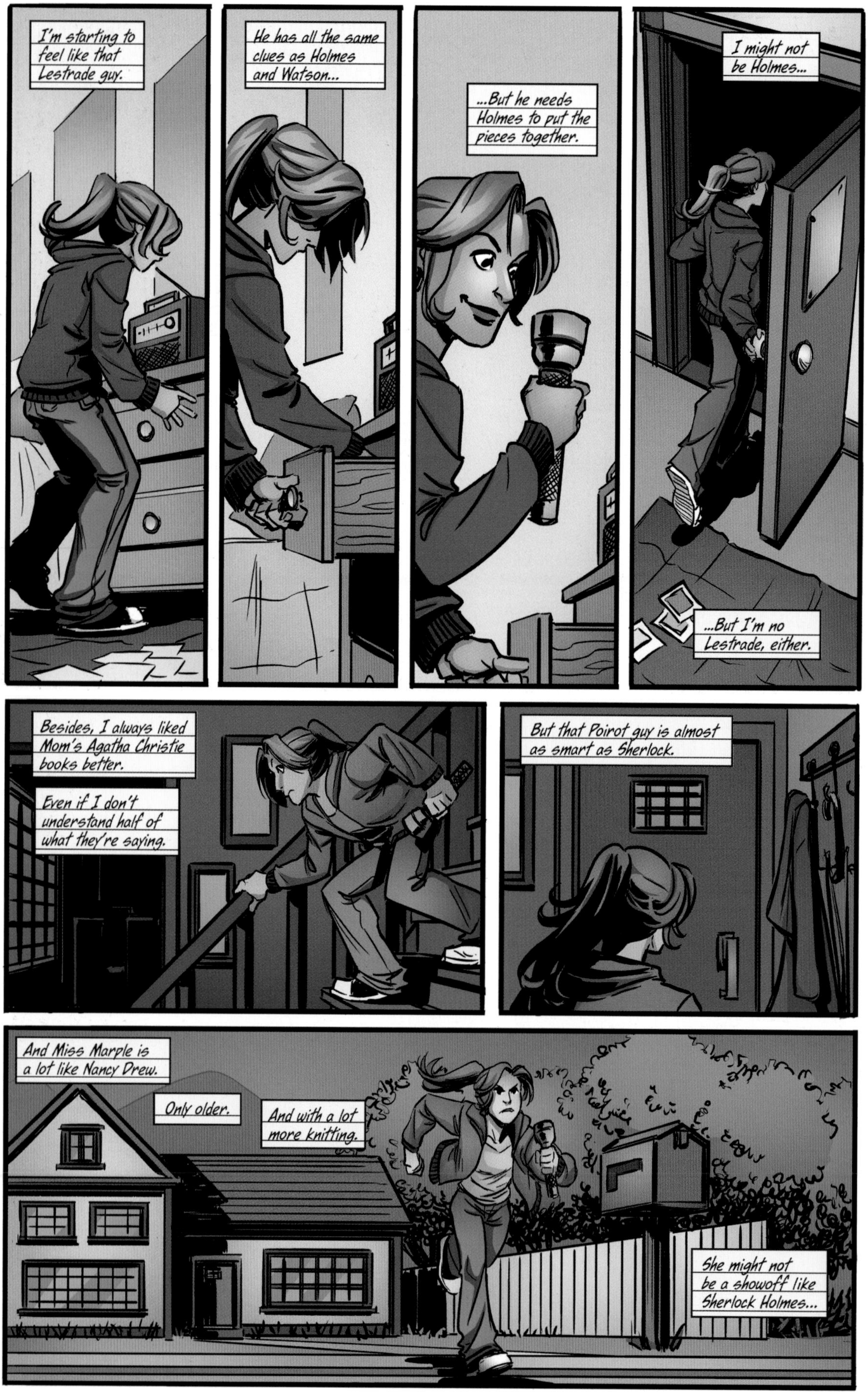
I'm starting to feel like that Lestrade guy.
He has all the same clues as Holmes and Watson...
...But he needs Holmes to put the pieces together.
I might not be Holmes...
...But I'm no Lestrade, either.
Besides, I always liked Mom's Agatha Christie books better.
Even if I don't understand half of what they're saying.
But that Poirot guy is almost as smart as Sherlock.
And Miss Marple is a lot like Nancy Drew.
Only older.
And with a lot more knitting.
She might not be a showoff like Sherlock Holmes...

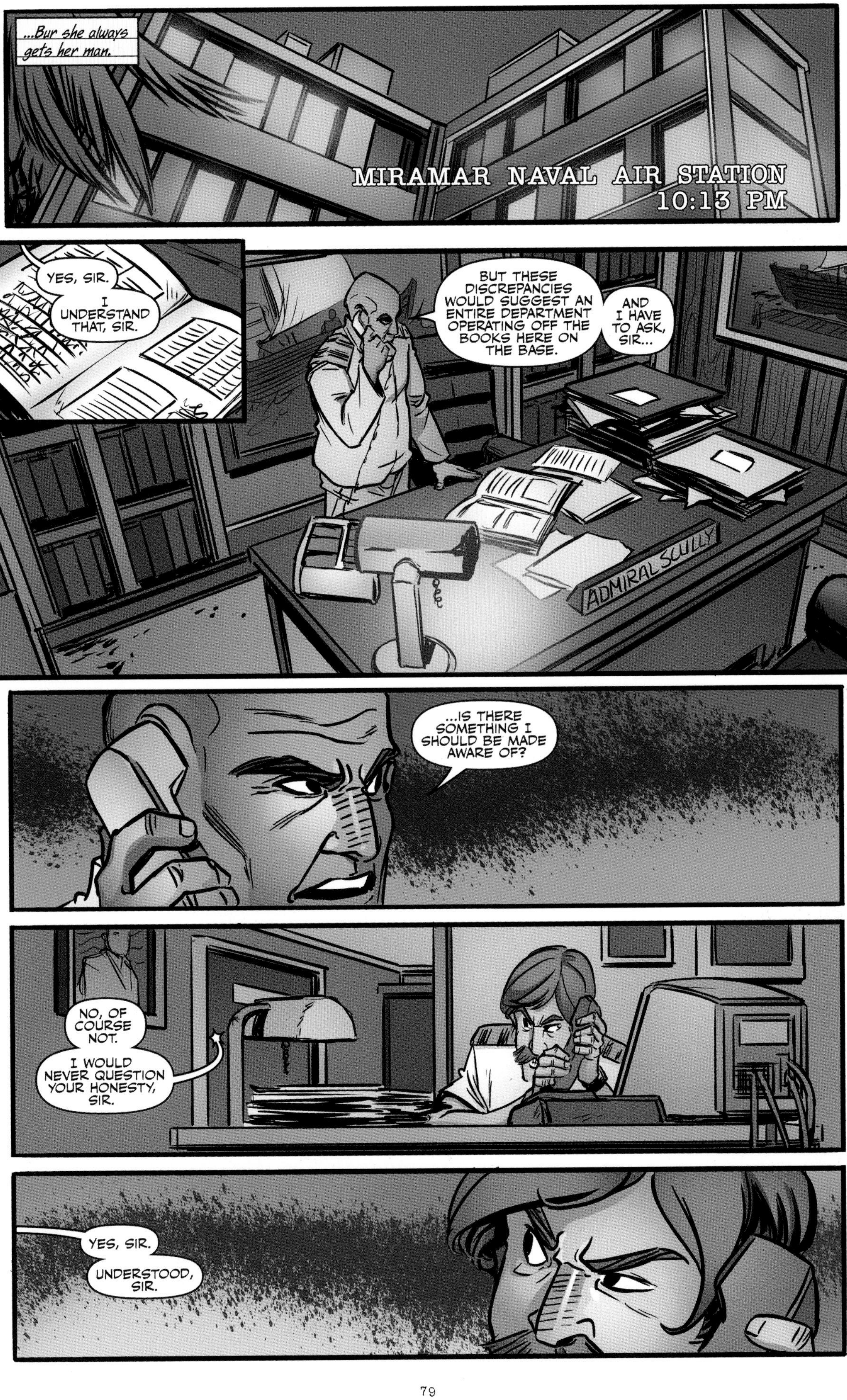
...Bur she always gets her man.
MIRAMAR NAVAL AIR STATION 10:13 PM
YES, SIR.
I UNDERSTAND THAT, SIR.
BUT THESE DISCREPANCIES WOULD SUGGEST AN ENTIRE DEPARTMENT OPERATING OFF THE BOOKS HERE ON THE BASE.
AND I HAVE TO ASK, SIR...
ADMIRAL SCULLY
...IS THERE SOMETHING I SHOULD BE MADE AWARE OF?
NO, OF COURSE NOT.
I WOULD NEVER QUESTION YOUR HONESTY, SIR.
YES, SIR.
UNDERSTOOD, SIR.

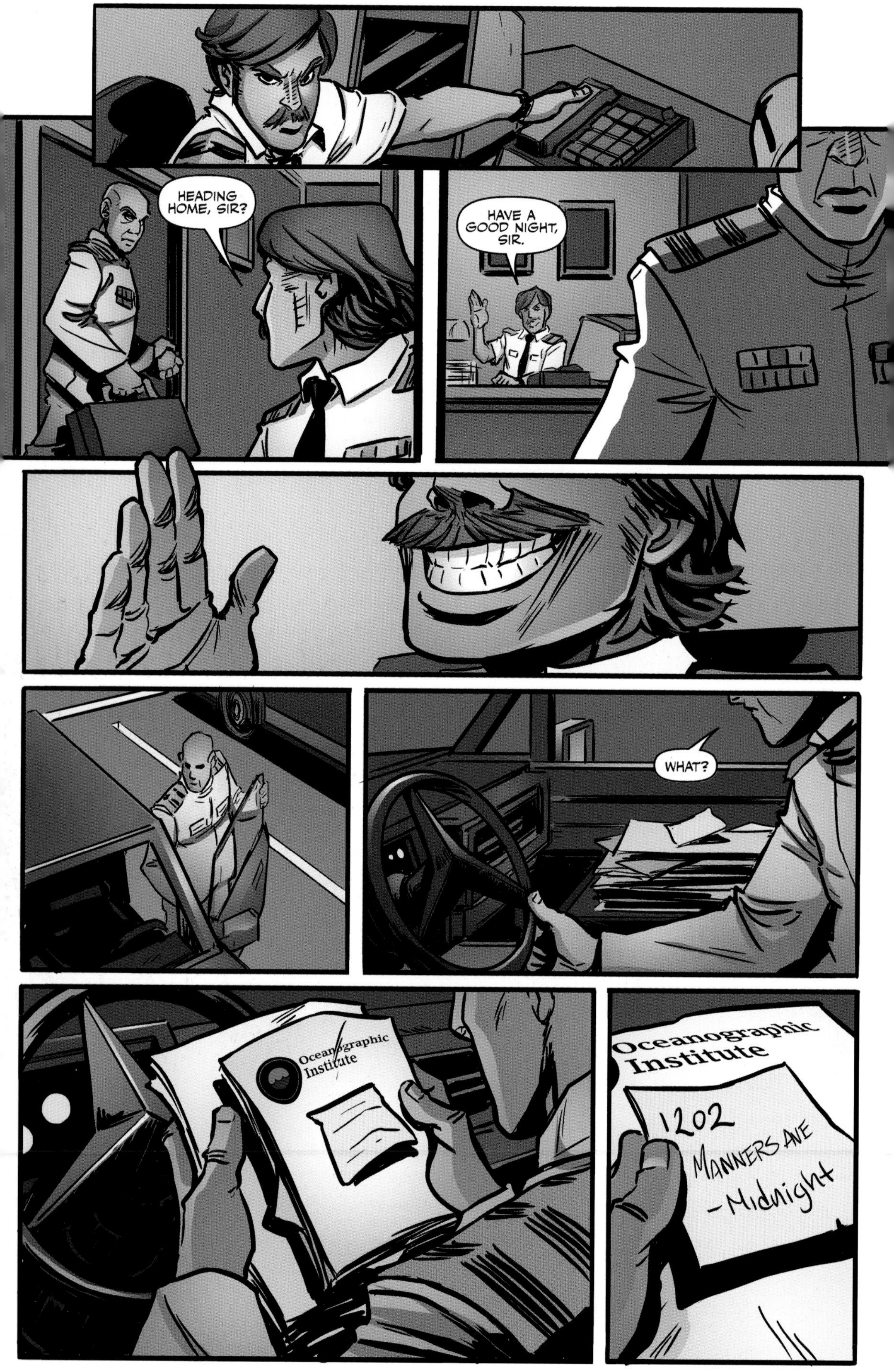
HEADING HOME, SIR?
HAVE A GOOD NIGHT, SIR.
WHAT?
Oceanographic Institute
Oceanographic Institute
1202 MANNERS AVE -Midnight

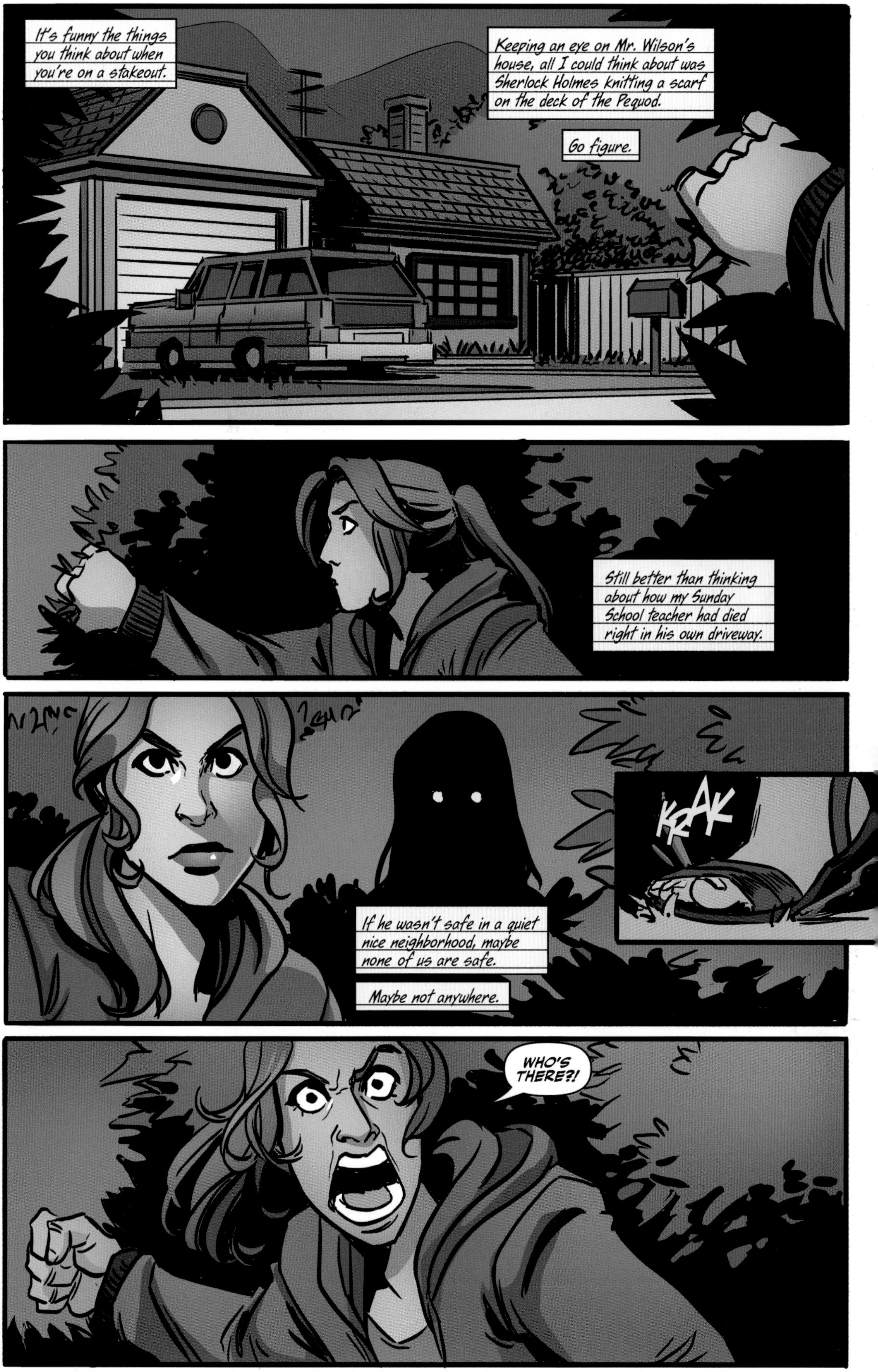
It's funny the things you think about when you're on a stakeout.
Keeping an eye on Mr. Wilson's house, all I could think about was Sherlock Holmes knitting a scarf on the deck of the Pequod.
Go figure.
Still better than thinking about how my Sunday School teacher had died right in his own driveway.
If he wasn't safe in a quiet nice neighborhood, maybe none of us are safe.
Maybe not anywhere.
KRAK
WHO'S THERE?!

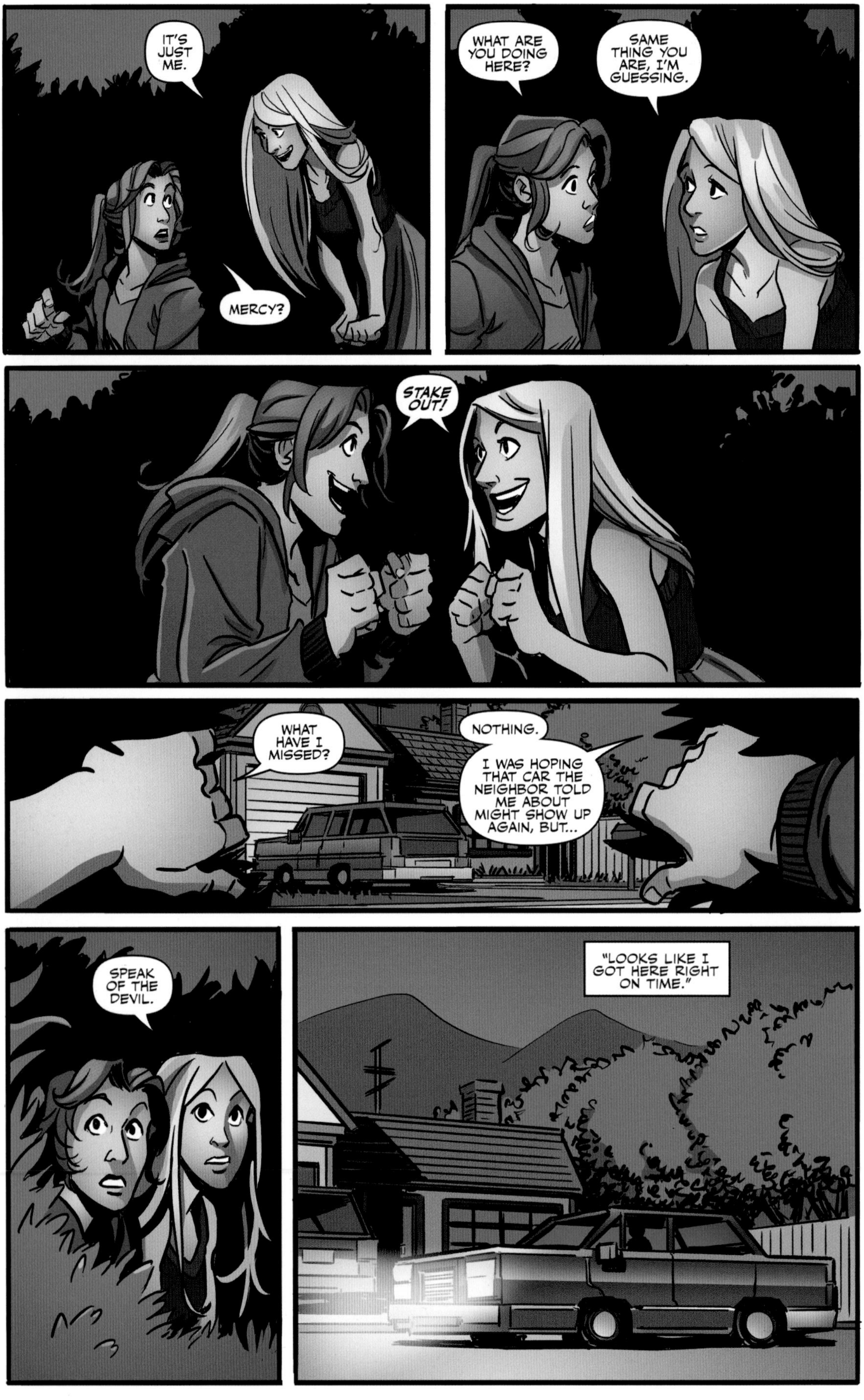
IT'S JUST ME.
MERCY?
WHAT ARE YOU DOING HERE?
SAME THING YOU ARE, I'M GUESSING.
STAKE OUT!
WHAT HAVE I MISSED?
NOTHING.
I WAS HOPING THAT CAR THE NEIGHBOR TOLD ME ABOUT MIGHT SHOW UP AGAIN, BUT...
SPEAK OF THE DEVIL.
"LOOKS LIKE I GOT HERE RIGHT ON TIME."

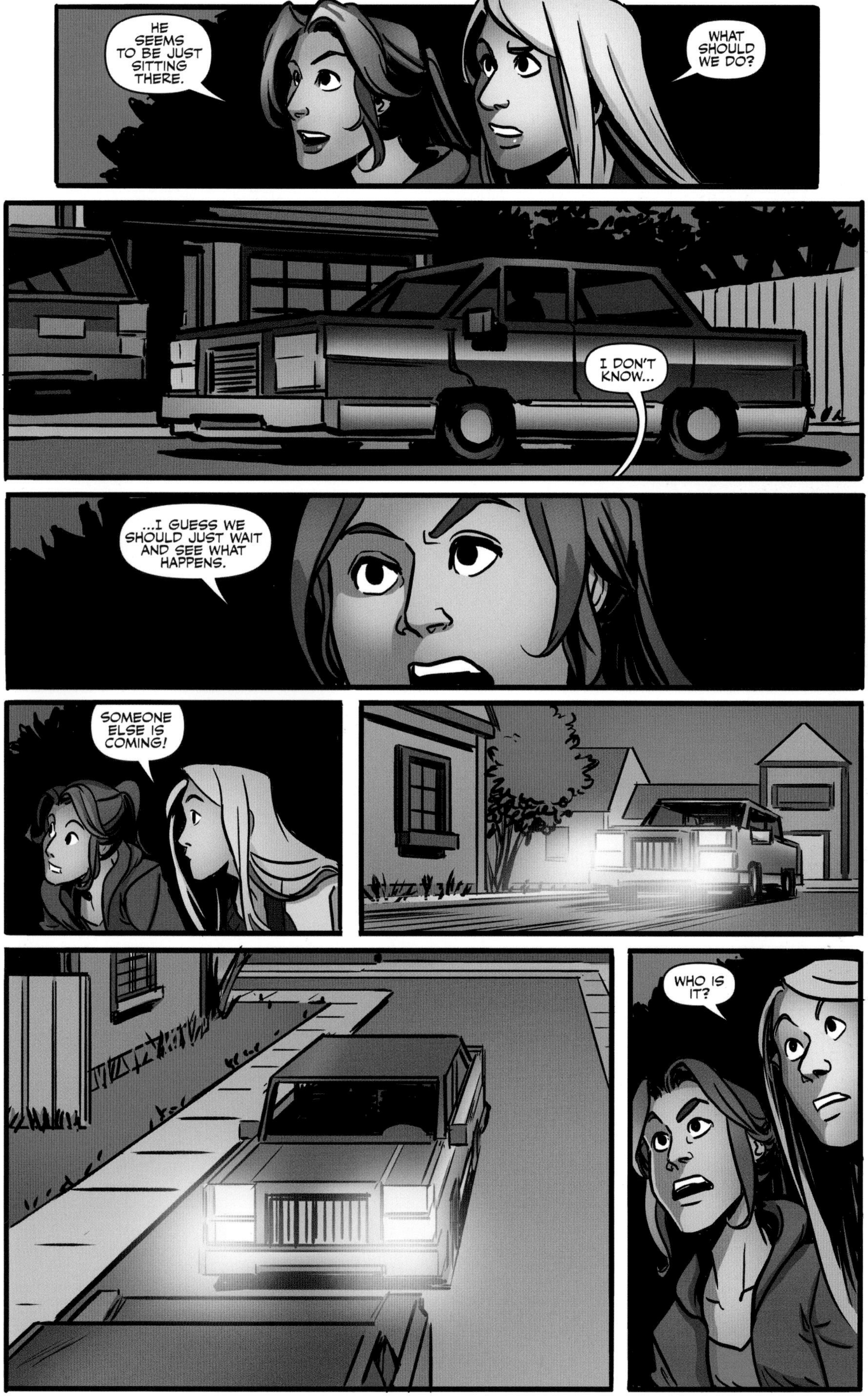
HE SEEMS TO BE JUST SITTING THERE.
WHAT SHOULD WE DO?
I DON'T KNOW...
...I GUESS WE SHOULD JUST WAIT AND SEE WHAT HAPPENS.
SOMEONE ELSE IS COMING!
WHO IS IT?

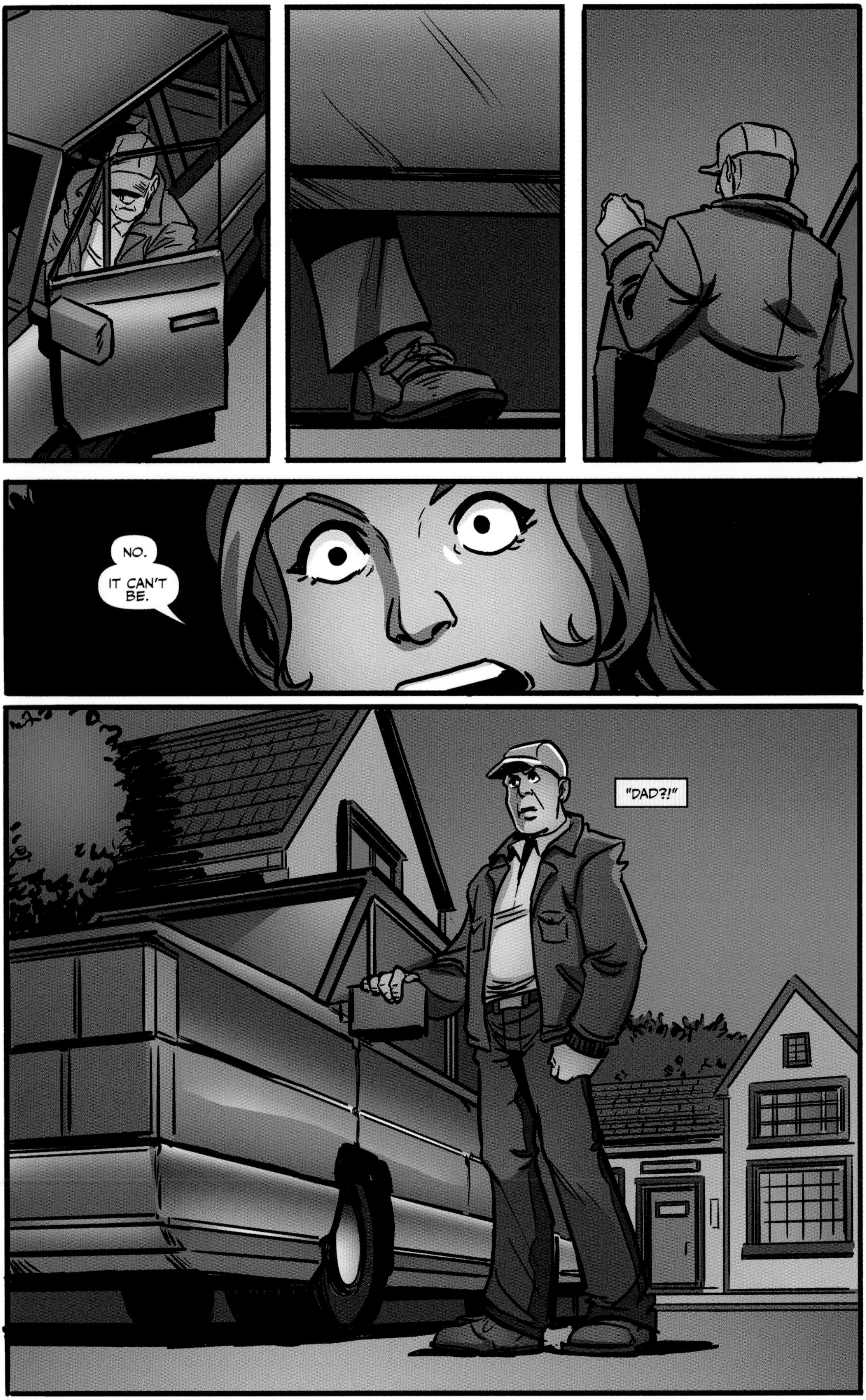
NO.
IT CAN'T BE.
"DAD?!"

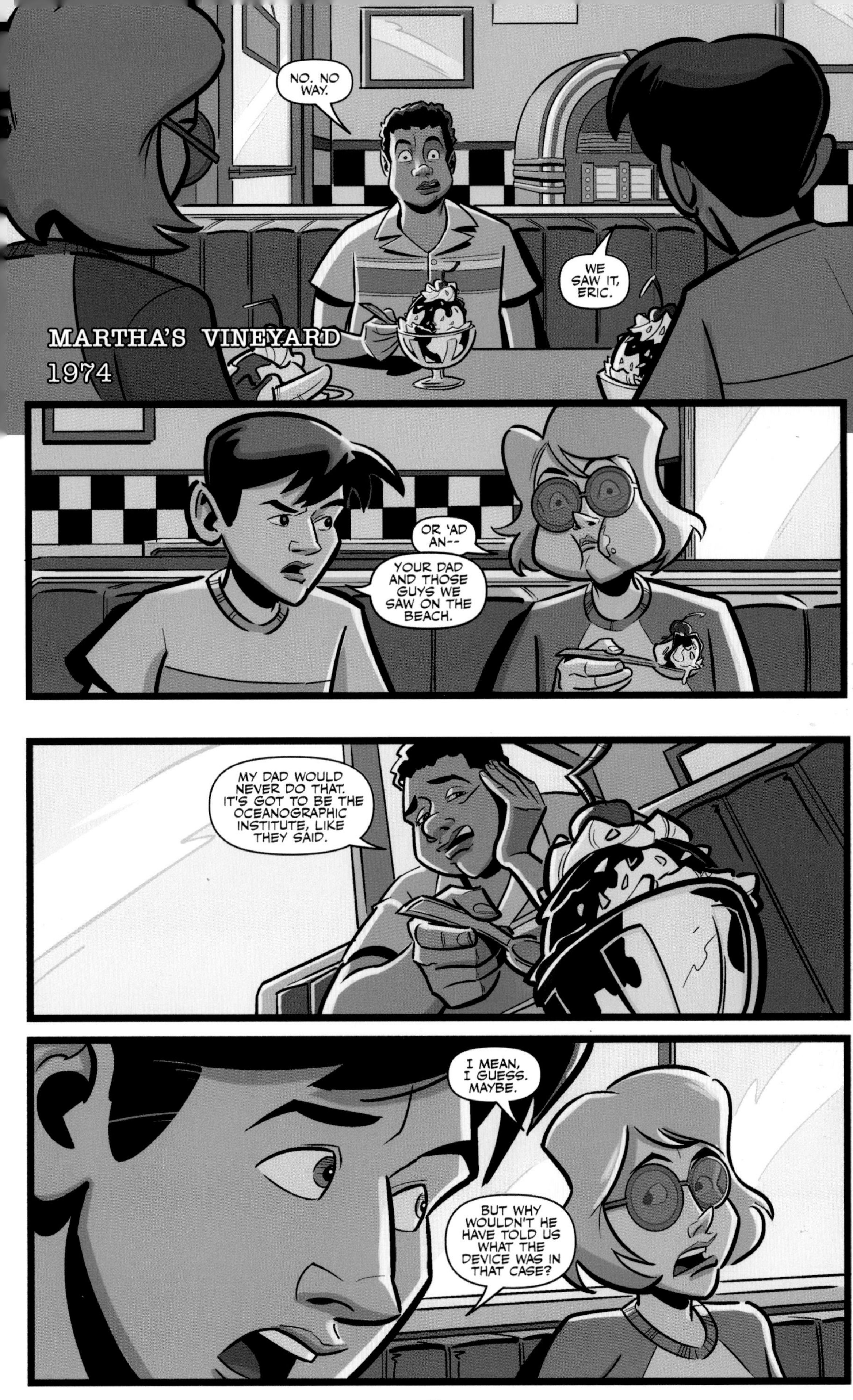
NO. NO WAY.
WE SAW IT, ERIC.
MARTHA'S VINEYARD
1974
OR 'AD AN--
YOUR DAD AND THOSE GUYS WE SAW ON THE BEACH.
MY DAD WOULD NEVER DO THAT. IT'S GOT TO BE THE OCEANOGRAPHIC INSTITUTE, LIKE THEY SAID.
I MEAN, I GUESS. MAYBE.
BUT WHY WOULDN'T HE HAVE TOLD US WHAT THE DEVICE WAS IN THAT CASE?

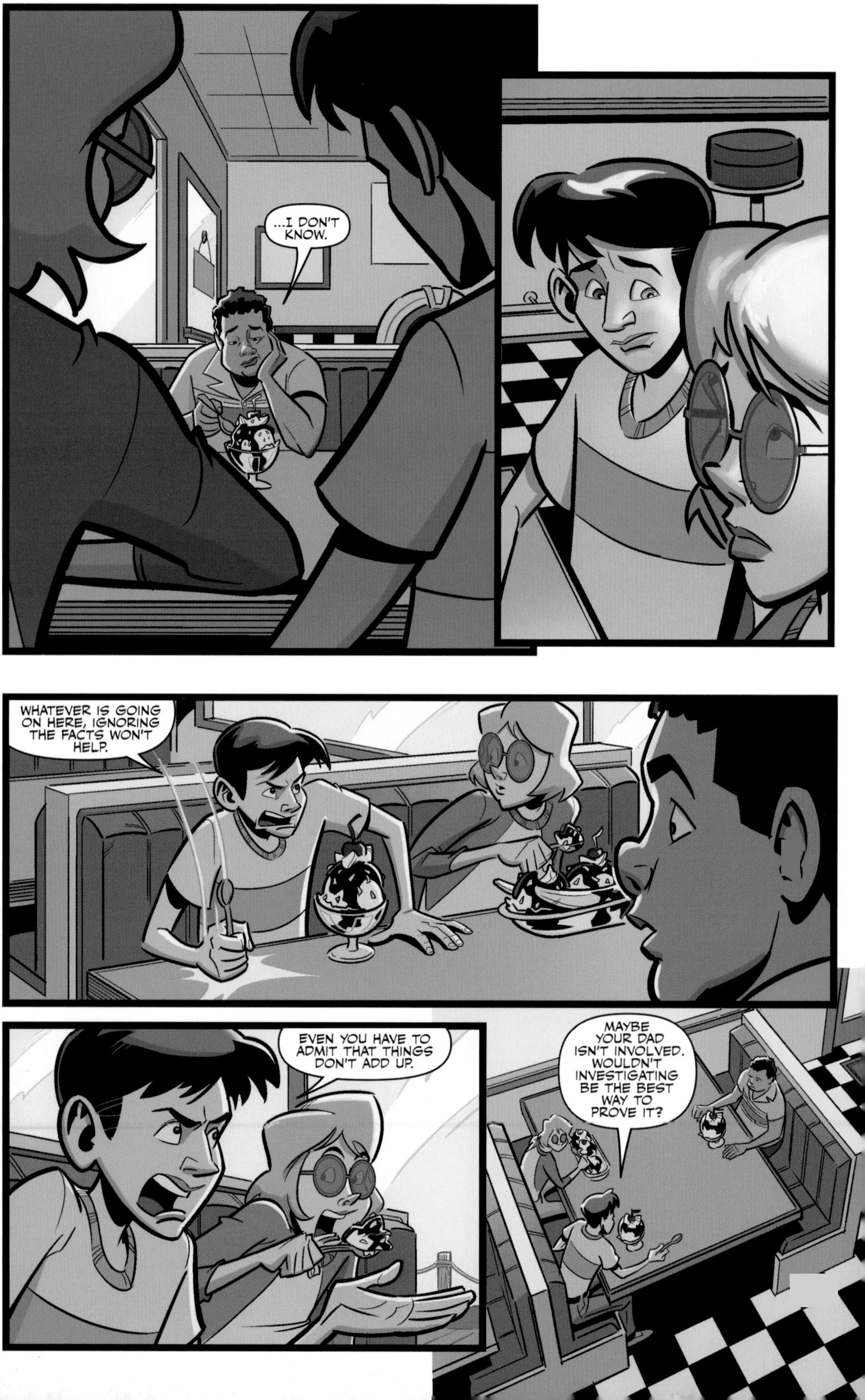
...I DON'T KNOW.
WHATEVER IS GOING ON HERE, IGNORING THE FACTS WON'T HELP.
EVEN YOU HAVE TO ADMIT THAT THINGS DON'T ADD UP.
MAYBE YOUR DAD ISN'T INVOLVED. WOULDN'T INVESTIGATING BE THE BEST WAY TO PROVE IT?

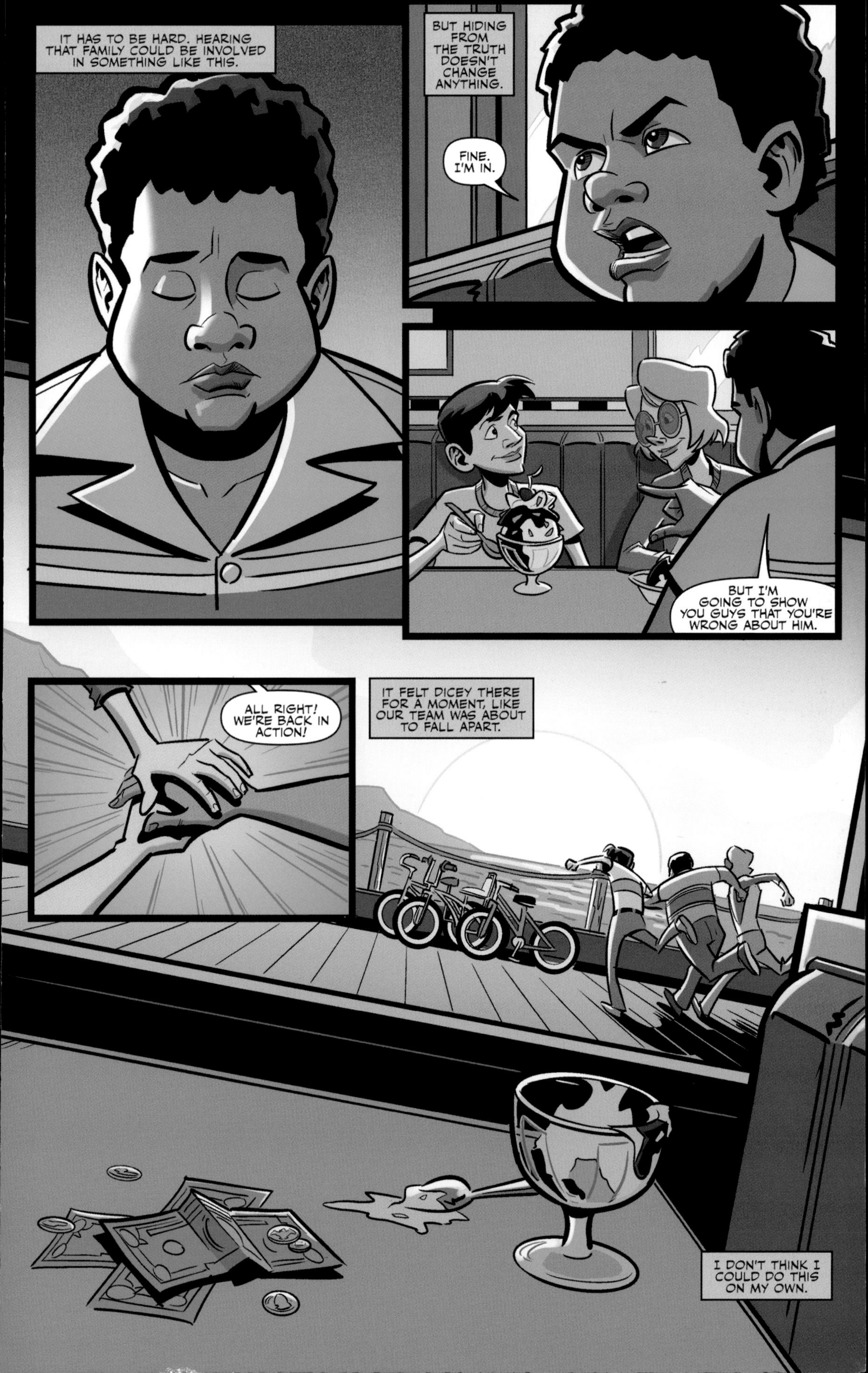
IT HAS TO BE HARD. HEARING THAT FAMILY COULD BE INVOLVED IN SOMETHING LIKE THIS.
BUT HIDING FROM THE TRUTH DOESN'T CHANGE ANYTHING.
FINE. I'M IN.
BUT I'M GOING TO SHOW YOU GUYS THAT YOU'RE WRONG ABOUT HIM.
ALL RIGHT! WE'RE BACK IN ACTION!
IT FELT DICEY THERE FOR A MOMENT, LIKE OUR TEAM WAS ABOUT TO FALL APART.
I DON'T THINK I COULD DO THIS ON MY OWN.

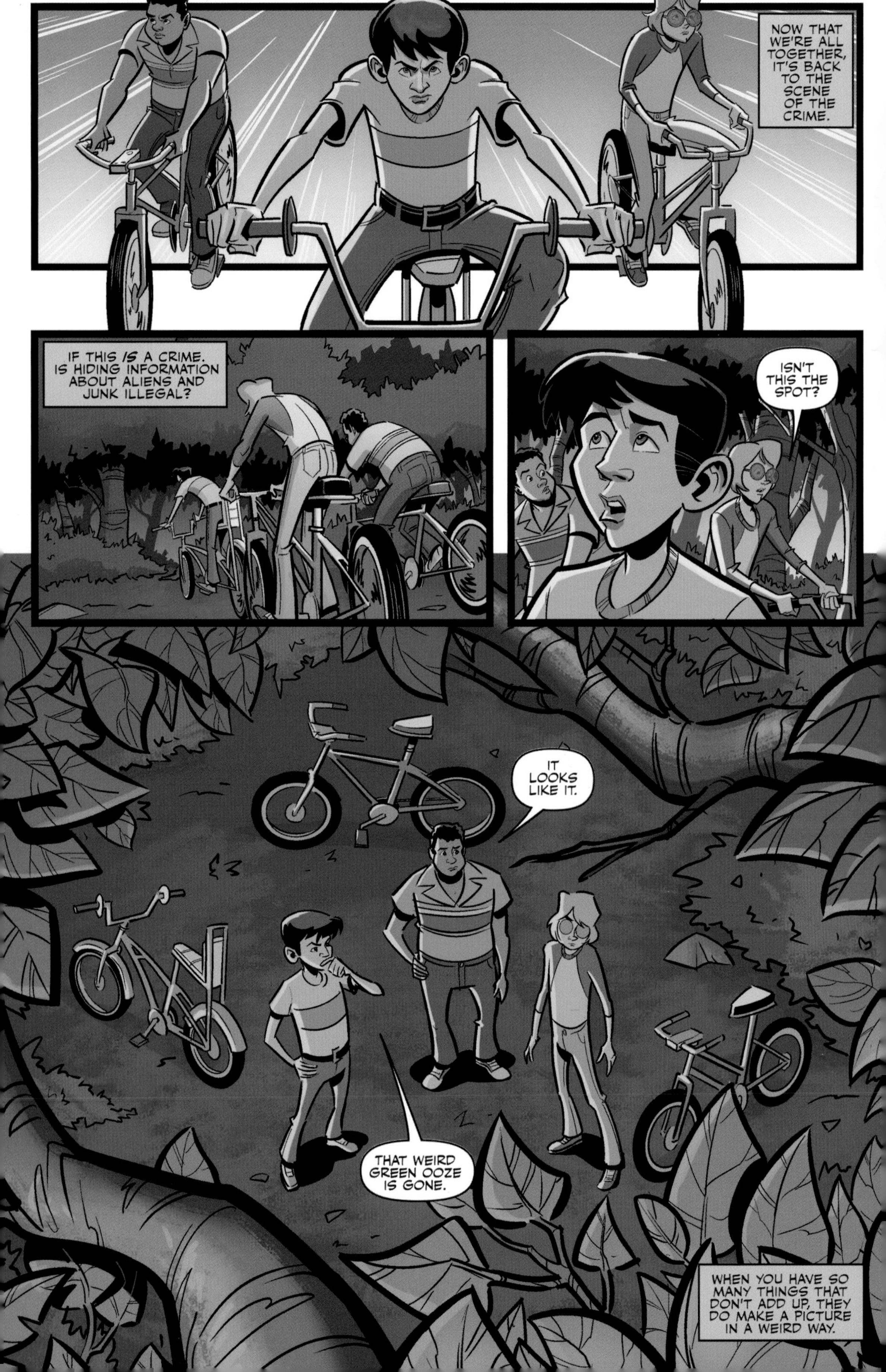
NOW THAT WE'RE ALL TOGETHER, IT'S BACK TO THE SCENE OF THE CRIME.
IF THIS *IS* A CRIME. IS HIDING INFORMATION ABOUT ALIENS AND JUNK ILLEGAL?
ISN'T THIS THE SPOT?
IT LOOKS LIKE IT.
THAT WEIRD GREEN OOZE IS GONE.
WHEN YOU HAVE SO MANY THINGS THAT DON'T ADD UP, THEY DO MAKE A PICTURE IN A WEIRD WAY.

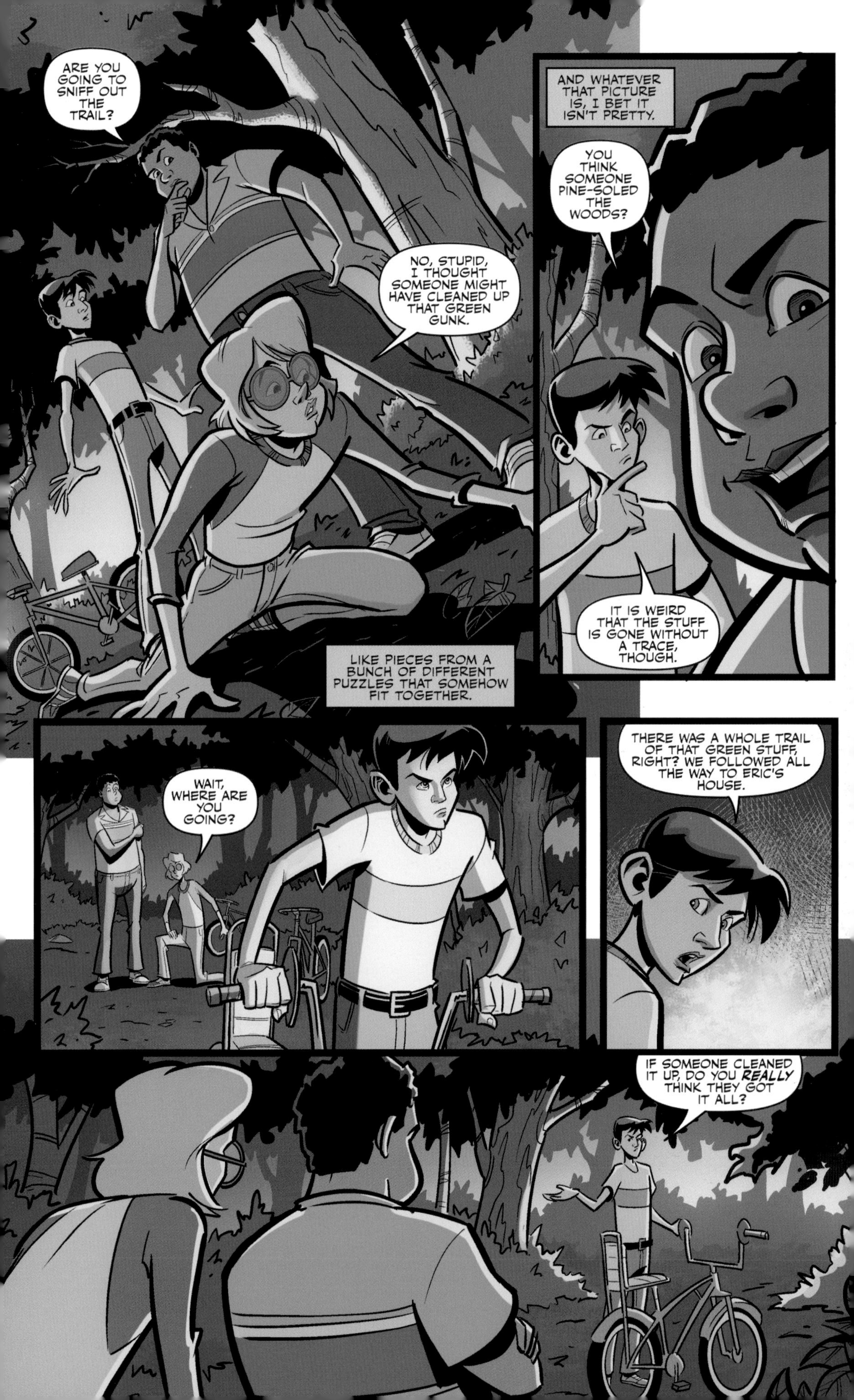
ARE YOU GOING TO SNIFF OUT THE TRAIL?
NO, STUPID, I THOUGHT SOMEONE MIGHT HAVE CLEANED UP THAT GREEN GUNK.
LIKE PIECES FROM A BUNCH OF DIFFERENT PUZZLES THAT SOMEHOW FIT TOGETHER.
AND WHATEVER THAT PICTURE IS, I BET IT ISN'T PRETTY.
YOU THINK SOMEONE PINE-SOLED THE WOODS?
IT IS WEIRD THAT THE STUFF IS GONE WITHOUT A TRACE, THOUGH.
WAIT, WHERE ARE YOU GOING?
THERE WAS A WHOLE TRAIL OF THAT GREEN STUFF, RIGHT? WE FOLLOWED ALL THE WAY TO ERIC'S HOUSE.
IF SOMEONE CLEANED IT UP, DO YOU *REALLY* THINK THEY GOT IT ALL?

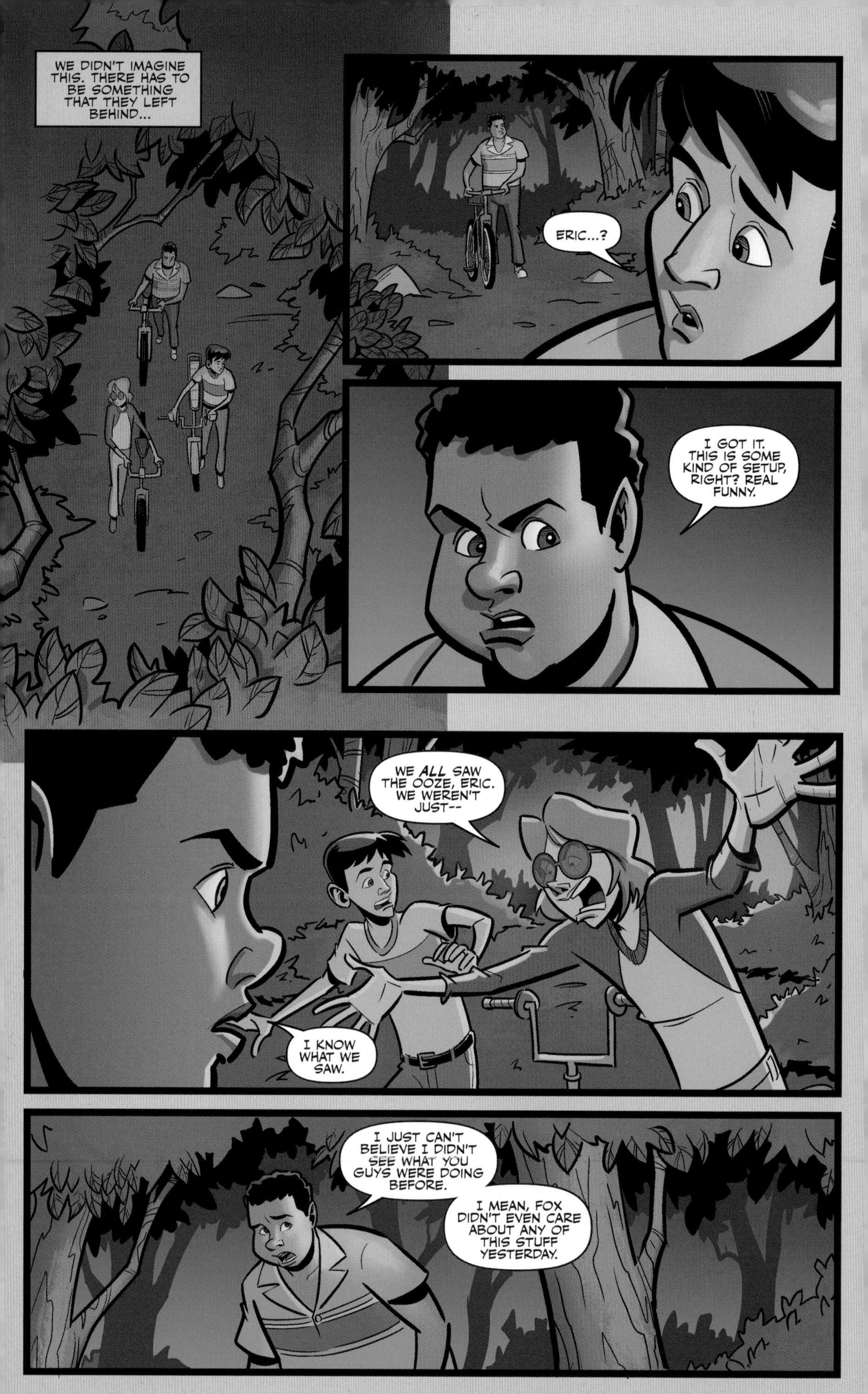
WE DIDN'T IMAGINE THIS. THERE HAS TO BE SOMETHING THAT THEY LEFT BEHIND...
ERIC...?
I GOT IT. THIS IS SOME KIND OF SETUP, RIGHT? REAL FUNNY.
WE *ALL* SAW THE OOZE, ERIC. WE WEREN'T JUST--
I KNOW WHAT WE SAW.
I JUST CAN'T BELIEVE I DIDN'T SEE WHAT YOU GUYS WERE DOING BEFORE.
I MEAN, FOX DIDN'T EVEN CARE ABOUT ANY OF THIS STUFF YESTERDAY.

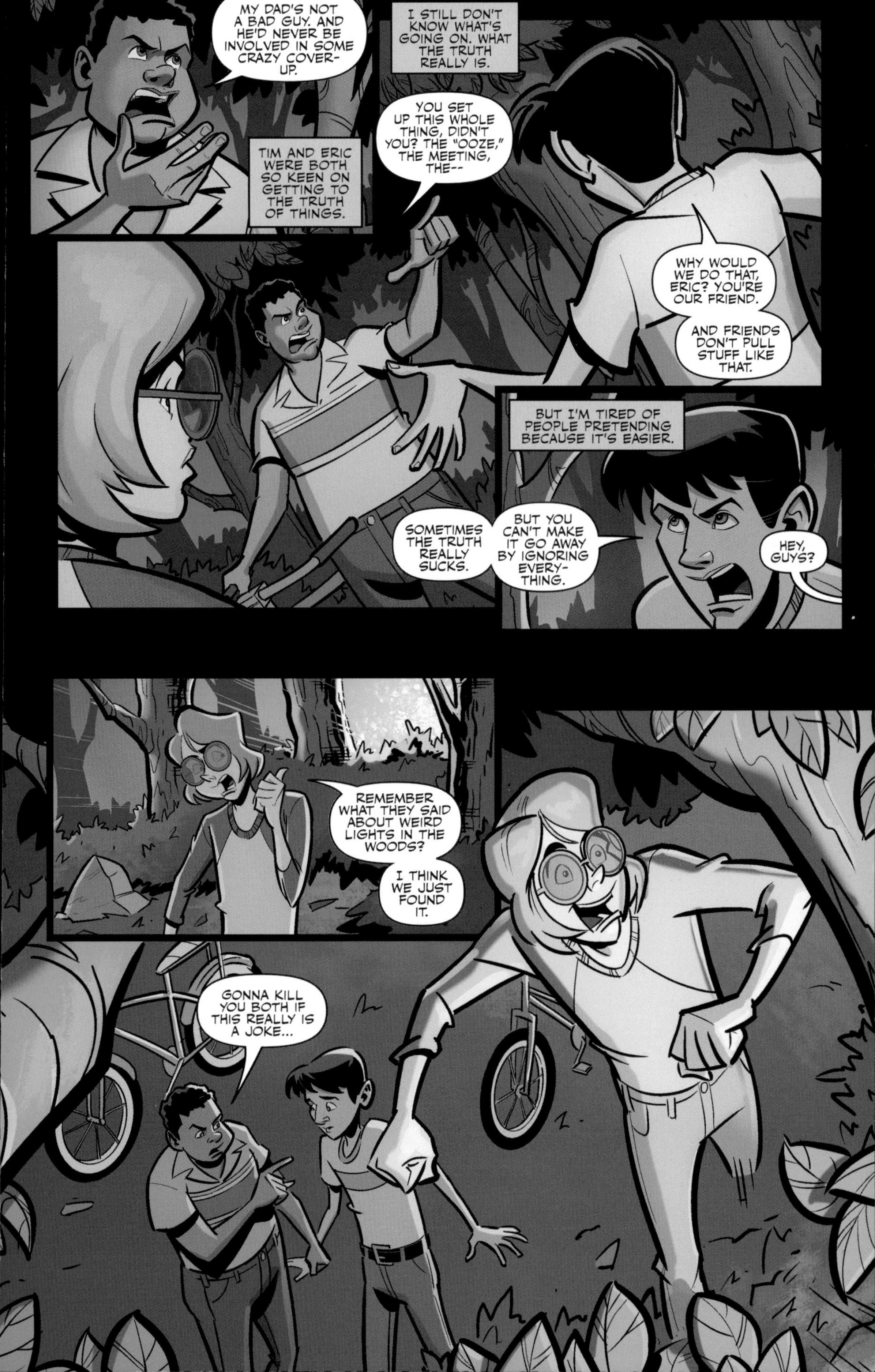
MY DAD'S NOT A BAD GUY. AND HE'D NEVER BE INVOLVED IN SOME CRAZY COVER-UP.
TIM AND ERIC WERE BOTH SO KEEN ON GETTING TO THE TRUTH OF THINGS.
I STILL DON'T KNOW WHAT'S GOING ON. WHAT THE TRUTH REALLY IS.
YOU SET UP THIS WHOLE THING, DIDN'T YOU? THE "OOZE," THE MEETING, THE--
WHY WOULD WE DO THAT, ERIC? YOU'RE OUR FRIEND.
AND FRIENDS DON'T PULL STUFF LIKE THAT.
BUT I'M TIRED OF PEOPLE PRETENDING BECAUSE IT'S EASIER.
SOMETIMES THE TRUTH REALLY SUCKS.
BUT YOU CAN'T MAKE IT GO AWAY BY IGNORING EVERY-THING.
HEY, GUYS?
REMEMBER WHAT THEY SAID ABOUT WEIRD LIGHTS IN THE WOODS?
I THINK WE JUST FOUND IT.
GONNA KILL YOU BOTH IF THIS REALLY IS A JOKE...

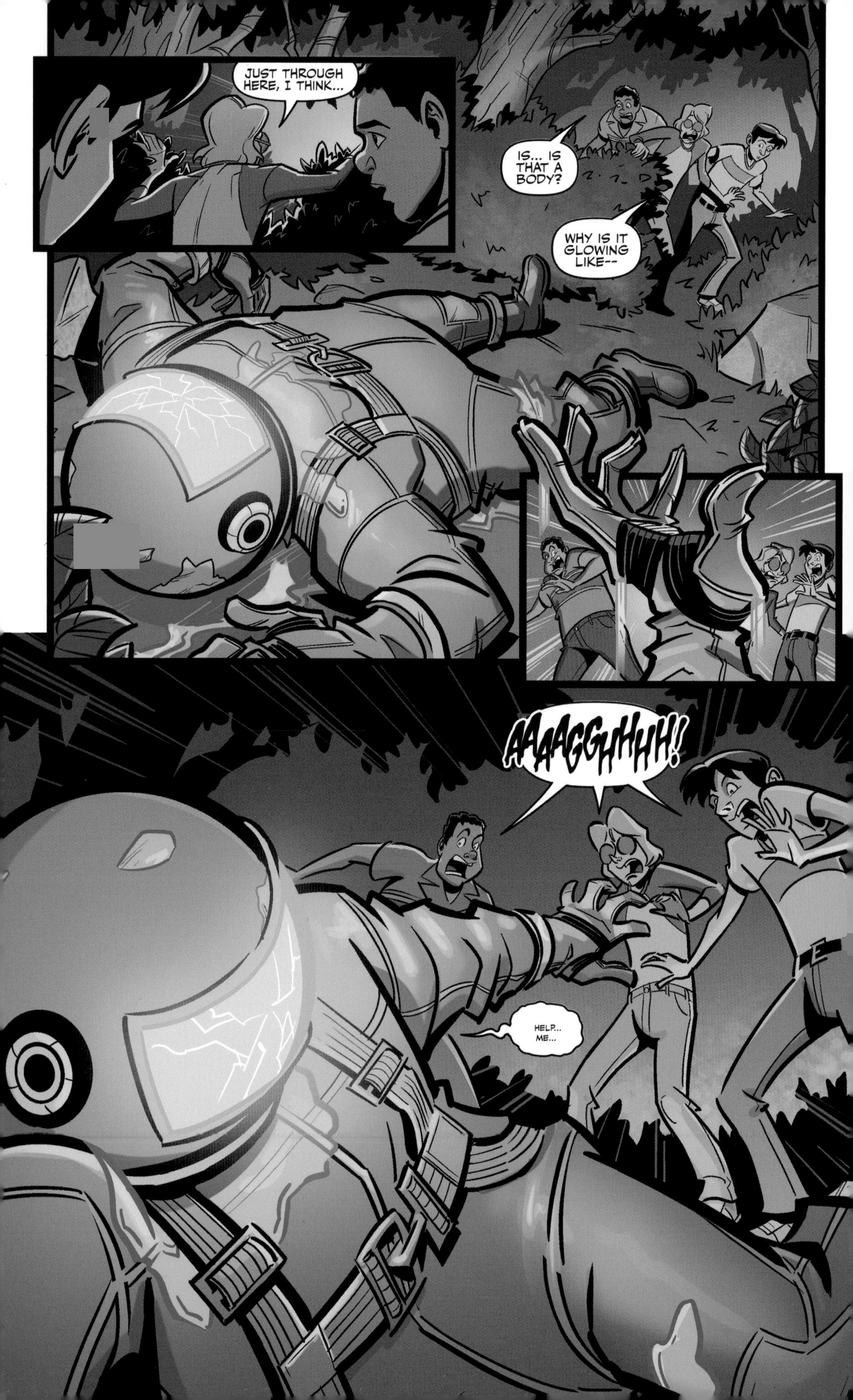
JUST THROUGH HERE, I THINK...
IS... IS THAT A BODY?
WHY IS IT GLOWING LIKE--
AAAAGGHHHH!
HELP... ME...

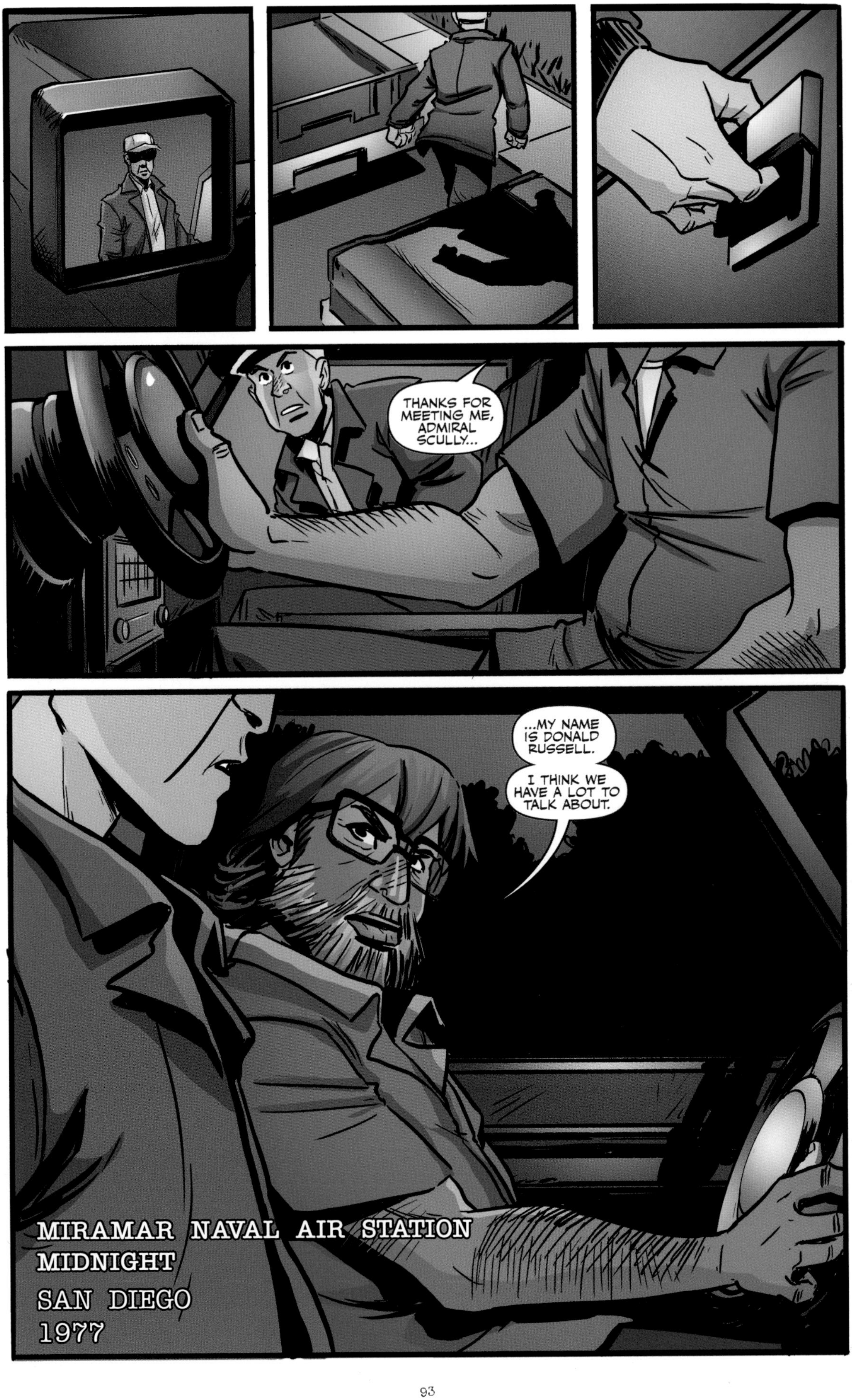
THANKS FOR MEETING ME, ADMIRAL SCULLY...
...MY NAME IS DONALD RUSSELL.
I THINK WE HAVE A LOT TO TALK ABOUT.
MIRAMAR NAVAL AIR STATION
MIDNIGHT
SAN DIEGO
1977

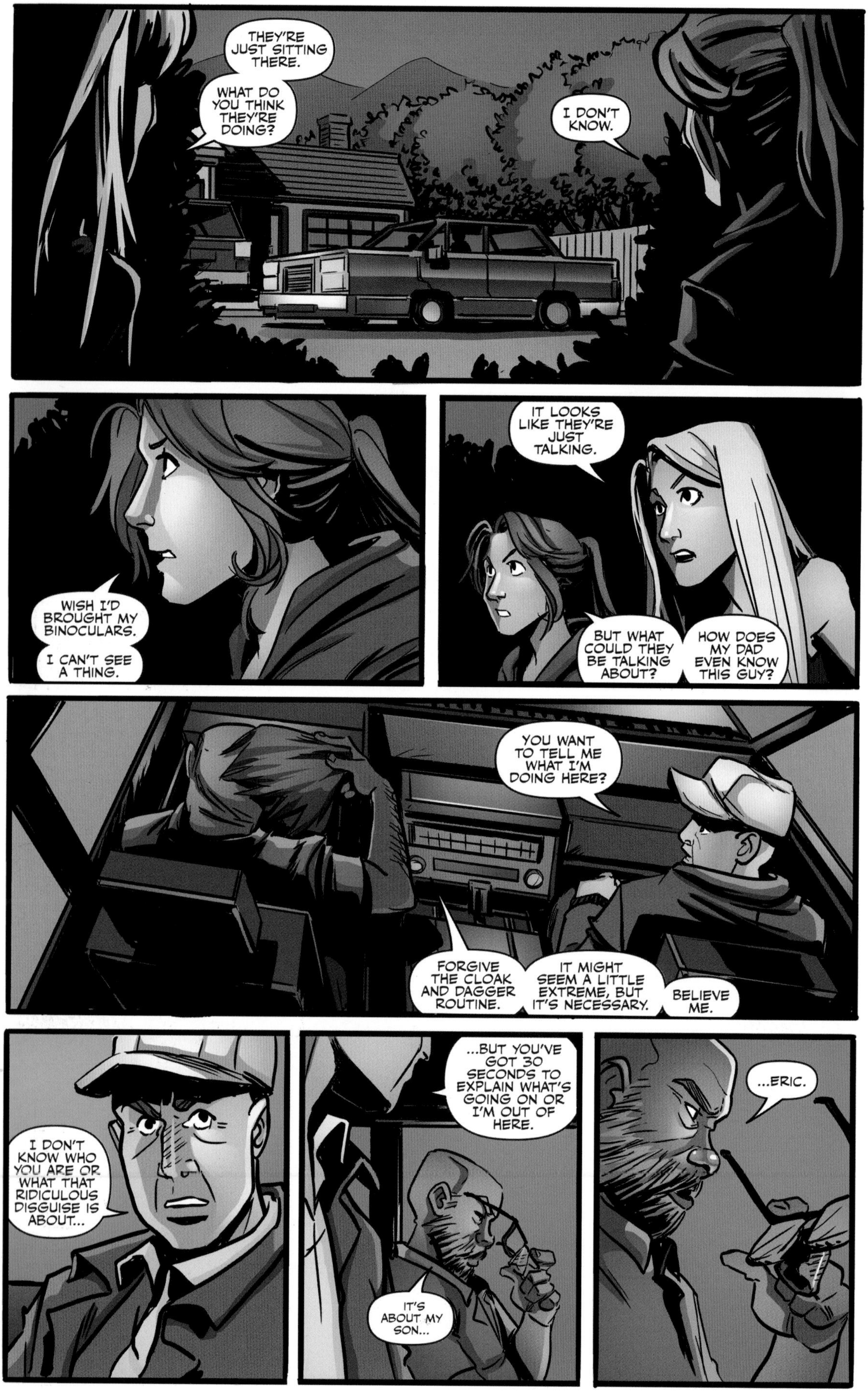
THEY'RE JUST SITTING THERE.
WHAT DO YOU THINK THEY'RE DOING?
I DON'T KNOW.
WISH I'D BROUGHT MY BINOCULARS.
I CAN'T SEE A THING.
IT LOOKS LIKE THEY'RE JUST TALKING.
BUT WHAT COULD THEY BE TALKING ABOUT?
HOW DOES MY DAD EVEN KNOW THIS GUY?
YOU WANT TO TELL ME WHAT I'M DOING HERE?
FORGIVE THE CLOAK AND DAGGER ROUTINE.
IT MIGHT SEEM A LITTLE EXTREME, BUT IT'S NECESSARY.
BELIEVE ME.
I DON'T KNOW WHO YOU ARE OR WHAT THAT RIDICULOUS DISGUISE IS ABOUT...
...BUT YOU'VE GOT 30 SECONDS TO EXPLAIN WHAT'S GOING ON OR I'M OUT OF HERE.
IT'S ABOUT MY SON...
...ERIC.

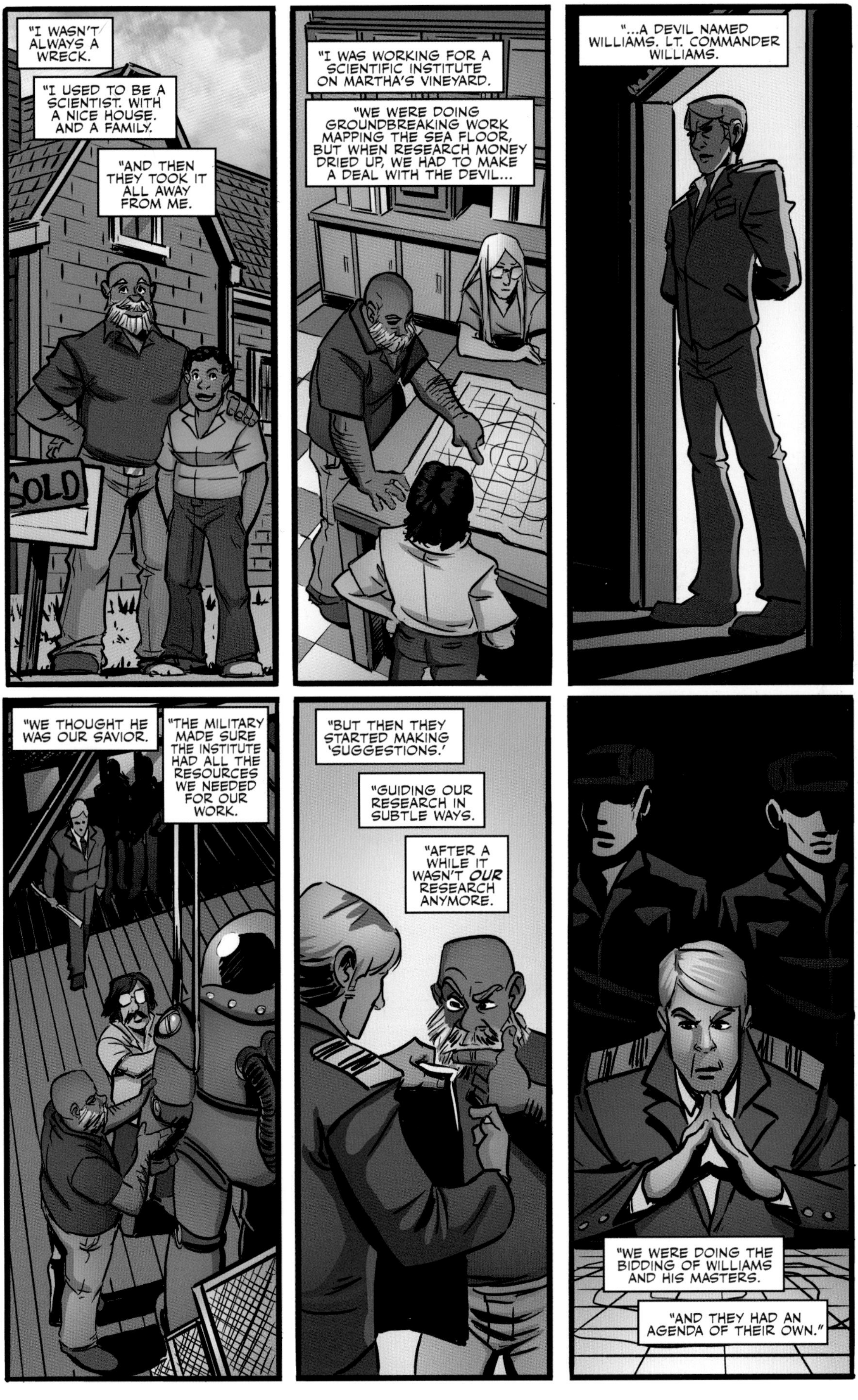
"I WASN'T ALWAYS A WRECK.
"I USED TO BE A SCIENTIST. WITH A NICE HOUSE. AND A FAMILY.
"AND THEN THEY TOOK IT ALL AWAY FROM ME.
SOLD
"I WAS WORKING FOR A SCIENTIFIC INSTITUTE ON MARTHA'S VINEYARD.
"WE WERE DOING GROUNDBREAKING WORK MAPPING THE SEA FLOOR, BUT WHEN RESEARCH MONEY DRIED UP, WE HAD TO MAKE A DEAL WITH THE DEVIL...
"...A DEVIL NAMED WILLIAMS. LT. COMMANDER WILLIAMS.
"WE THOUGHT HE WAS OUR SAVIOR.
"THE MILITARY MADE SURE THE INSTITUTE HAD ALL THE RESOURCES WE NEEDED FOR OUR WORK.
"BUT THEN THEY STARTED MAKING 'SUGGESTIONS.'
"GUIDING OUR RESEARCH IN SUBTLE WAYS.
"AFTER A WHILE IT WASN'T *OUR* RESEARCH ANYMORE.
"WE WERE DOING THE BIDDING OF WILLIAMS AND HIS MASTERS.
"AND THEY HAD AN AGENDA OF THEIR OWN."

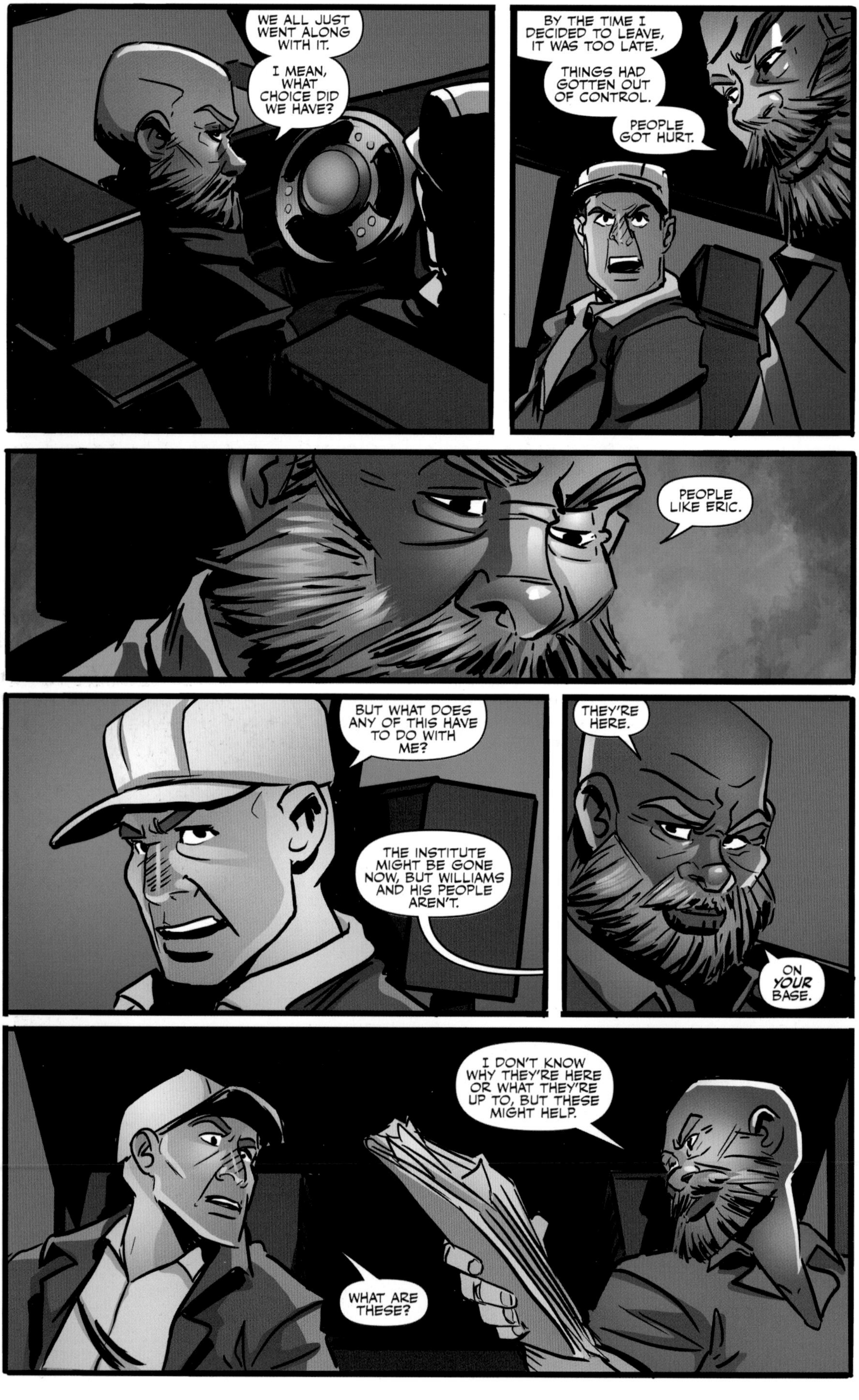
WE ALL JUST WENT ALONG WITH IT.
I MEAN, WHAT CHOICE DID WE HAVE?
BY THE TIME I DECIDED TO LEAVE, IT WAS TOO LATE.
THINGS HAD GOTTEN OUT OF CONTROL.
PEOPLE GOT HURT.
PEOPLE LIKE ERIC.
BUT WHAT DOES ANY OF THIS HAVE TO DO WITH ME?
THE INSTITUTE MIGHT BE GONE NOW, BUT WILLIAMS AND HIS PEOPLE AREN'T.
THEY'RE HERE.
ON *YOUR* BASE.
I DON'T KNOW WHY THEY'RE HERE OR WHAT THEY'RE UP TO, BUT THESE MIGHT HELP.
WHAT ARE THESE?

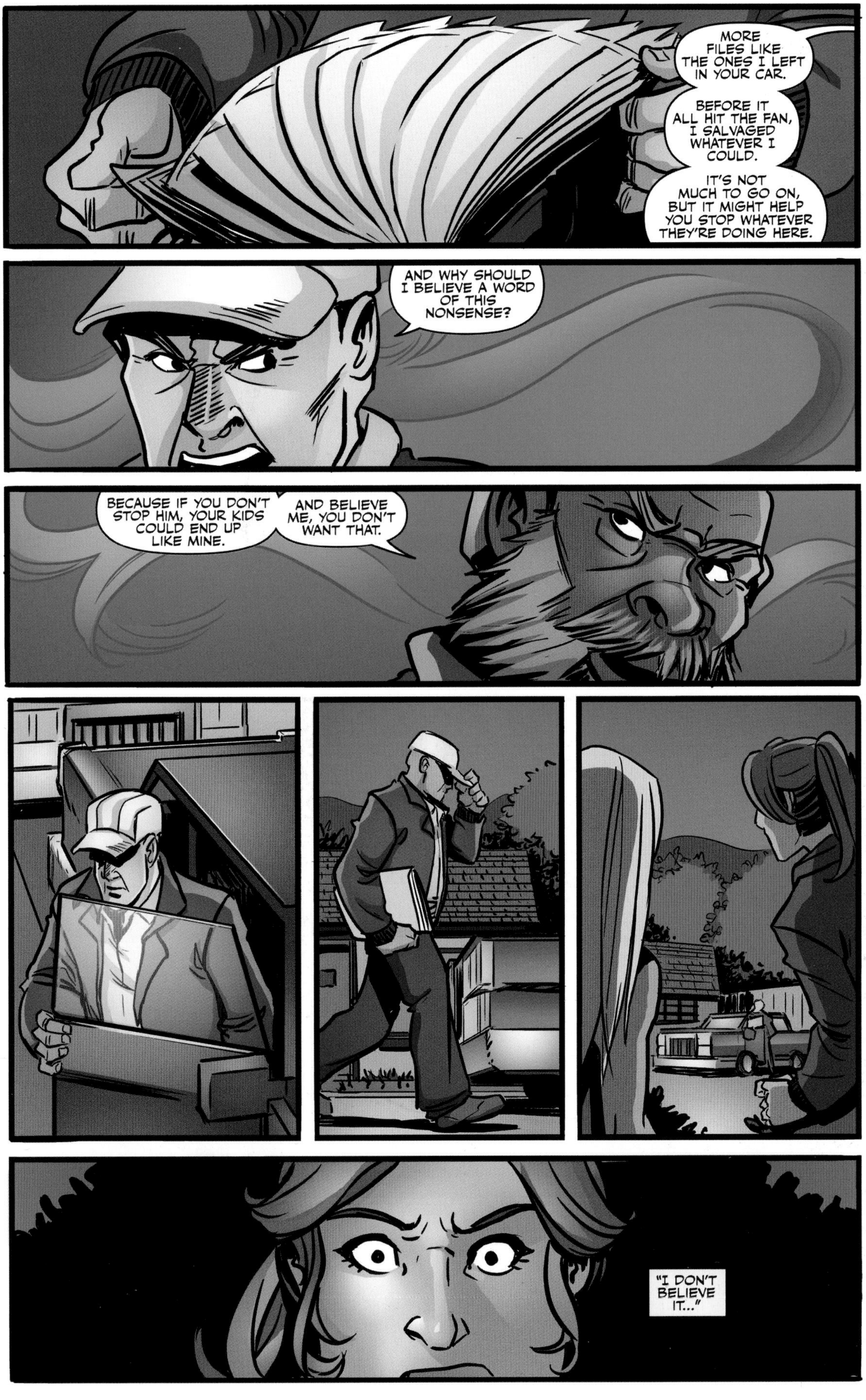
MORE FILES LIKE THE ONES I LEFT IN YOUR CAR.
BEFORE IT ALL HIT THE FAN, I SALVAGED WHATEVER I COULD.
IT'S NOT MUCH TO GO ON, BUT IT MIGHT HELP YOU STOP WHATEVER THEY'RE DOING HERE.
AND WHY SHOULD I BELIEVE A WORD OF THIS NONSENSE?
BECAUSE IF YOU DON'T STOP HIM, YOUR KIDS COULD END UP LIKE MINE.
AND BELIEVE ME, YOU DON'T WANT THAT.
"I DON'T BELIEVE IT..."

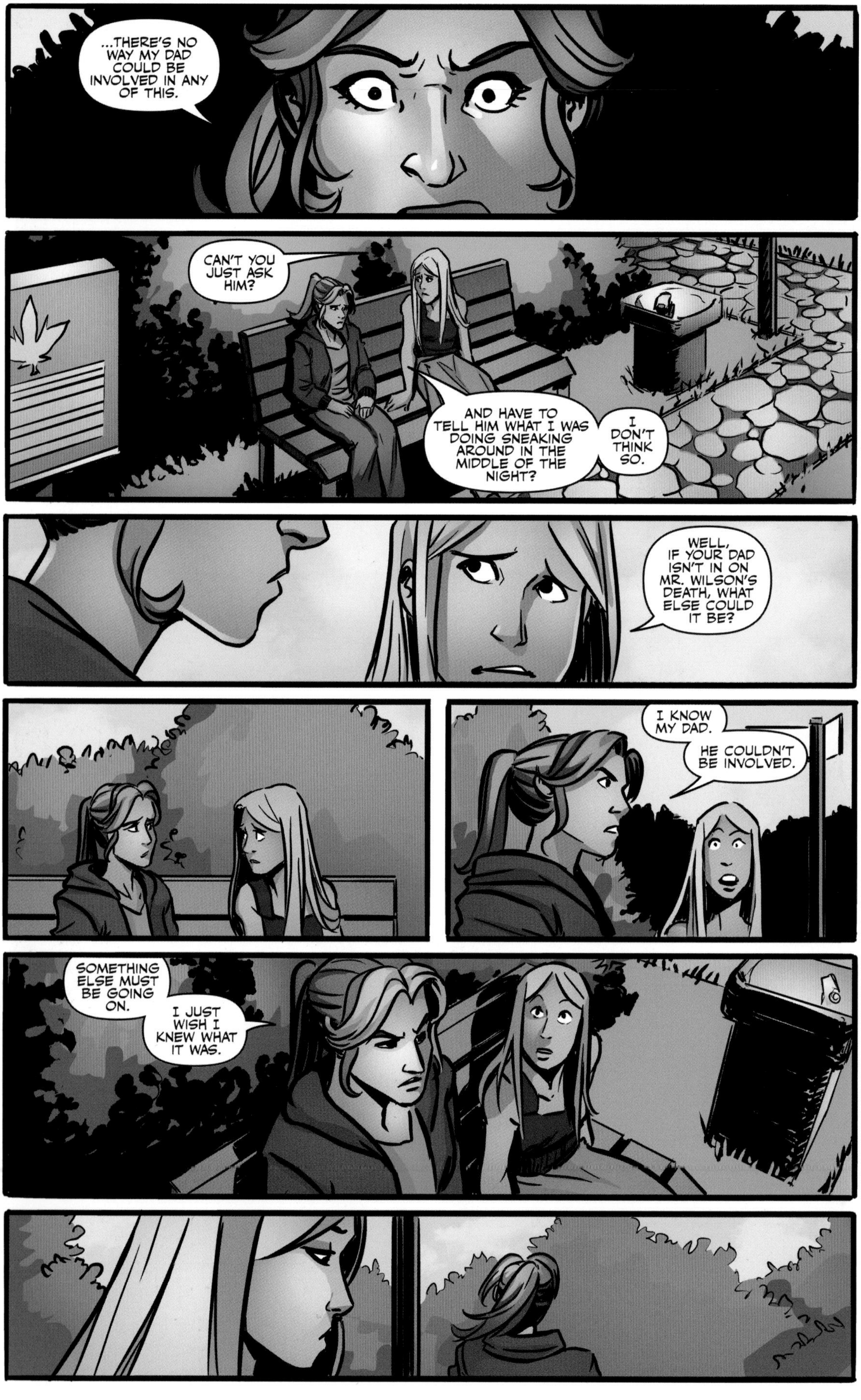
...THERE'S NO WAY MY DAD COULD BE INVOLVED IN ANY OF THIS.
CAN'T YOU JUST ASK HIM?
AND HAVE TO TELL HIM WHAT I WAS DOING SNEAKING AROUND IN THE MIDDLE OF THE NIGHT?
I DON'T THINK SO.
WELL, IF YOUR DAD ISN'T IN ON MR. WILSON'S DEATH, WHAT ELSE COULD IT BE?
I KNOW MY DAD.
HE COULDN'T BE INVOLVED.
SOMETHING ELSE MUST BE GOING ON.
I JUST WISH I KNEW WHAT IT WAS.

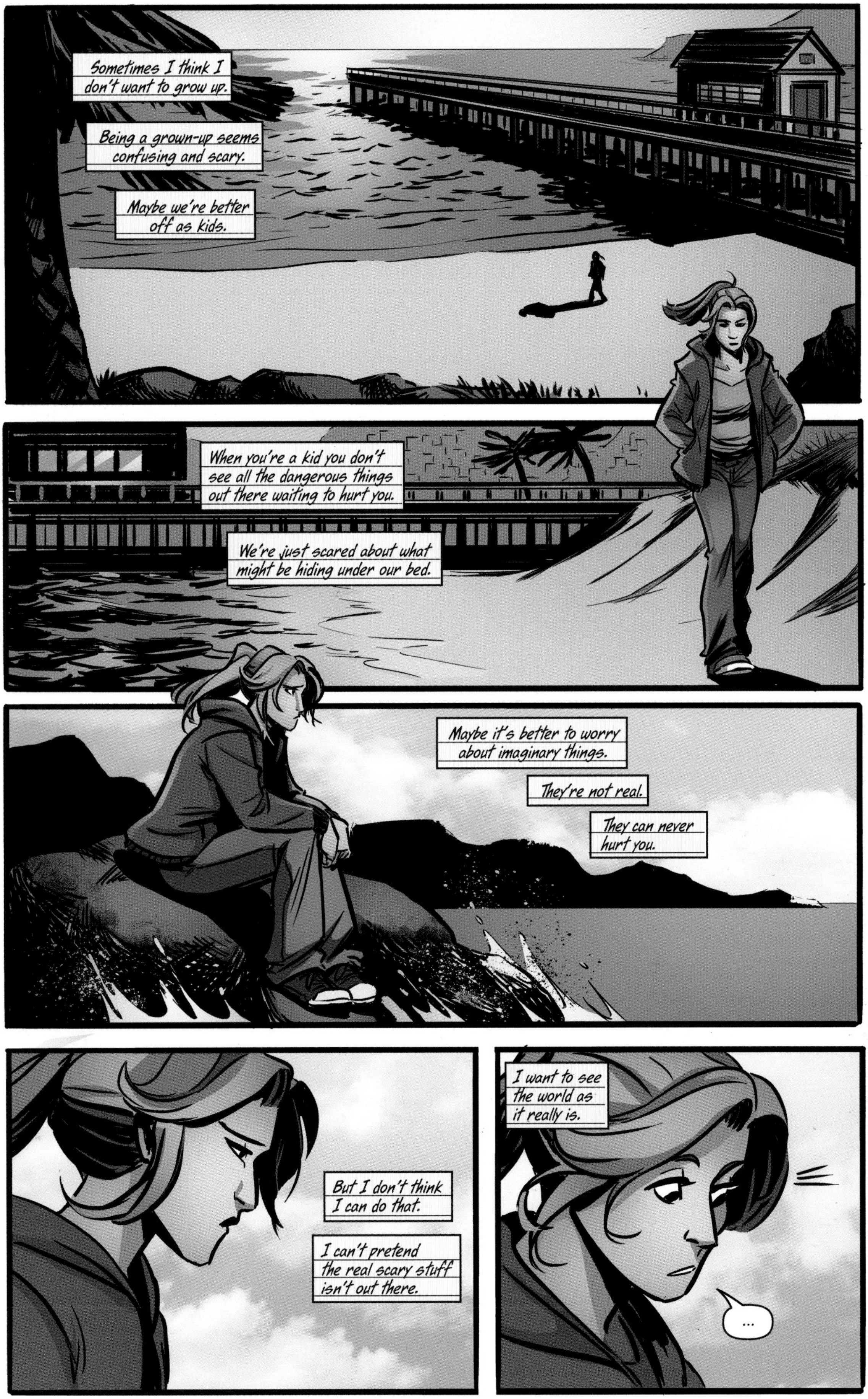
Sometimes I think I don't want to grow up.
Being a grown-up seems confusing and scary.
Maybe we're better off as kids.
When you're a kid you don't see all the dangerous things out there waiting to hurt you.
We're just scared about what might be hiding under our bed.
Maybe it's better to worry about imaginary things.
They're not real.
They can never hurt you.
But I don't think I can do that.
I can't pretend the real scary stuff isn't out there.
I want to see the world as it really is.
...

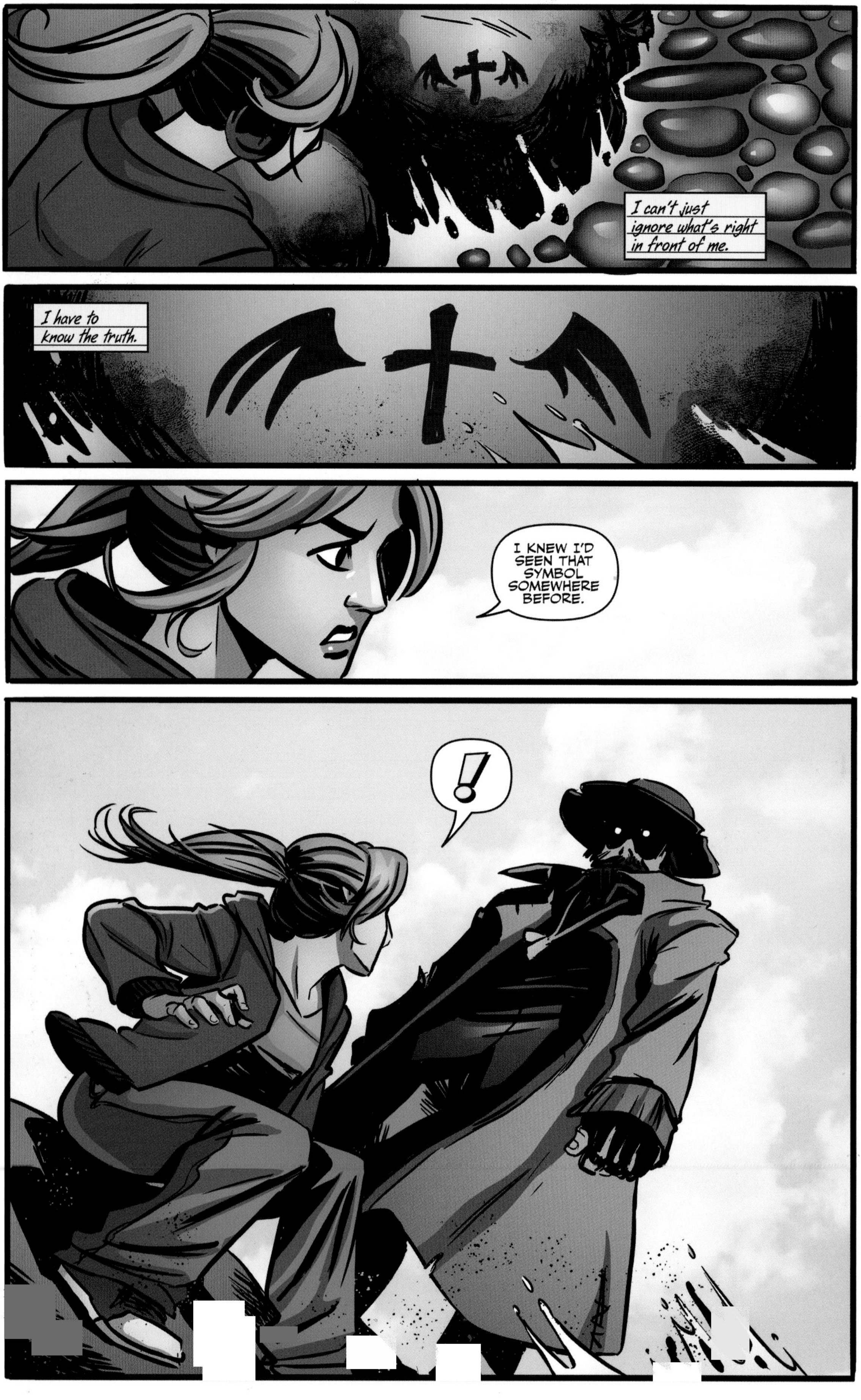
I can't just ignore what's right in front of me.
I have to know the truth.
I KNEW I'D SEEN THAT SYMBOL SOMEWHERE BEFORE.
!

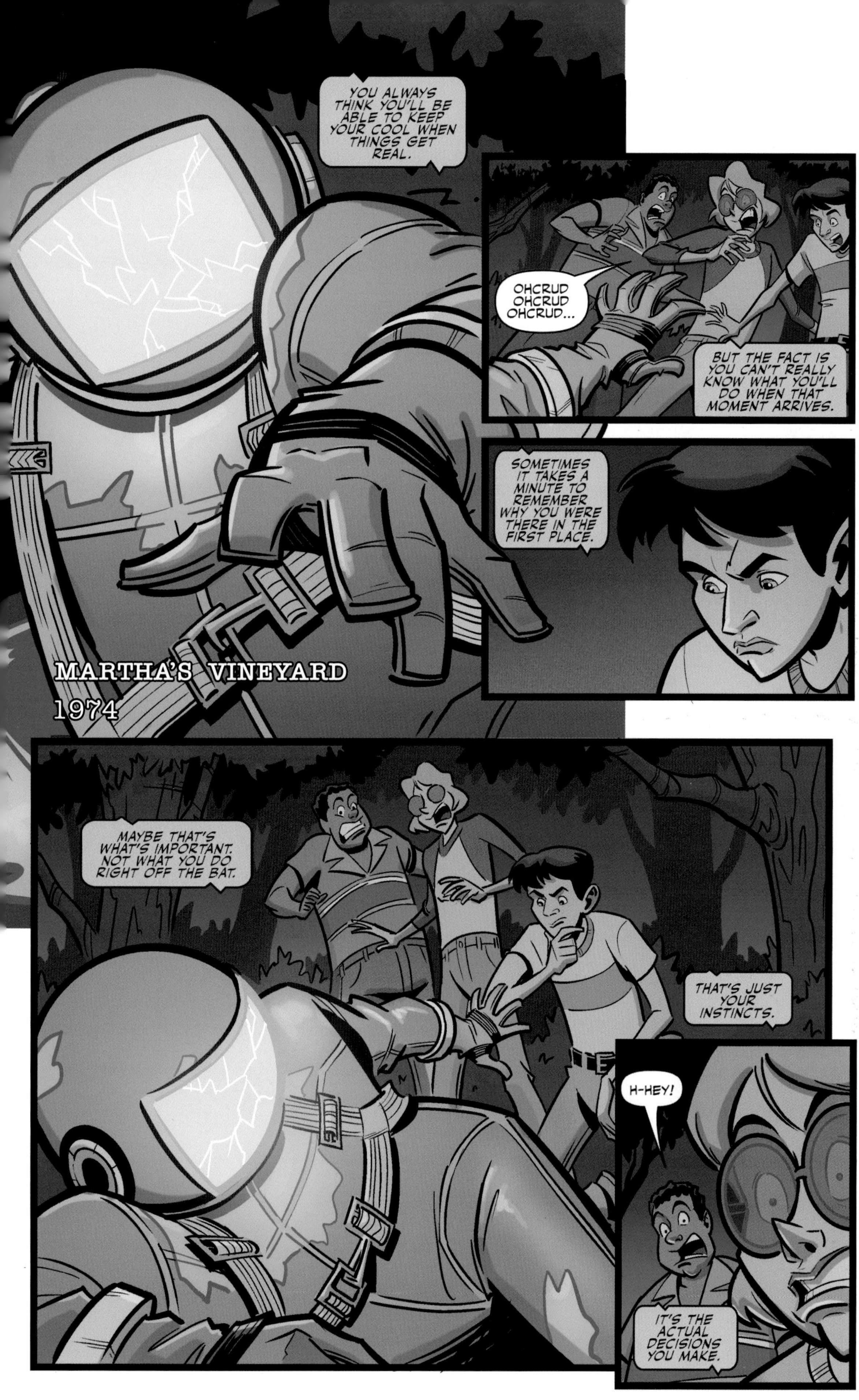
YOU ALWAYS THINK YOU'LL BE ABLE TO KEEP YOUR COOL WHEN THINGS GET REAL.
OHCRUD OHCRUD OHCRUD...
BUT THE FACT IS YOU CAN'T REALLY KNOW WHAT YOU'LL DO WHEN THAT MOMENT ARRIVES.
SOMETIMES IT TAKES A MINUTE TO REMEMBER WHY YOU WERE THERE IN THE FIRST PLACE.
MARTHA'S VINEYARD
1974
MAYBE THAT'S WHAT'S IMPORTANT. NOT WHAT YOU DO RIGHT OFF THE BAT.
THAT'S JUST YOUR INSTINCTS.
H-HEY!
IT'S THE ACTUAL DECISIONS YOU MAKE.

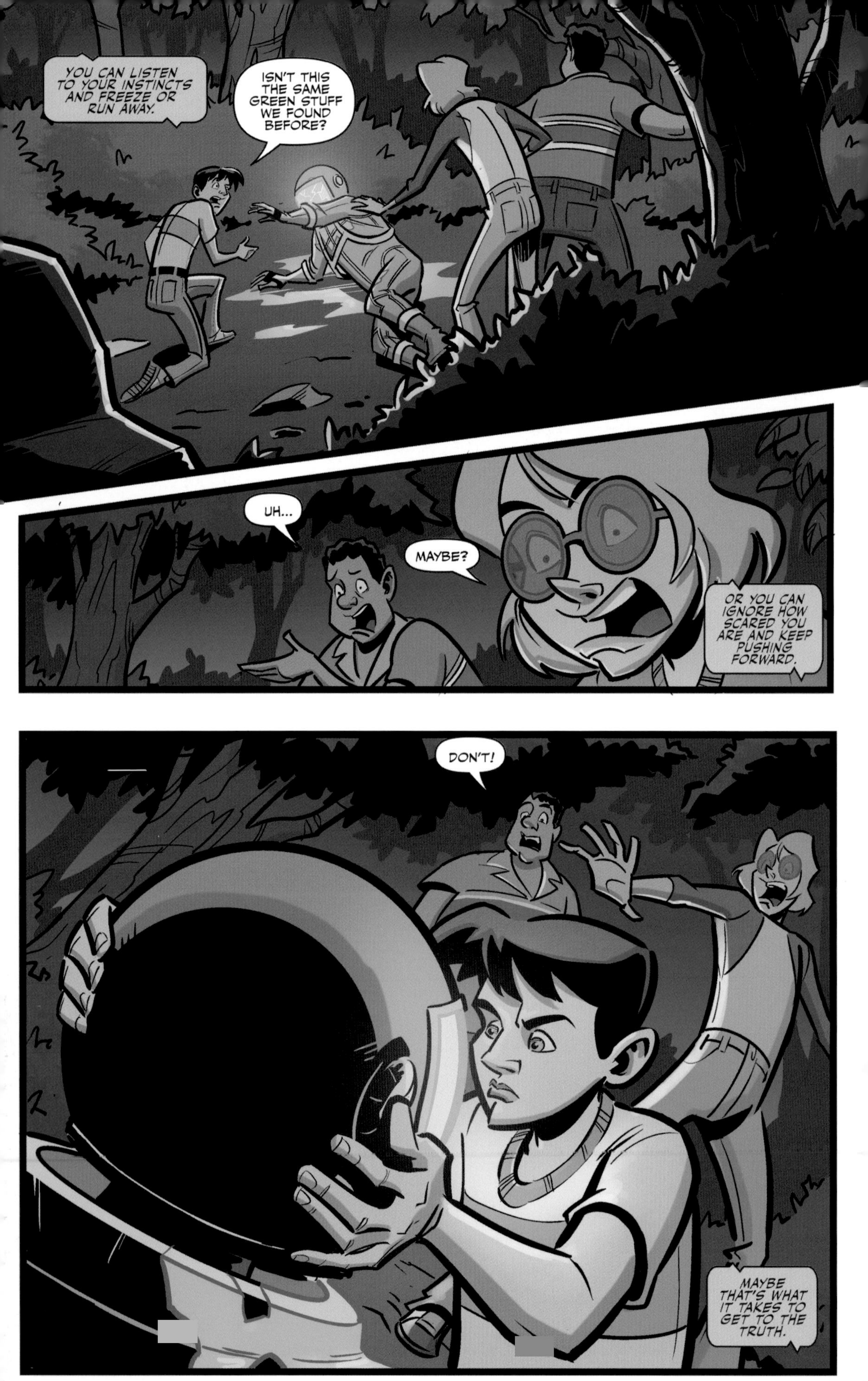
YOU CAN LISTEN TO YOUR INSTINCTS AND FREEZE OR RUN AWAY.
ISN'T THIS THE SAME GREEN STUFF WE FOUND BEFORE?
UH...
MAYBE?
OR YOU CAN IGNORE HOW SCARED YOU ARE AND KEEP PUSHING FORWARD.
DON'T!
MAYBE THAT'S WHAT IT TAKES TO GET TO THE TRUTH.

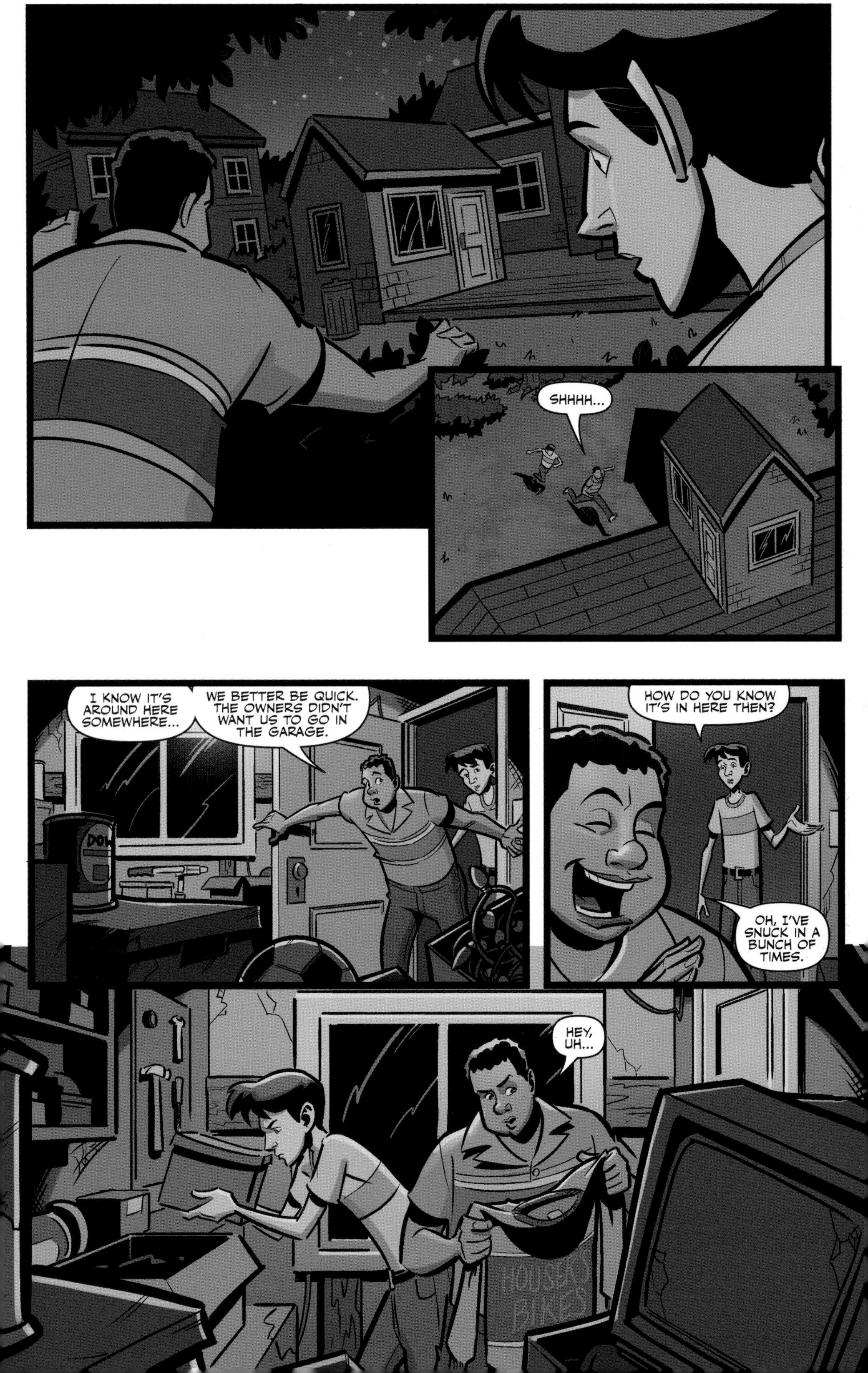
SHHHH...
I KNOW IT'S AROUND HERE SOMEWHERE...
WE BETTER BE QUICK. THE OWNERS DIDN'T WANT US TO GO IN THE GARAGE.
HOW DO YOU KNOW IT'S IN HERE THEN?
OH, I'VE SNUCK IN A BUNCH OF TIMES.
HEY, UH...
HOUSER'S BIKES

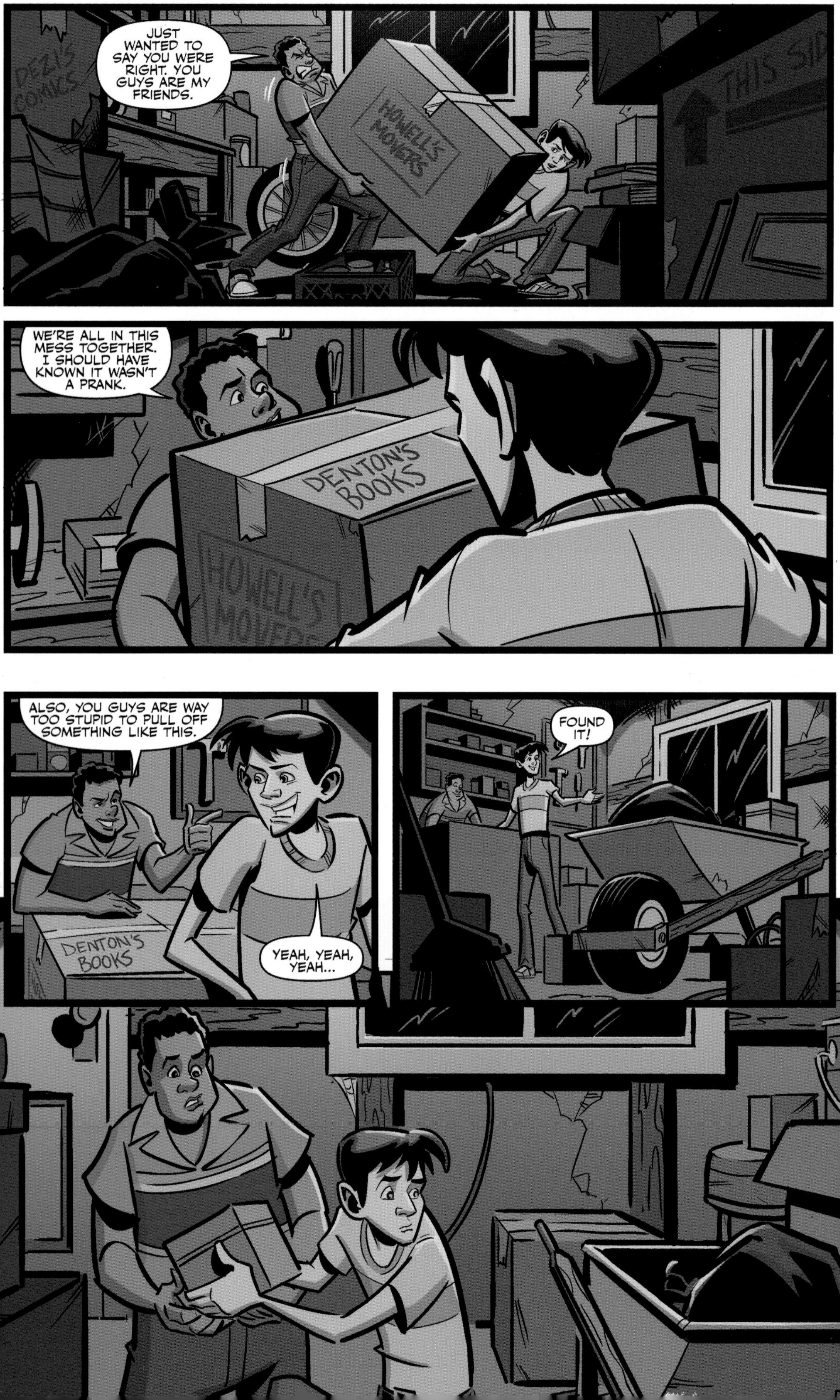
DEZI'S COMICS
JUST WANTED TO SAY YOU WERE RIGHT. YOU GUYS ARE MY FRIENDS.
HOWELL'S MOVERS
THIS SID
WE'RE ALL IN THIS MESS TOGETHER. I SHOULD HAVE KNOWN IT WASN'T A PRANK.
DENTON'S BOOKS
HOWELL'S MOVERS
ALSO, YOU GUYS ARE WAY TOO STUPID TO PULL OFF SOMETHING LIKE THIS.
DENTON'S BOOKS
YEAH, YEAH, YEAH...
FOUND IT!

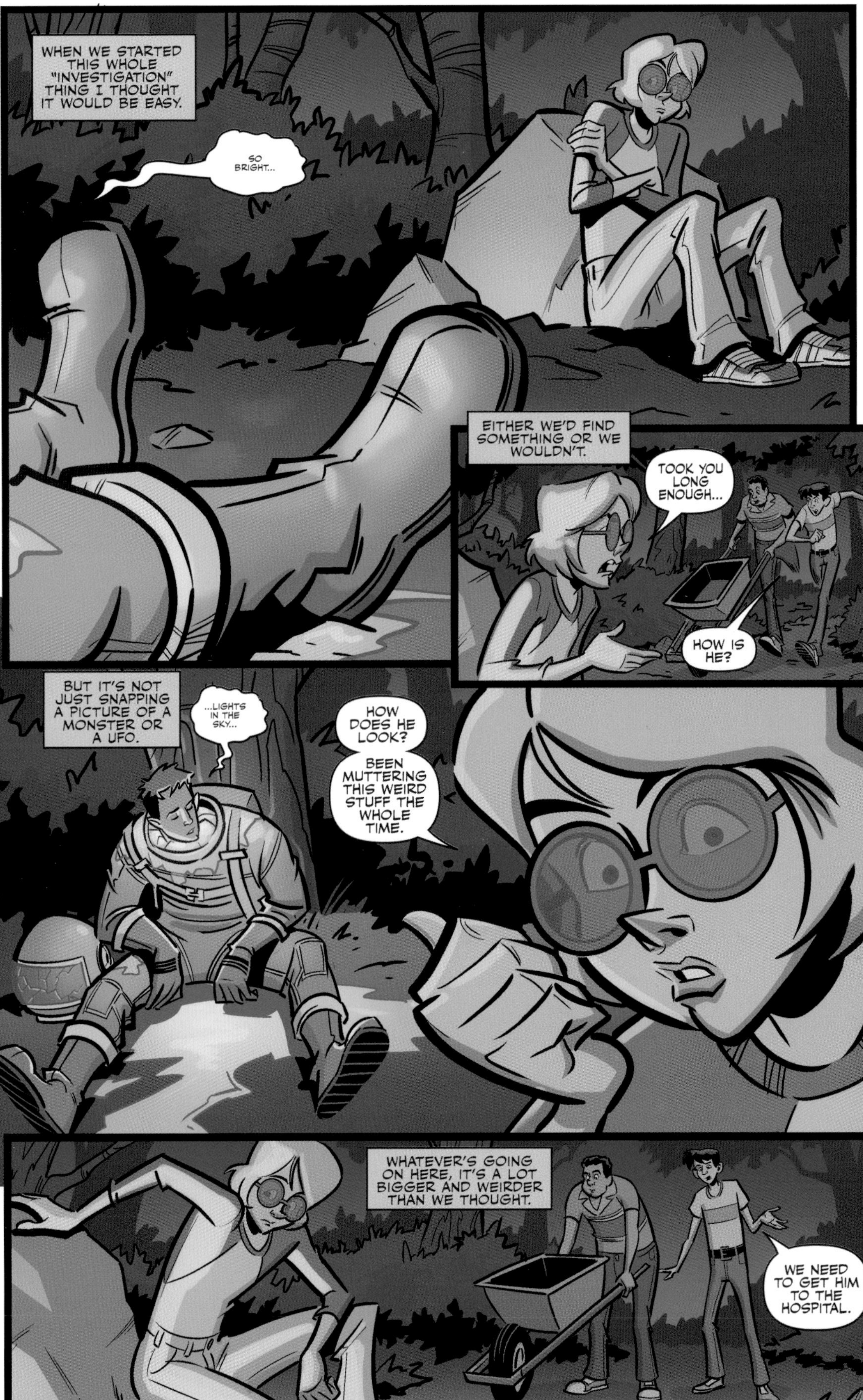
WHEN WE STARTED THIS WHOLE "INVESTIGATION" THING I THOUGHT IT WOULD BE EASY.
SO BRIGHT...
EITHER WE'D FIND SOMETHING OR WE WOULDN'T.
TOOK YOU LONG ENOUGH...
HOW IS HE?
BUT IT'S NOT JUST SNAPPING A PICTURE OF A MONSTER OR A UFO.
...LIGHTS IN THE SKY...
HOW DOES HE LOOK?
BEEN MUTTERING THIS WEIRD STUFF THE WHOLE TIME.
WHATEVER'S GOING ON HERE, IT'S A LOT BIGGER AND WEIRDER THAN WE THOUGHT.
WE NEED TO GET HIM TO THE HOSPITAL.

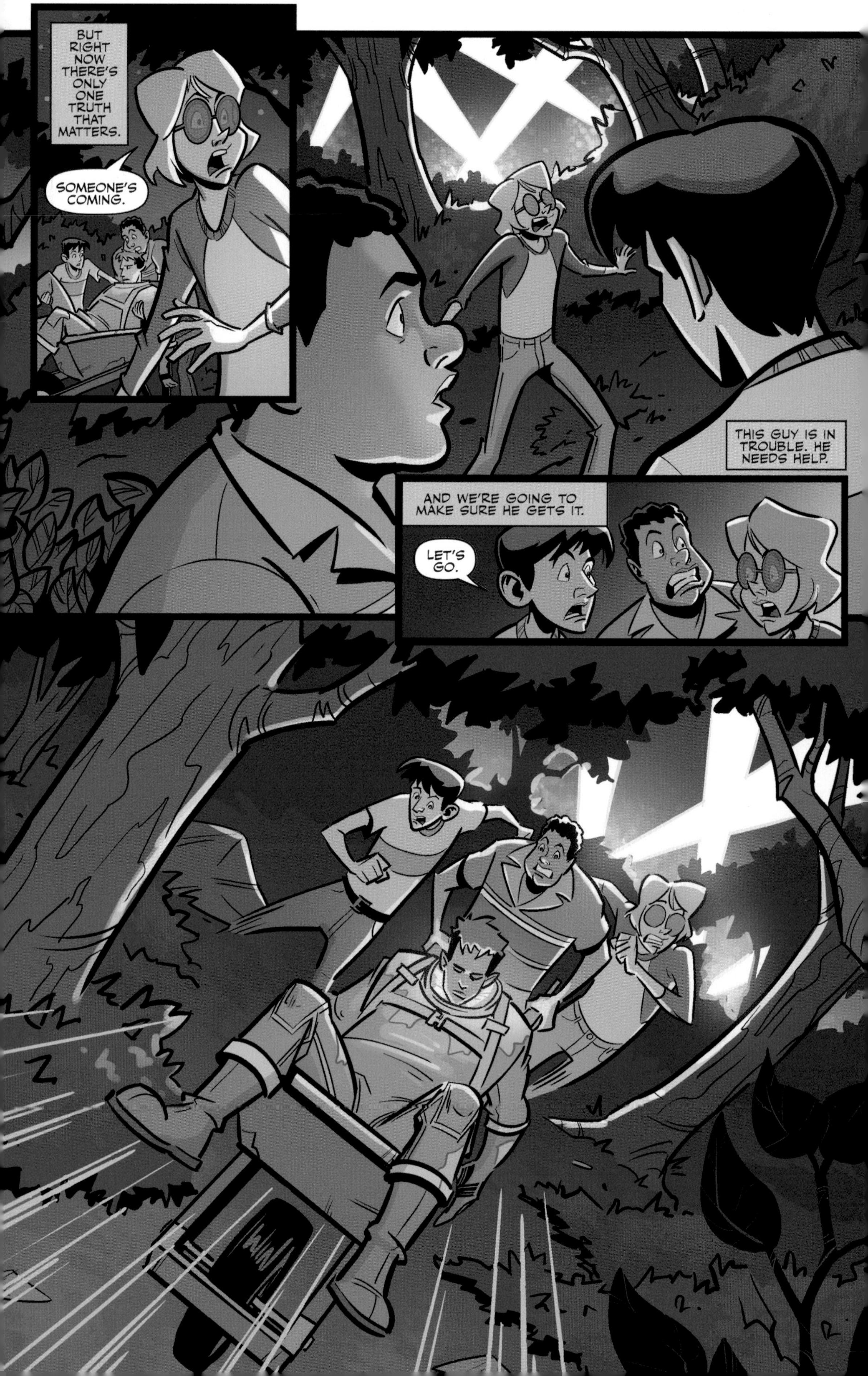
BUT RIGHT NOW THERE'S ONLY ONE TRUTH THAT MATTERS.
SOMEONE'S COMING.
THIS GUY IS IN TROUBLE. HE NEEDS HELP.
AND WE'RE GOING TO MAKE SURE HE GETS IT.
LET'S GO.

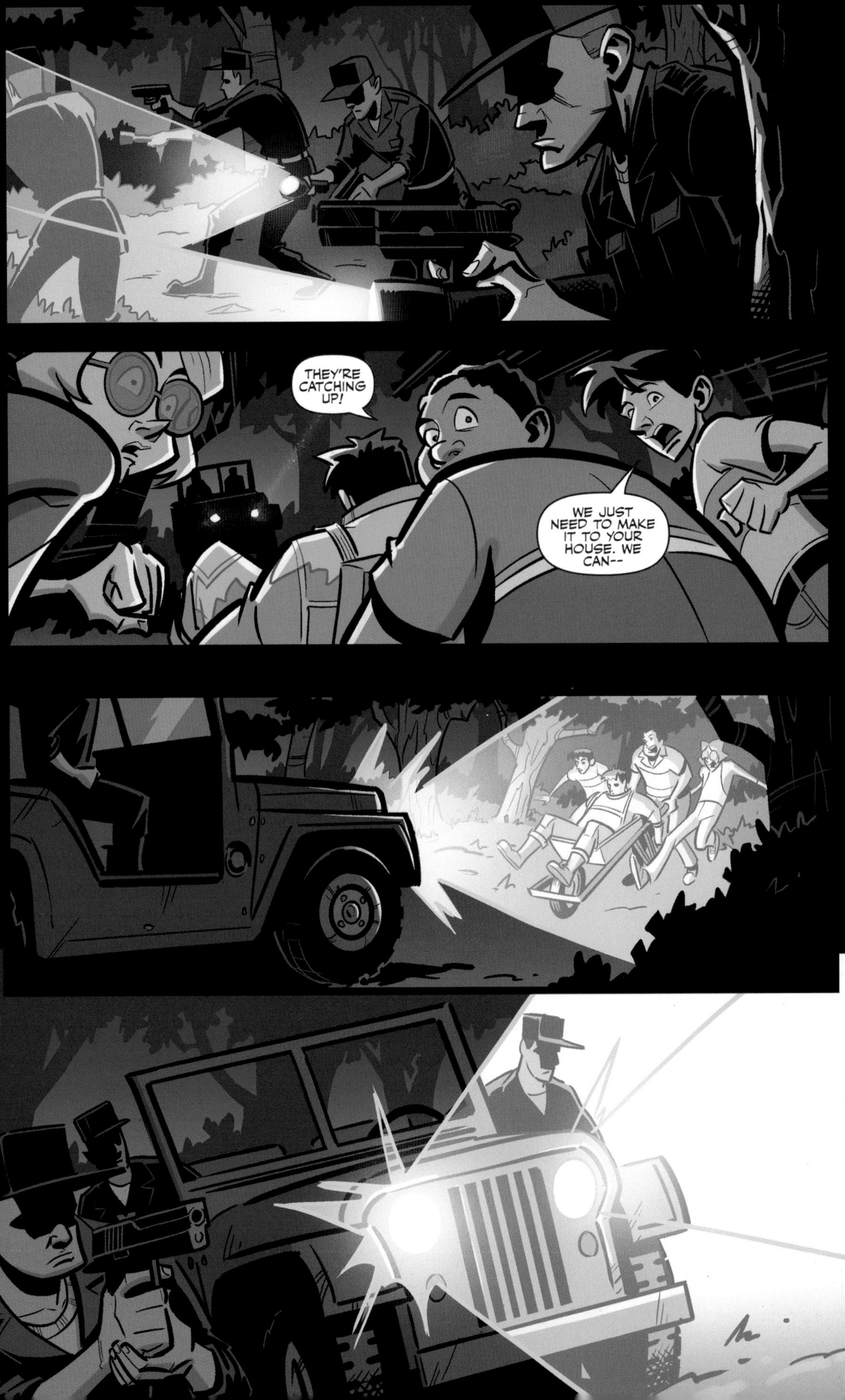
THEY'RE CATCHING UP!
WE JUST NEED TO MAKE IT TO YOUR HOUSE. WE CAN--

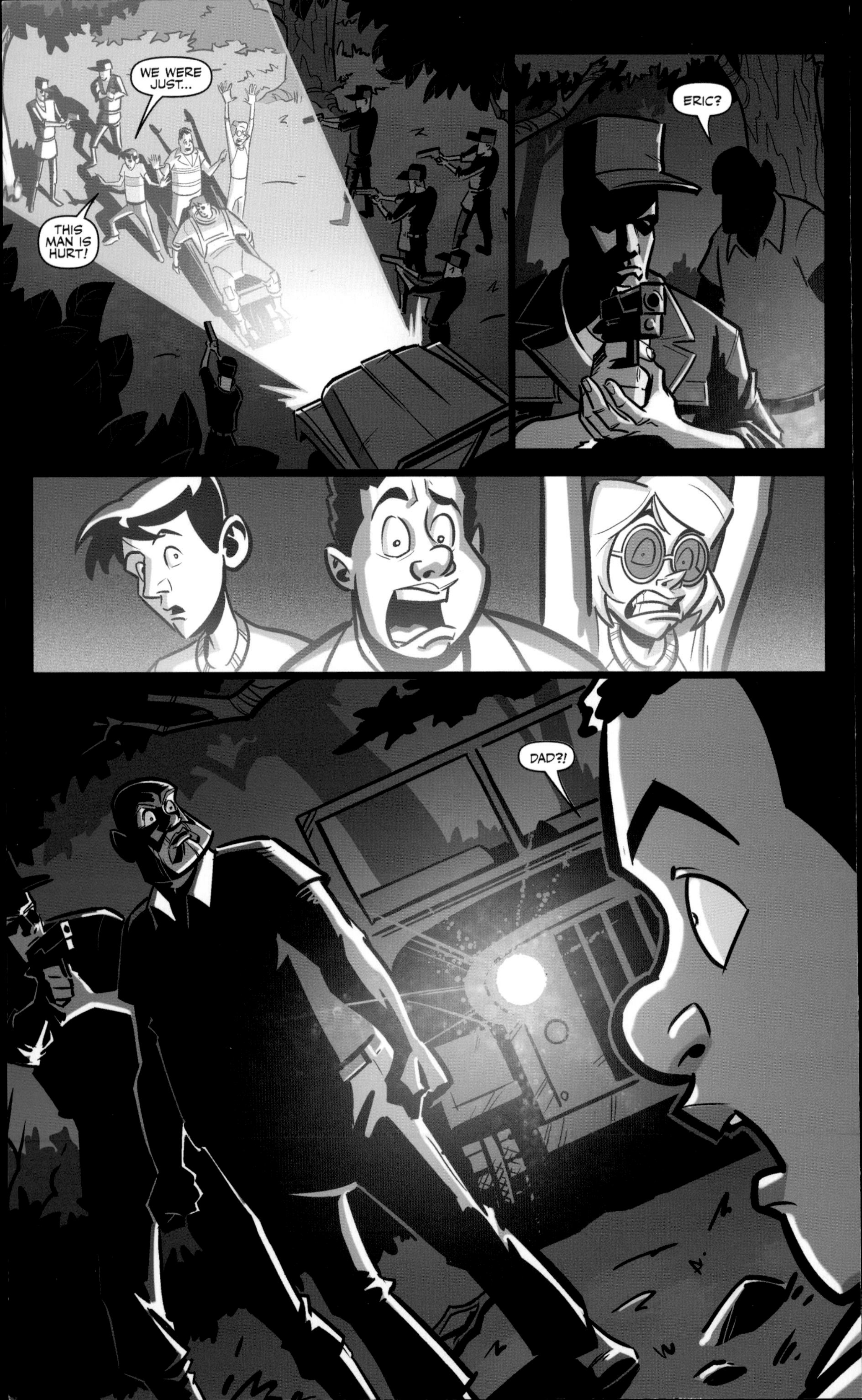
WE WERE JUST...
THIS MAN IS HURT!
ERIC?
DAD?!

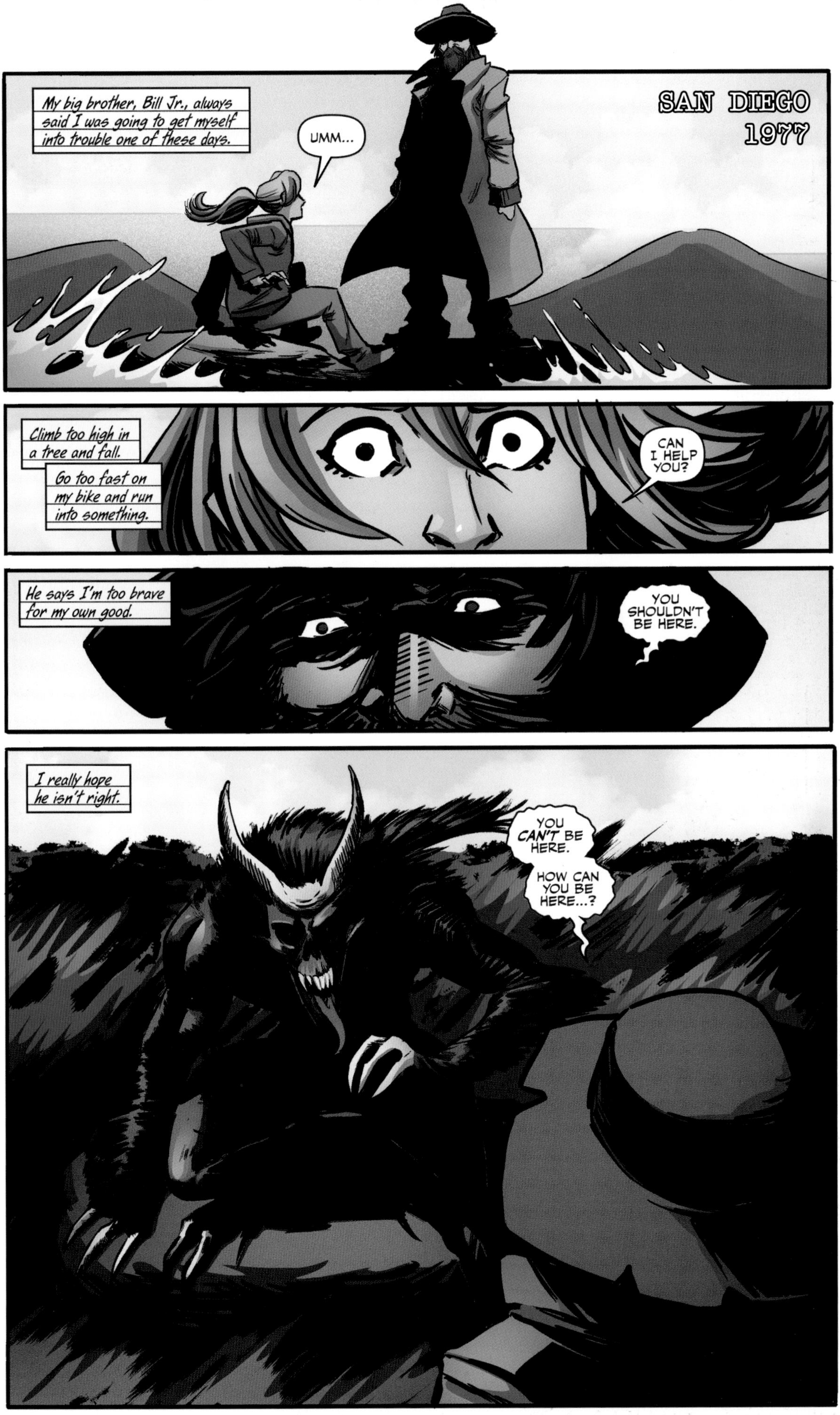
My big brother, Bill Jr., always said I was going to get myself into trouble one of these days.
SAN DIEGO 1977
UMM...
Climb too high in a tree and fall.
Go too fast on my bike and run into something.
CAN I HELP YOU?
He says I'm too brave for my own good.
YOU SHOULDN'T BE HERE.
I really hope he isn't right.
YOU CAN'T BE HERE.
HOW CAN YOU BE HERE...?

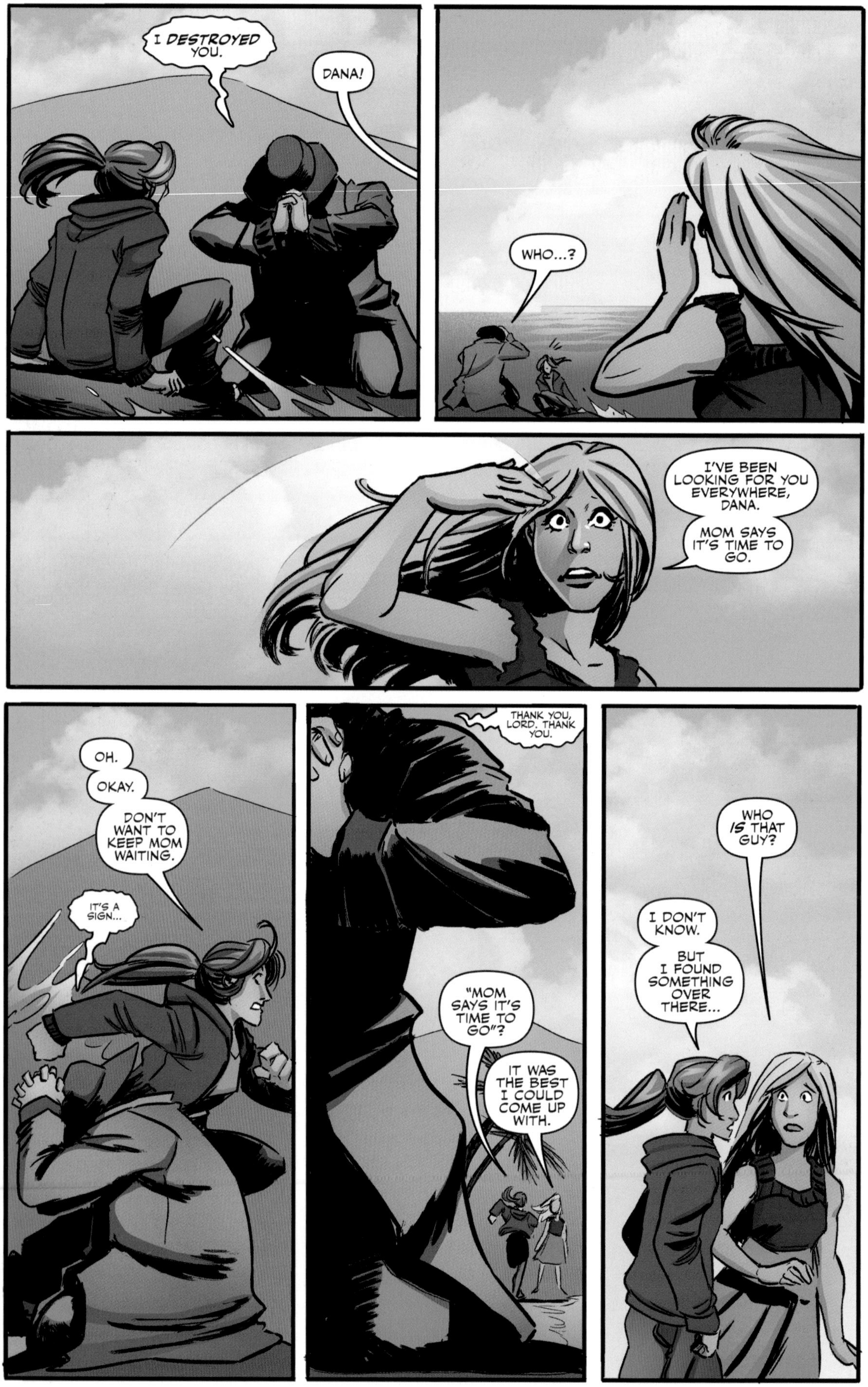
I DESTROYED YOU.
DANA!
WHO...?
I'VE BEEN LOOKING FOR YOU EVERYWHERE, DANA.
MOM SAYS IT'S TIME TO GO.
OH.
OKAY.
DON'T WANT TO KEEP MOM WAITING.
IT'S A SIGN...
THANK YOU, LORD. THANK YOU.
"MOM SAYS IT'S TIME TO GO"?
IT WAS THE BEST I COULD COME UP WITH.
WHO IS THAT GUY?
I DON'T KNOW.
BUT I FOUND SOMETHING OVER THERE...

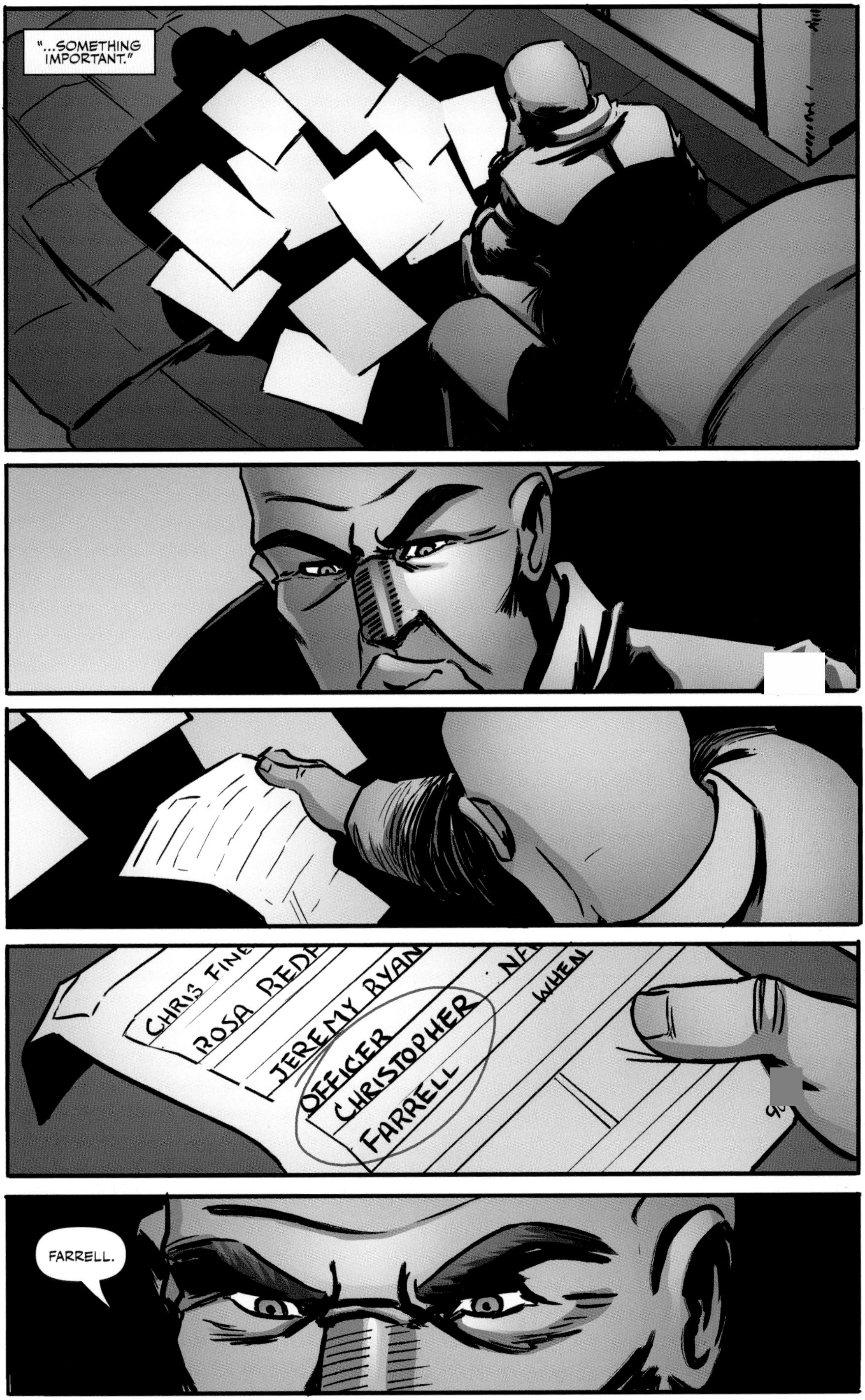
"...SOMETHING IMPORTANT."
JEREMY RYAN
OFFICER CHRISTOPHER FARRELL
WHEN
FARRELL.

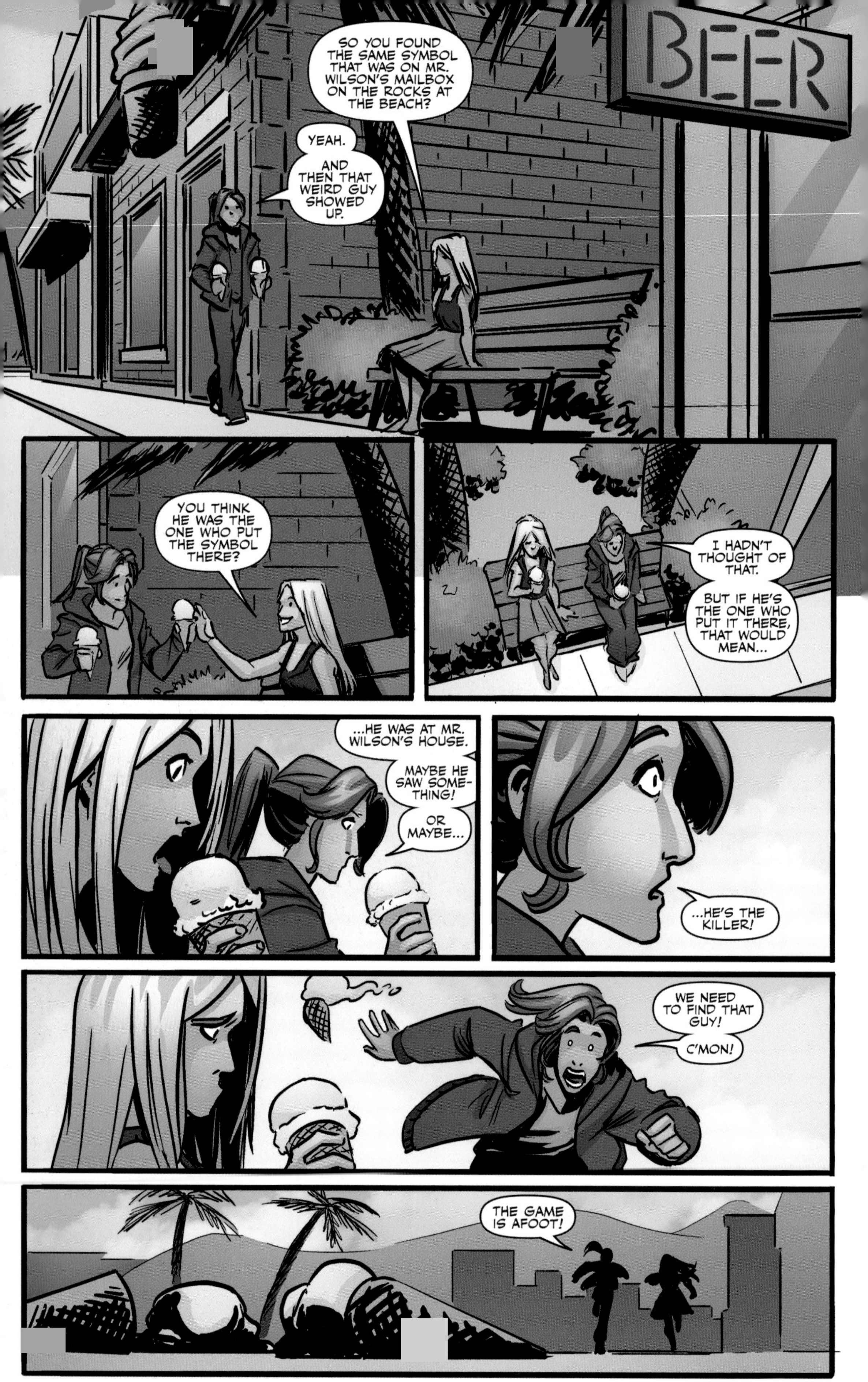
SO YOU FOUND THE SAME SYMBOL THAT WAS ON MR. WILSON'S MAILBOX ON THE ROCKS AT THE BEACH?
YEAH.
AND THEN THAT WEIRD GUY SHOWED UP.
YOU THINK HE WAS THE ONE WHO PUT THE SYMBOL THERE?
I HADN'T THOUGHT OF THAT.
BUT IF HE'S THE ONE WHO PUT IT THERE, THAT WOULD MEAN...
...HE WAS AT MR. WILSON'S HOUSE.
MAYBE HE SAW SOME-THING!
OR MAYBE...
...HE'S THE KILLER!
WE NEED TO FIND THAT GUY!
C'MON!
THE GAME IS AFOOT!

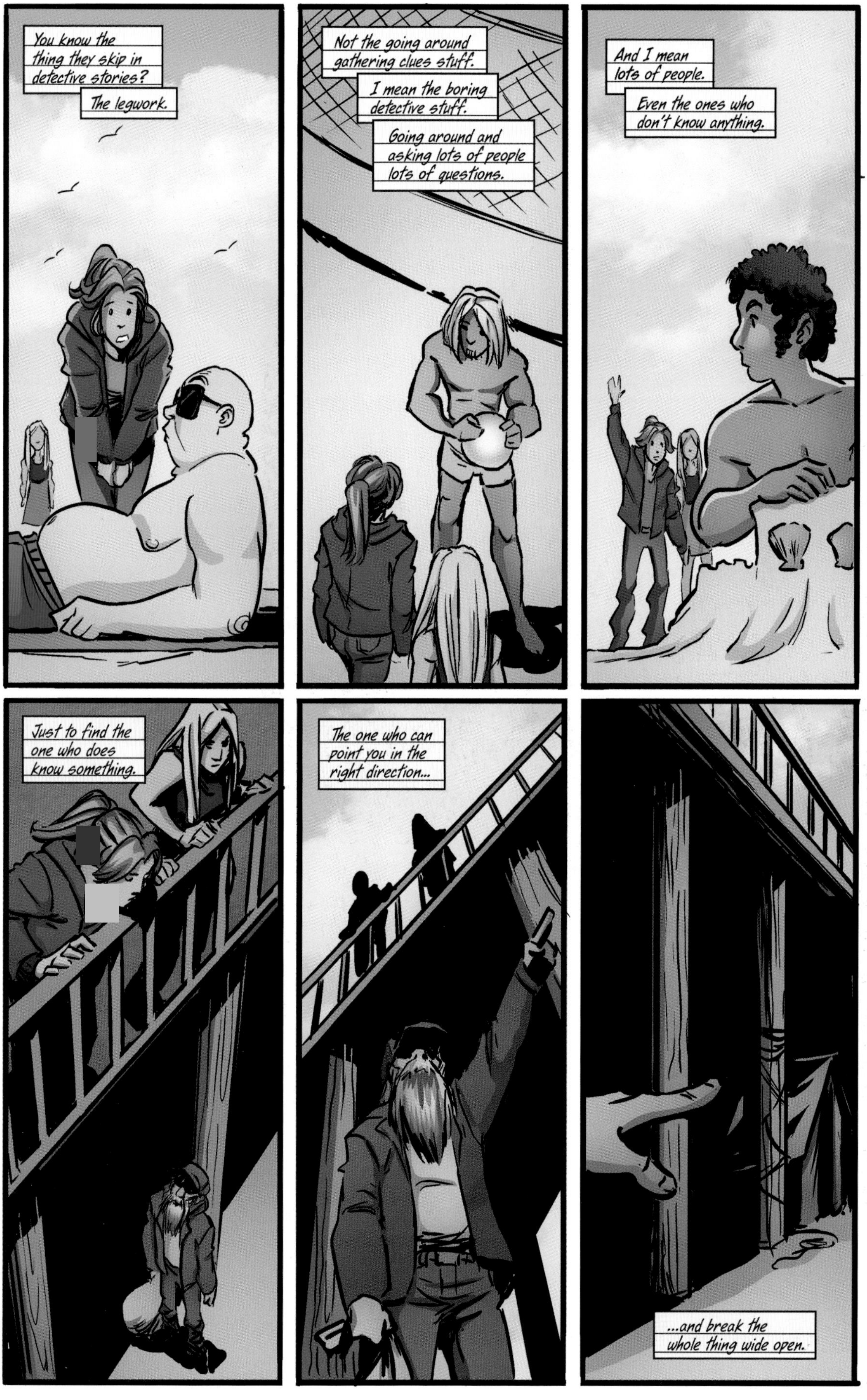
You know the thing they skip in detective stories?
The legwork.
Not the going around gathering clues stuff.
I mean the boring detective stuff.
Going around and asking lots of people lots of questions.
And I mean lots of people.
Even the ones who don't know anything.
Just to find the one who does know something.
The one who can point you in the right direction...
...and break the whole thing wide open.

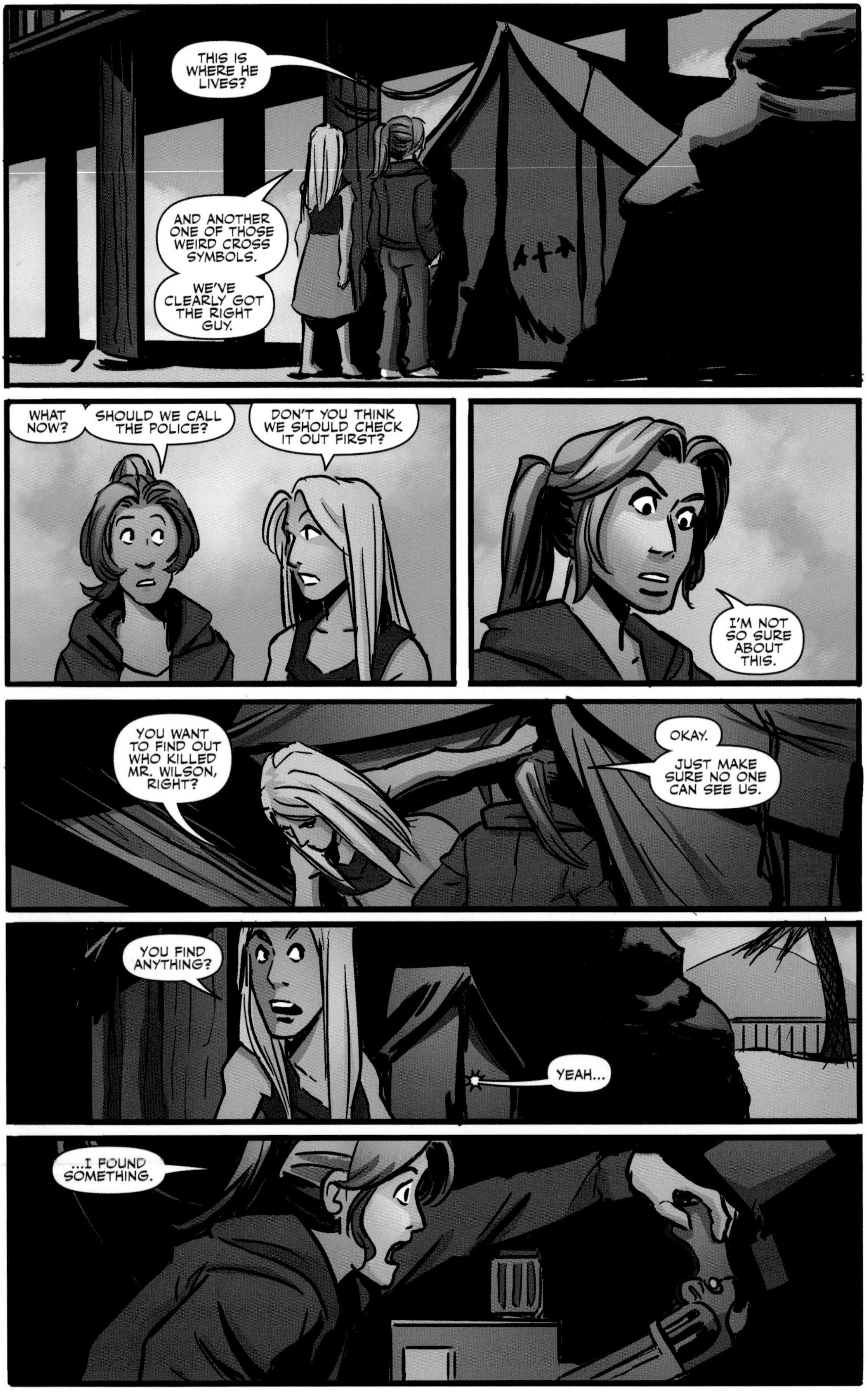
THIS IS WHERE HE LIVES?
AND ANOTHER ONE OF THOSE WEIRD CROSS SYMBOLS.
WE'VE CLEARLY GOT THE RIGHT GUY.
WHAT NOW?
SHOULD WE CALL THE POLICE?
DON'T YOU THINK WE SHOULD CHECK IT OUT FIRST?
I'M NOT SO SURE ABOUT THIS.
YOU WANT TO FIND OUT WHO KILLED MR. WILSON, RIGHT?
OKAY.
JUST MAKE SURE NO ONE CAN SEE US.
YOU FIND ANYTHING?
YEAH...
...I FOUND SOMETHING.

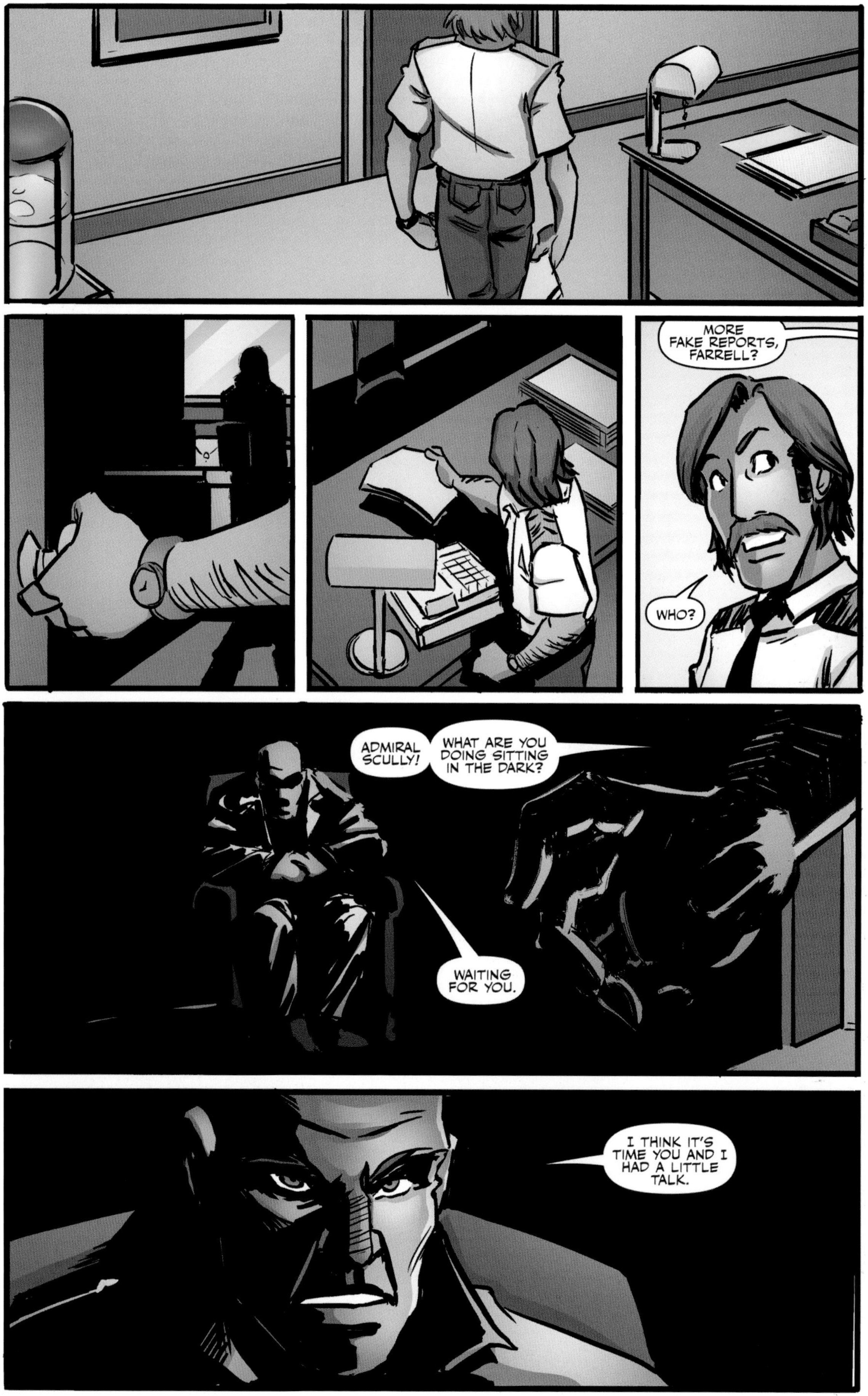

MORE FAKE REPORTS, FARRELL?
WHO?
ADMIRAL SCULLY!
WHAT ARE YOU DOING SITTING IN THE DARK?
WAITING FOR YOU.
I THINK IT'S TIME YOU AND I HAD A LITTLE TALK.

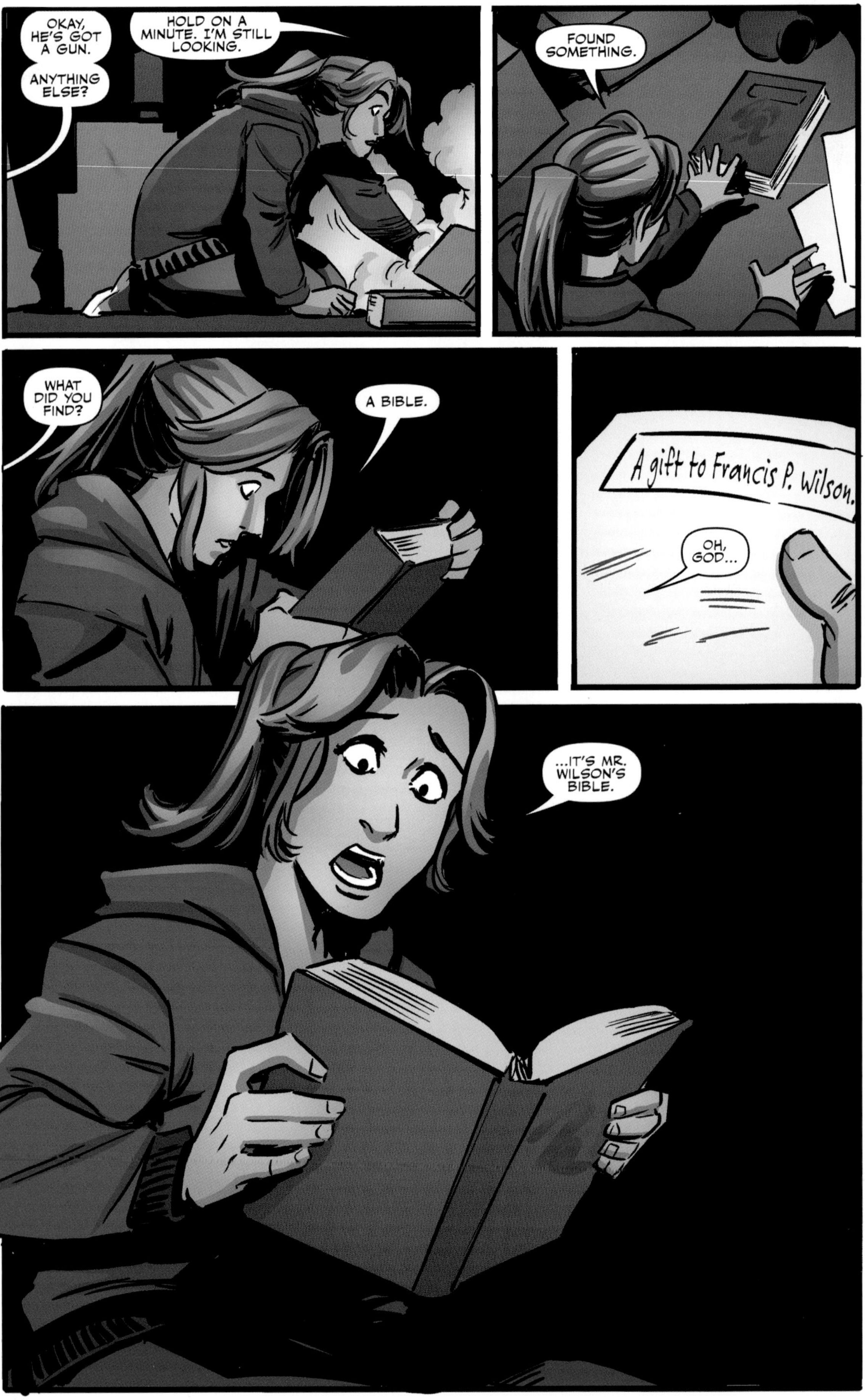
OKAY, HE'S GOT A GUN.
ANYTHING ELSE?
HOLD ON A MINUTE. I'M STILL LOOKING.
FOUND SOMETHING.
WHAT DID YOU FIND?
A BIBLE.
A gift to Francis P. Wilson.
OH, GOD...
...IT'S MR. WILSON'S BIBLE.

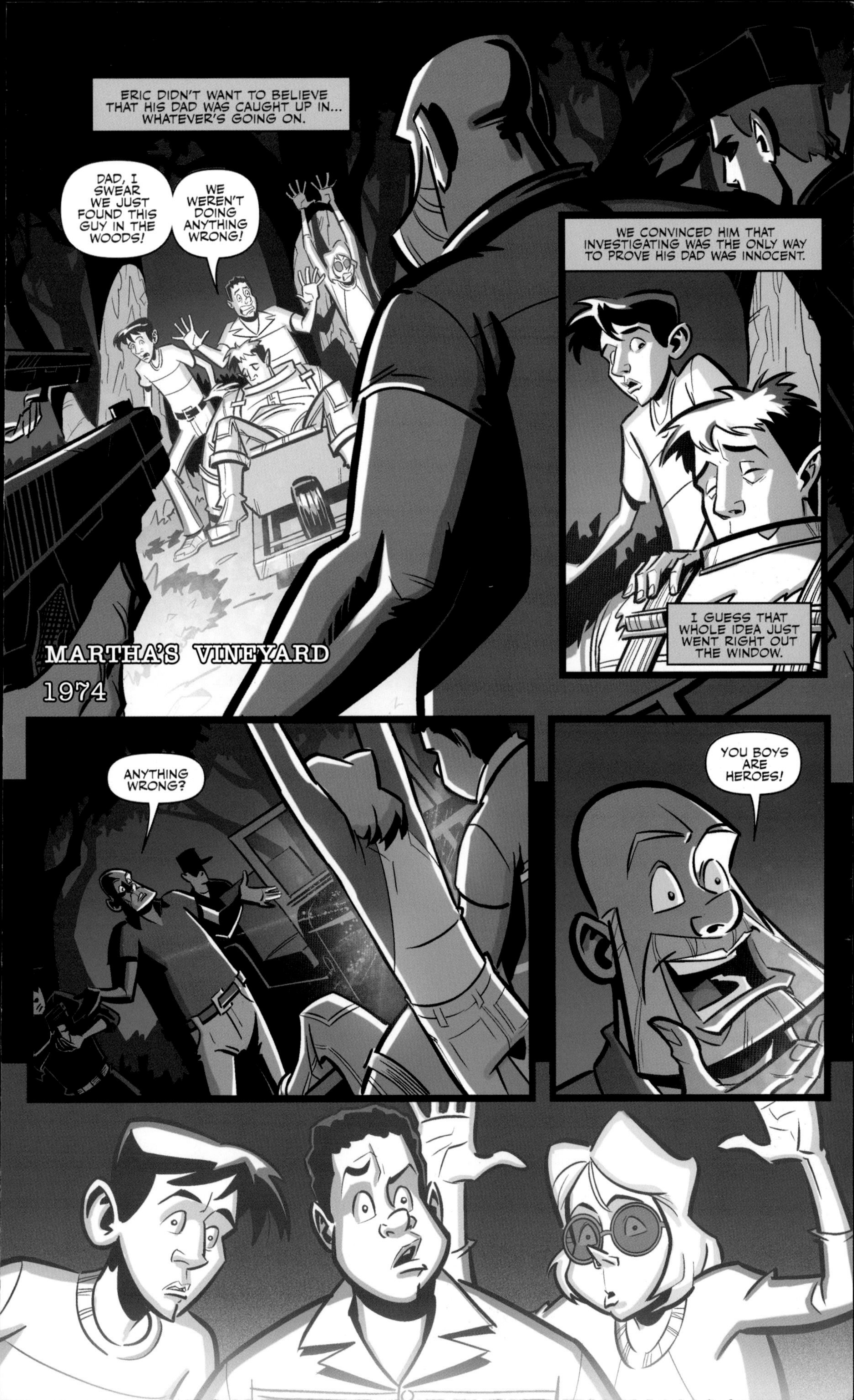
ERIC DIDN'T WANT TO BELIEVE THAT HIS DAD WAS CAUGHT UP IN... WHATEVER'S GOING ON.
DAD, I SWEAR WE JUST FOUND THIS GUY IN THE WOODS!
WE WEREN'T DOING ANYTHING WRONG!
WE CONVINCED HIM THAT INVESTIGATING WAS THE ONLY WAY TO PROVE HIS DAD WAS INNOCENT.
I GUESS THAT WHOLE IDEA JUST WENT RIGHT OUT THE WINDOW.
MARTHA'S VINEYARD
1974
ANYTHING WRONG?
YOU BOYS ARE HEROES!

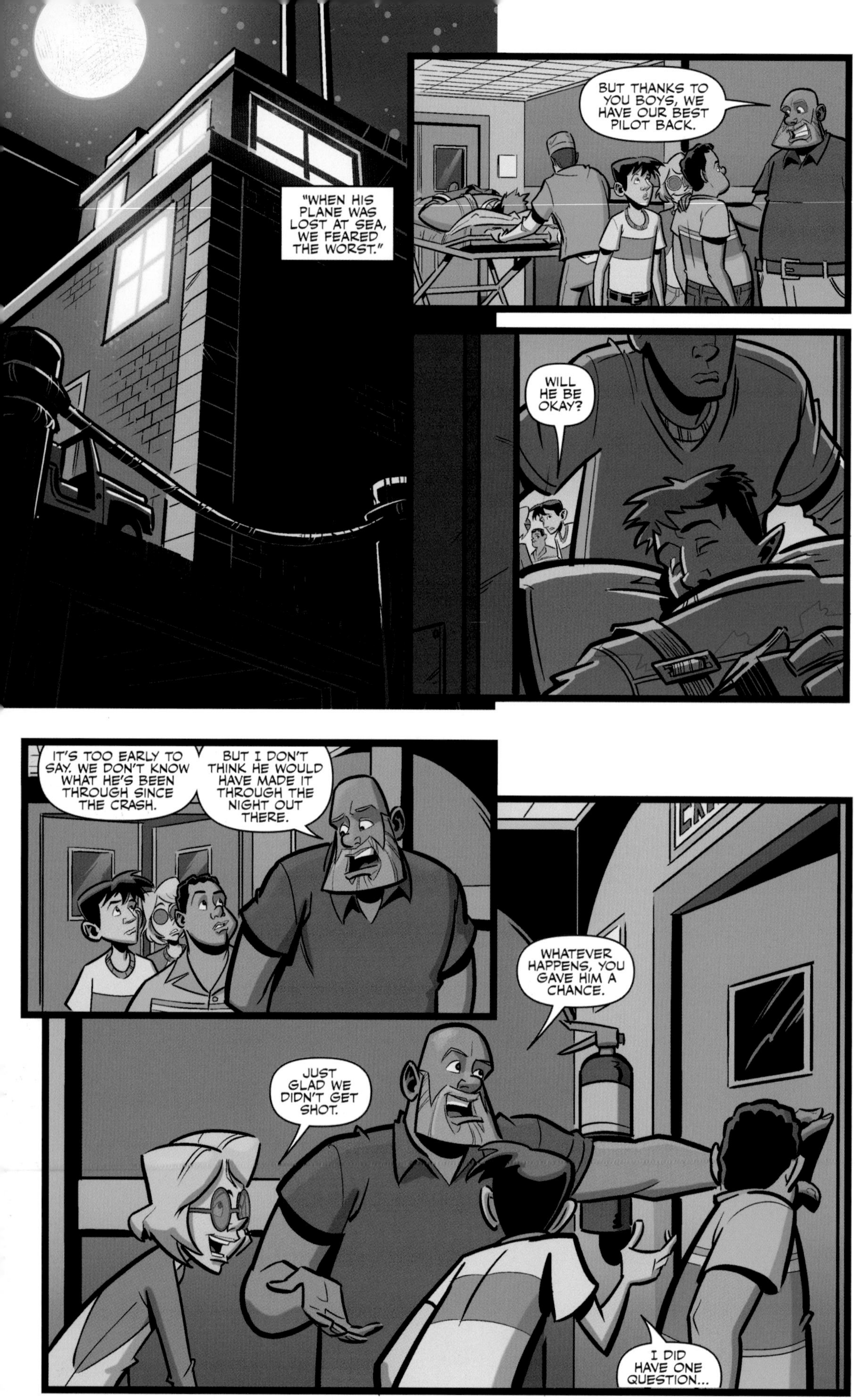
"WHEN HIS PLANE WAS LOST AT SEA, WE FEARED THE WORST."
BUT THANKS TO YOU BOYS, WE HAVE OUR BEST PILOT BACK.
WILL HE BE OKAY?
IT'S TOO EARLY TO SAY. WE DON'T KNOW WHAT HE'S BEEN THROUGH SINCE THE CRASH.
BUT I DON'T THINK HE WOULD HAVE MADE IT THROUGH THE NIGHT OUT THERE.
WHATEVER HAPPENS, YOU GAVE HIM A CHANCE.
JUST GLAD WE DIDN'T GET SHOT.
I DID HAVE ONE QUESTION...

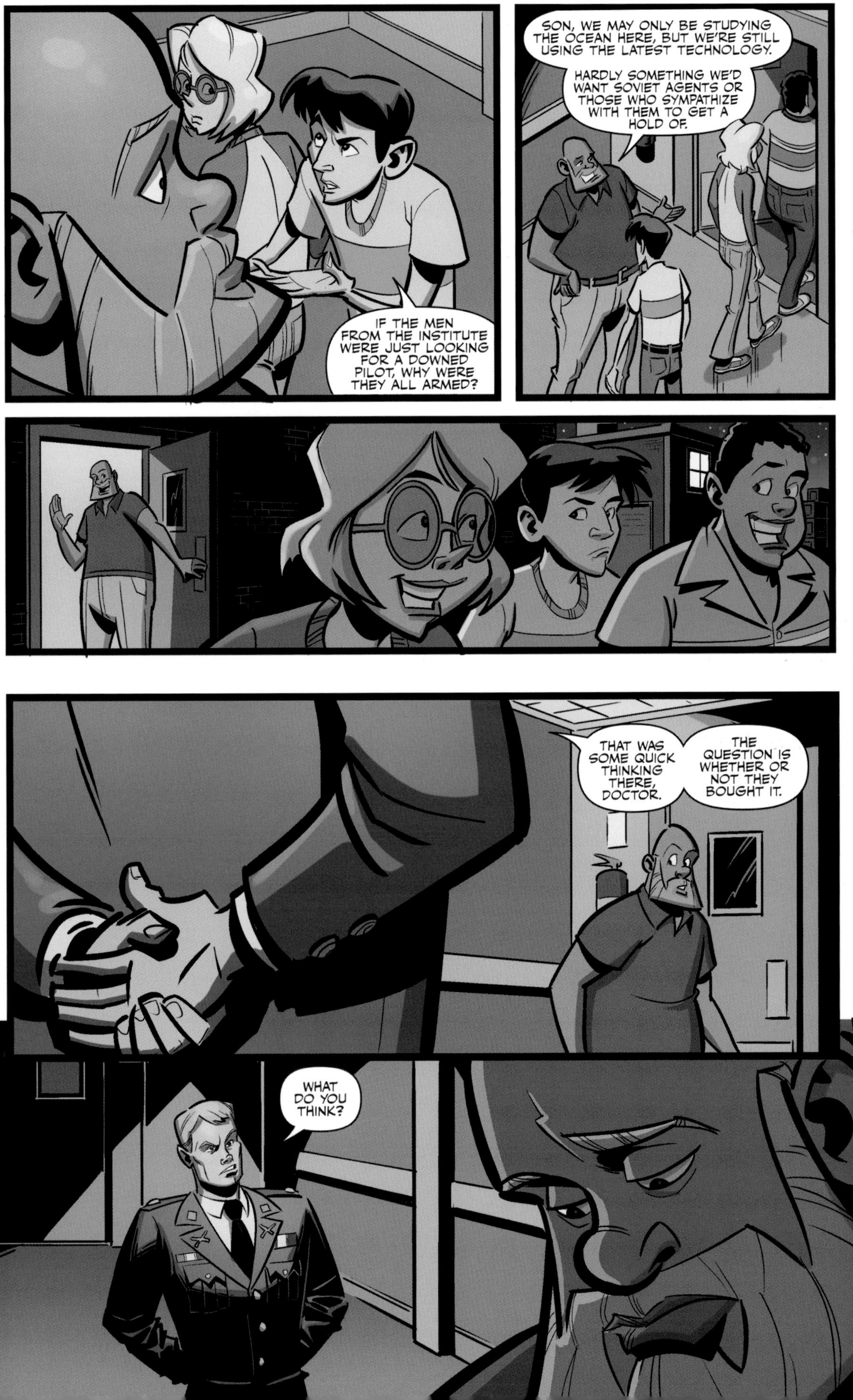
IF THE MEN FROM THE INSTITUTE WERE JUST LOOKING FOR A DOWNED PILOT, WHY WERE THEY ALL ARMED?
SON, WE MAY ONLY BE STUDYING THE OCEAN HERE, BUT WE'RE STILL USING THE LATEST TECHNOLOGY.
HARDLY SOMETHING WE'D WANT SOVIET AGENTS OR THOSE WHO SYMPATHIZE WITH THEM TO GET A HOLD OF.
THAT WAS SOME QUICK THINKING THERE, DOCTOR.
THE QUESTION IS WHETHER OR NOT THEY BOUGHT IT.
WHAT DO YOU THINK?

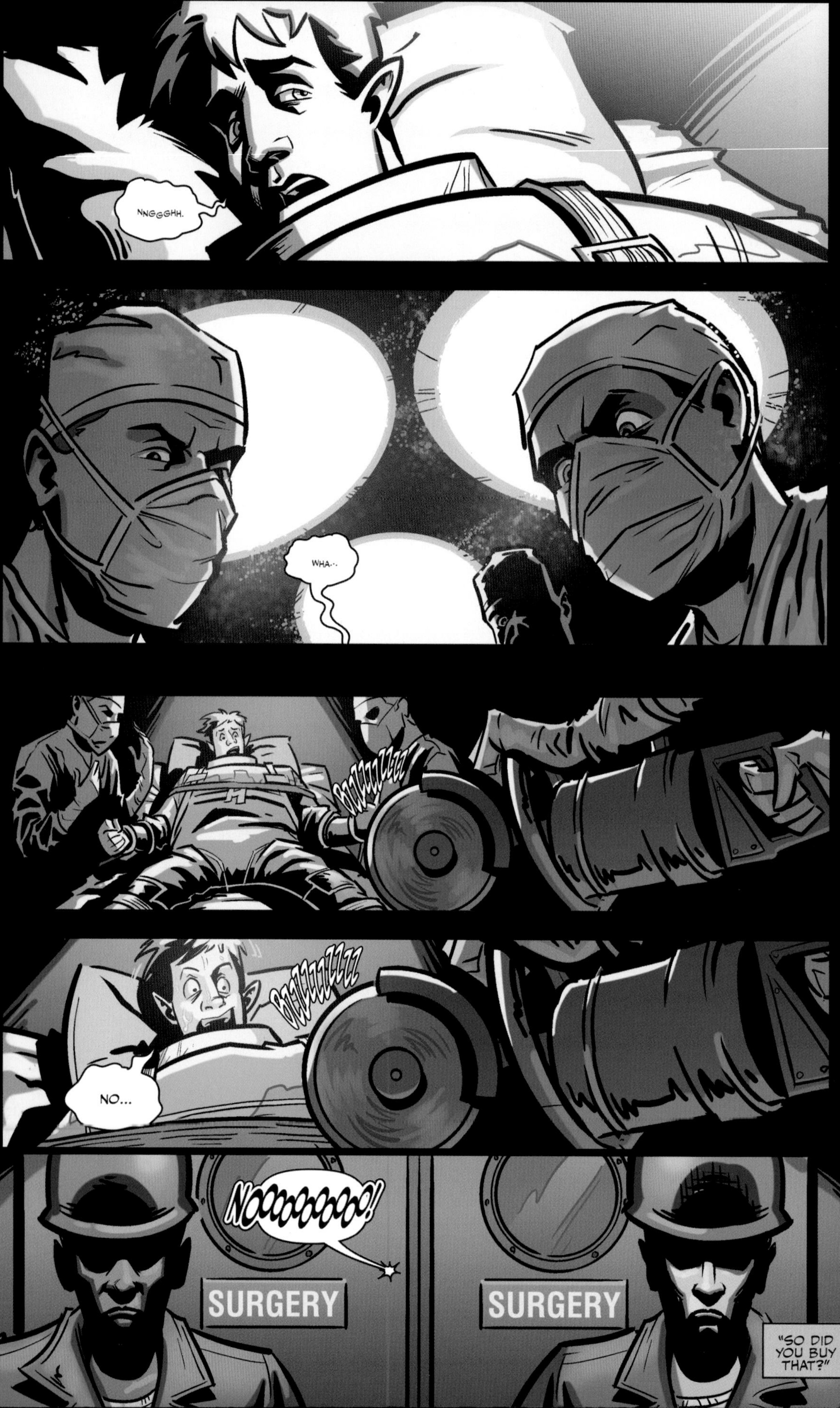
NNGGGHH.
WHA...
BRZZZZZZZZZ
BRZZZZZZZZZ
NO...
NOOOOOOOOO!
SURGERY
SURGERY
"SO DID YOU BUY THAT?"

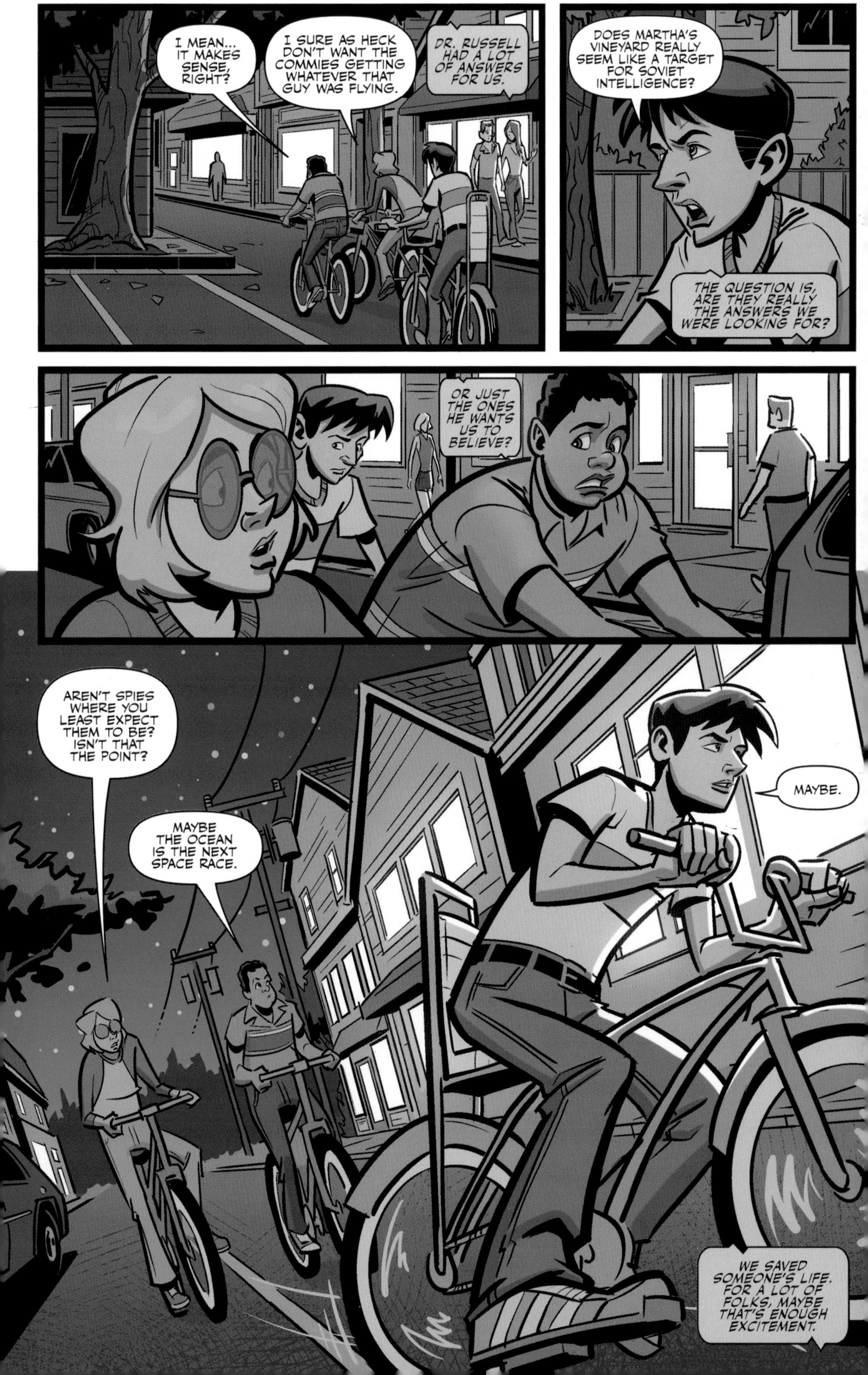
I MEAN... IT MAKES SENSE, RIGHT?
I SURE AS HECK DON'T WANT THE COMMIES GETTING WHATEVER THAT GUY WAS FLYING.
DR. RUSSELL HAD A LOT OF ANSWERS FOR US.
DOES MARTHA'S VINEYARD REALLY SEEM LIKE A TARGET FOR SOVIET INTELLIGENCE?
THE QUESTION IS, ARE THEY REALLY THE ANSWERS WE WERE LOOKING FOR?
OR JUST THE ONES HE WANTS US TO BELIEVE?
AREN'T SPIES WHERE YOU LEAST EXPECT THEM TO BE? ISN'T THAT THE POINT?
MAYBE THE OCEAN IS THE NEXT SPACE RACE.
MAYBE.
WE SAVED SOMEONE'S LIFE. FOR A LOT OF FOLKS, MAYBE THAT'S ENOUGH EXCITEMENT.

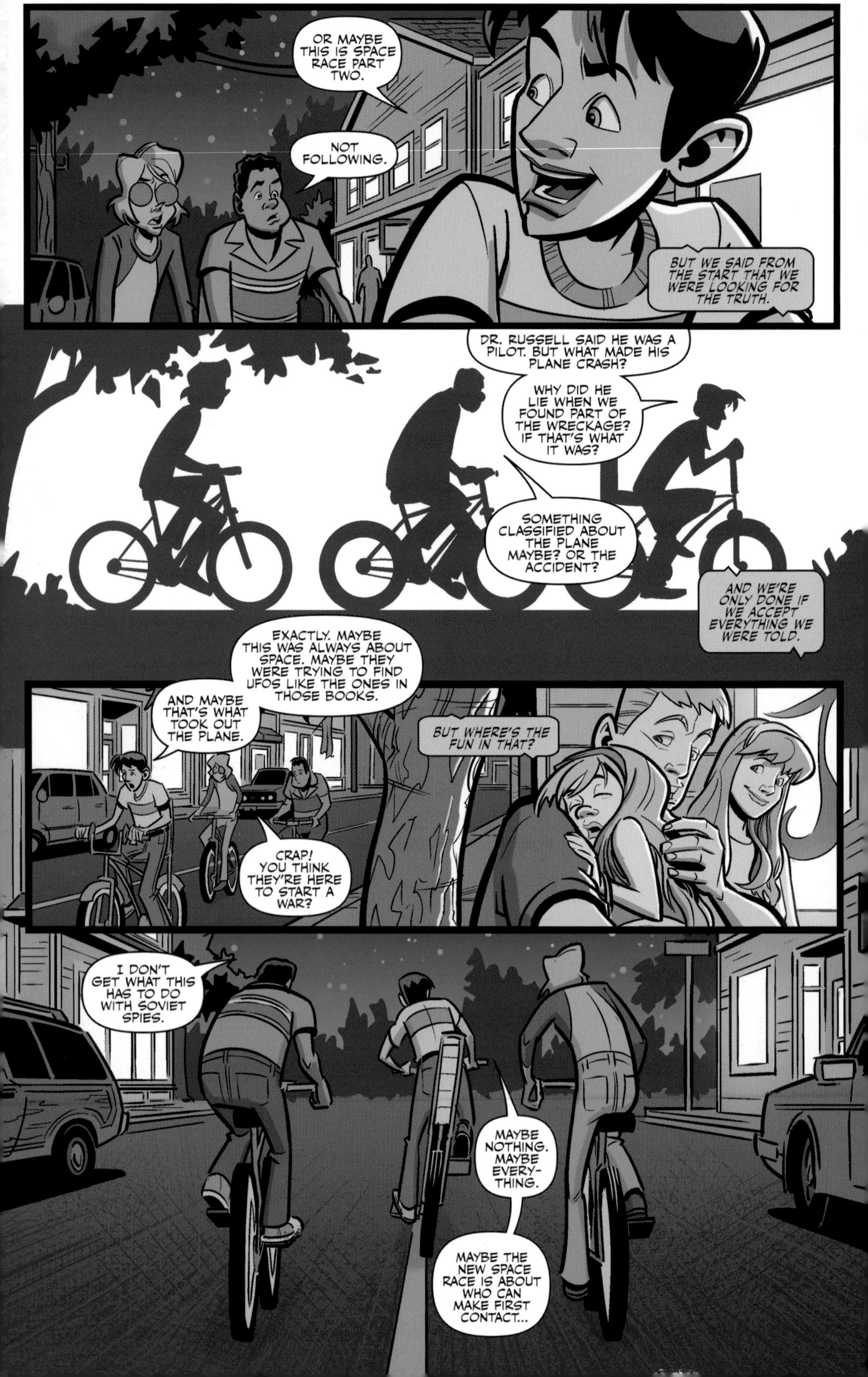
OR MAYBE THIS IS SPACE RACE PART TWO.
NOT FOLLOWING.
BUT WE SAID FROM THE START THAT WE WERE LOOKING FOR THE TRUTH.
DR. RUSSELL SAID HE WAS A PILOT. BUT WHAT MADE HIS PLANE CRASH?
WHY DID HE LIE WHEN WE FOUND PART OF THE WRECKAGE? IF THAT'S WHAT IT WAS?
SOMETHING CLASSIFIED ABOUT THE PLANE MAYBE? OR THE ACCIDENT?
AND WE'RE ONLY DONE IF WE ACCEPT EVERYTHING WE WERE TOLD.
EXACTLY. MAYBE THIS WAS ALWAYS ABOUT SPACE. MAYBE THEY WERE TRYING TO FIND UFOS LIKE THE ONES IN THOSE BOOKS.
AND MAYBE THAT'S WHAT TOOK OUT THE PLANE.
BUT WHERE'S THE FUN IN THAT?
CRAP! YOU THINK THEY'RE HERE TO START A WAR?
I DON'T GET WHAT THIS HAS TO DO WITH SOVIET SPIES.
MAYBE NOTHING. MAYBE EVERY-THING.
MAYBE THE NEW SPACE RACE IS ABOUT WHO CAN MAKE FIRST CONTACT...

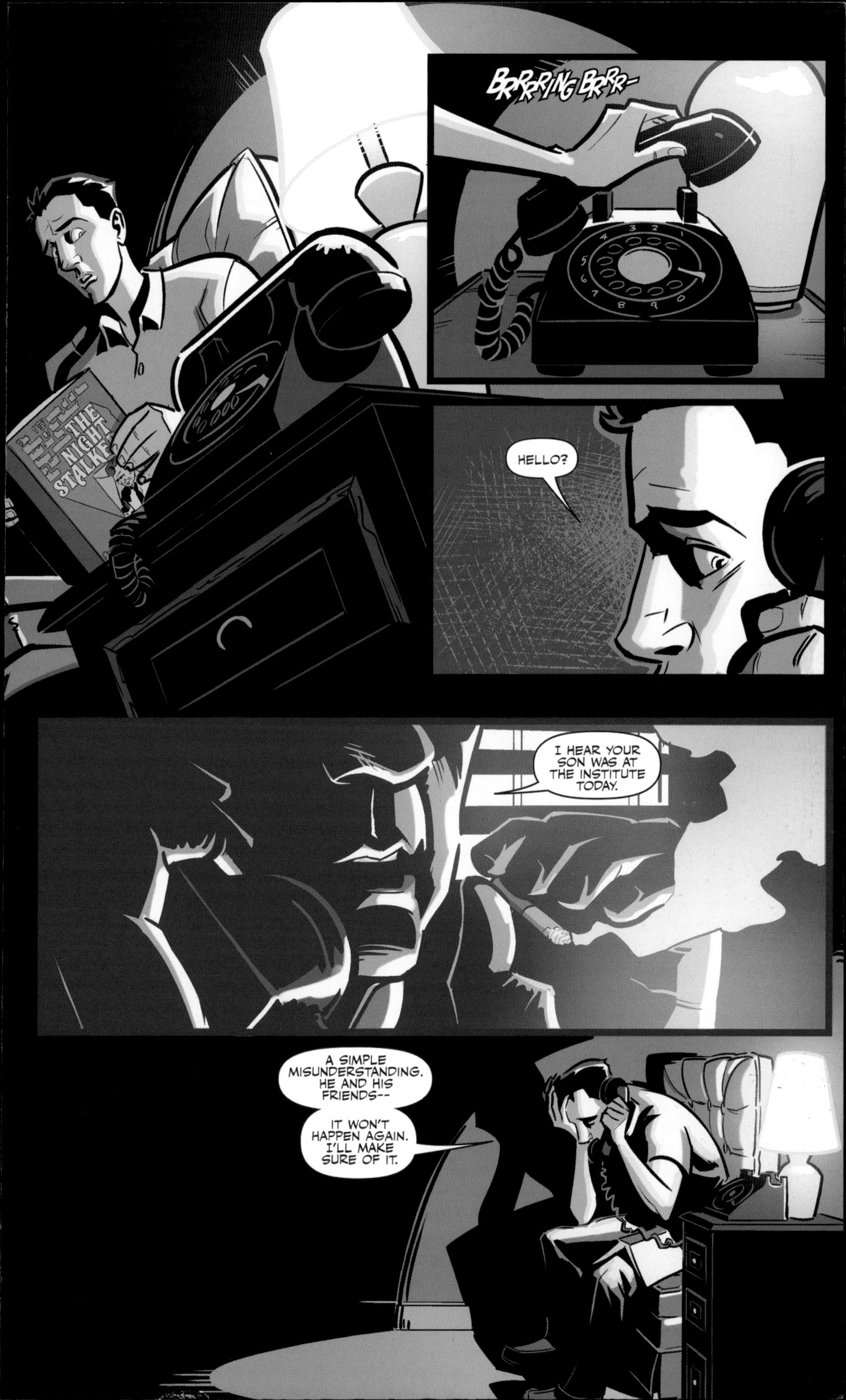
BRRRRING BRRR-
THE NIGHT STALKER
HELLO?
I HEAR YOUR SON WAS AT THE INSTITUTE TODAY.
A SIMPLE MISUNDERSTANDING. HE AND HIS FRIENDS--
IT WON'T HAPPEN AGAIN. I'LL MAKE SURE OF IT.

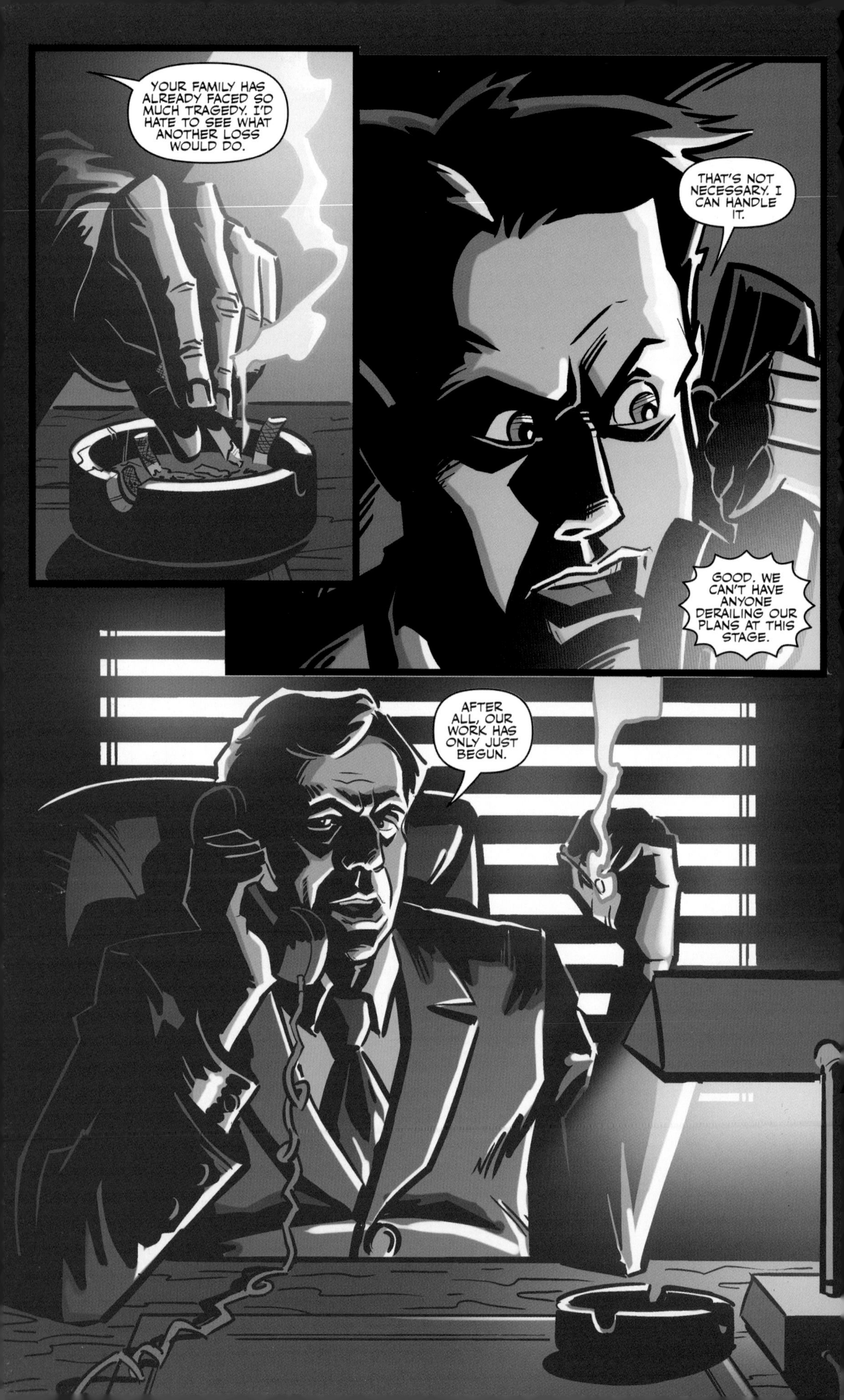
YOUR FAMILY HAS ALREADY FACED SO MUCH TRAGEDY. I'D HATE TO SEE WHAT ANOTHER LOSS WOULD DO.
THAT'S NOT NECESSARY. I CAN HANDLE IT.
GOOD. WE CAN'T HAVE ANYONE DERAILING OUR PLANS AT THIS STAGE.
AFTER ALL, OUR WORK HAS ONLY JUST BEGUN.

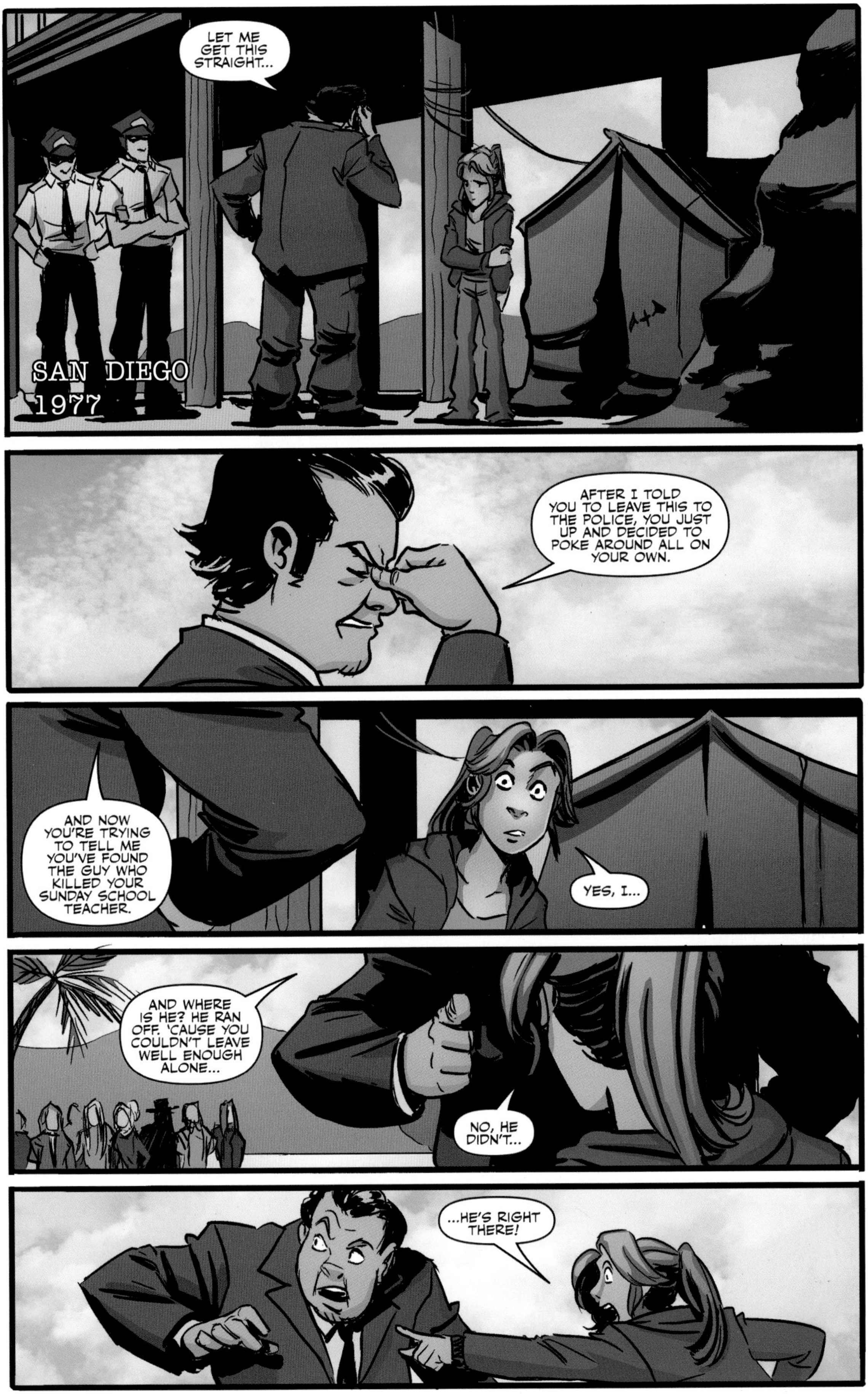
LET ME GET THIS STRAIGHT...
SAN DIEGO 1977
AFTER I TOLD YOU TO LEAVE THIS TO THE POLICE, YOU JUST UP AND DECIDED TO POKE AROUND ALL ON YOUR OWN.
AND NOW YOU'RE TRYING TO TELL ME YOU'VE FOUND THE GUY WHO KILLED YOUR SUNDAY SCHOOL TEACHER.
YES, I...
AND WHERE IS HE? HE RAN OFF. 'CAUSE YOU COULDN'T LEAVE WELL ENOUGH ALONE...
NO, HE DIDN'T...
...HE'S RIGHT THERE!

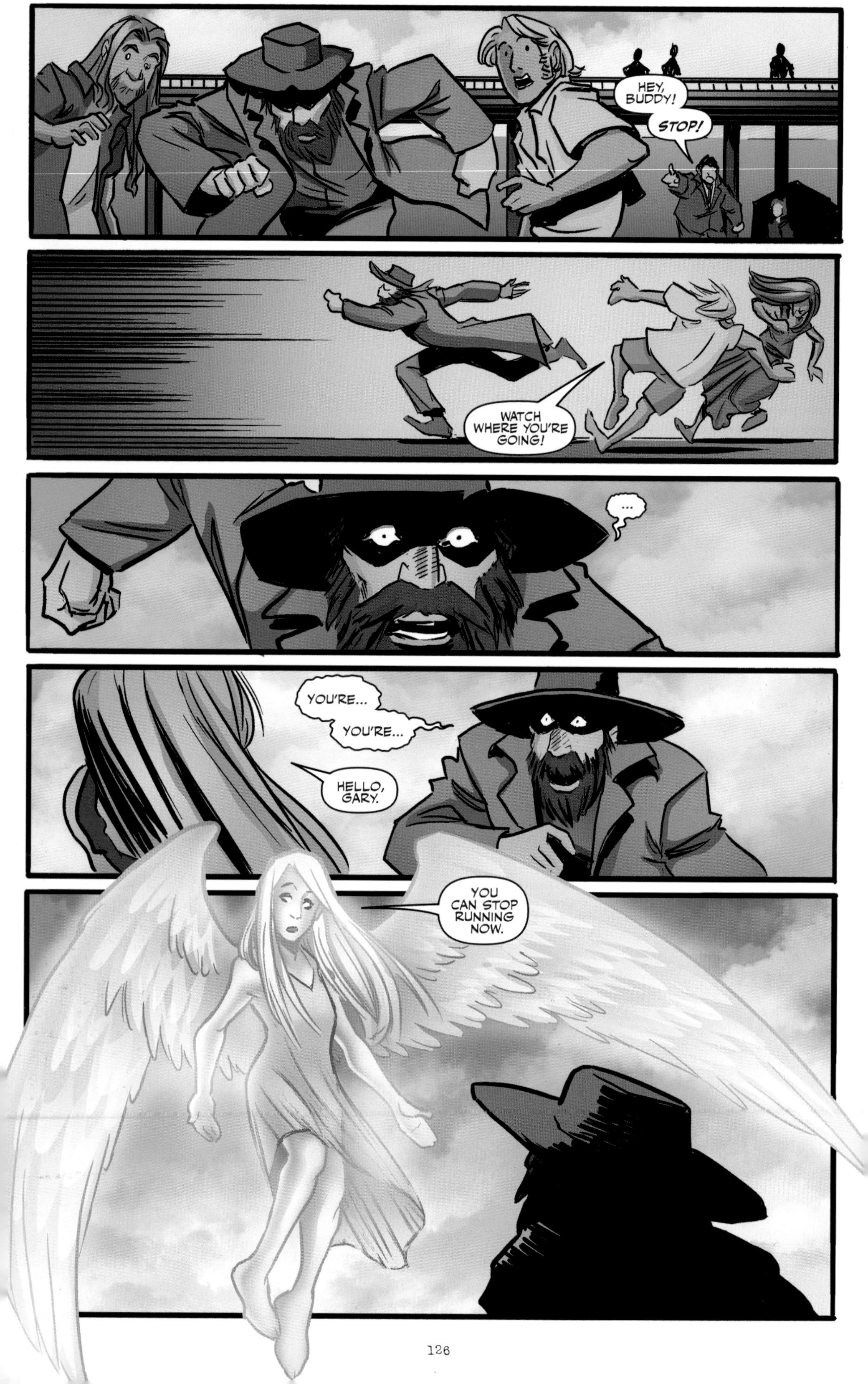
HEY, BUDDY!
STOP!
WATCH WHERE YOU'RE GOING!
...
YOU'RE...
YOU'RE...
HELLO, GARY.
YOU CAN STOP RUNNING NOW.

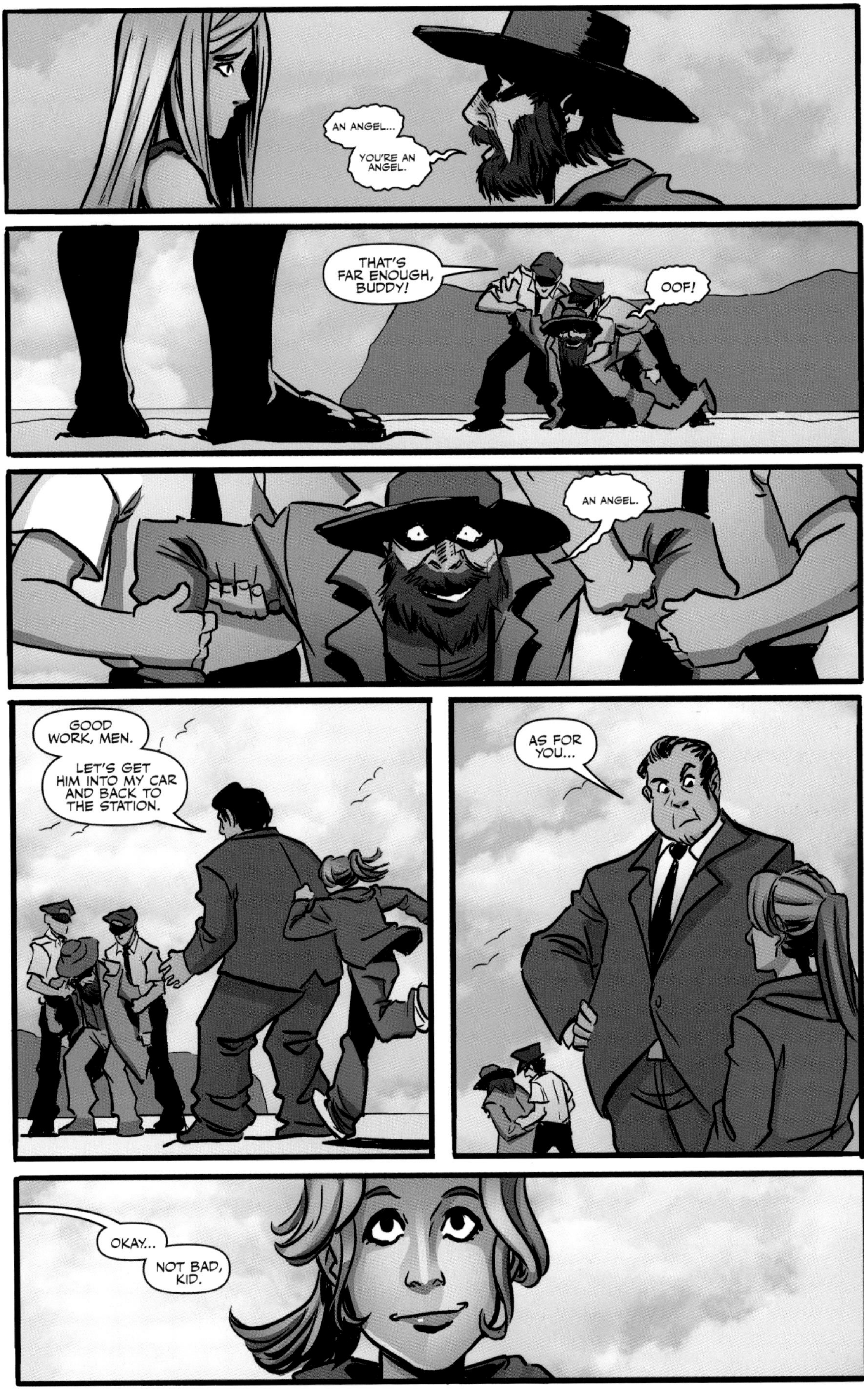
AN ANGEL...
YOU'RE AN ANGEL.
THAT'S FAR ENOUGH, BUDDY!
OOF!
AN ANGEL.
GOOD WORK, MEN.
LET'S GET HIM INTO MY CAR AND BACK TO THE STATION.
AS FOR YOU...
OKAY...
NOT BAD, KID.

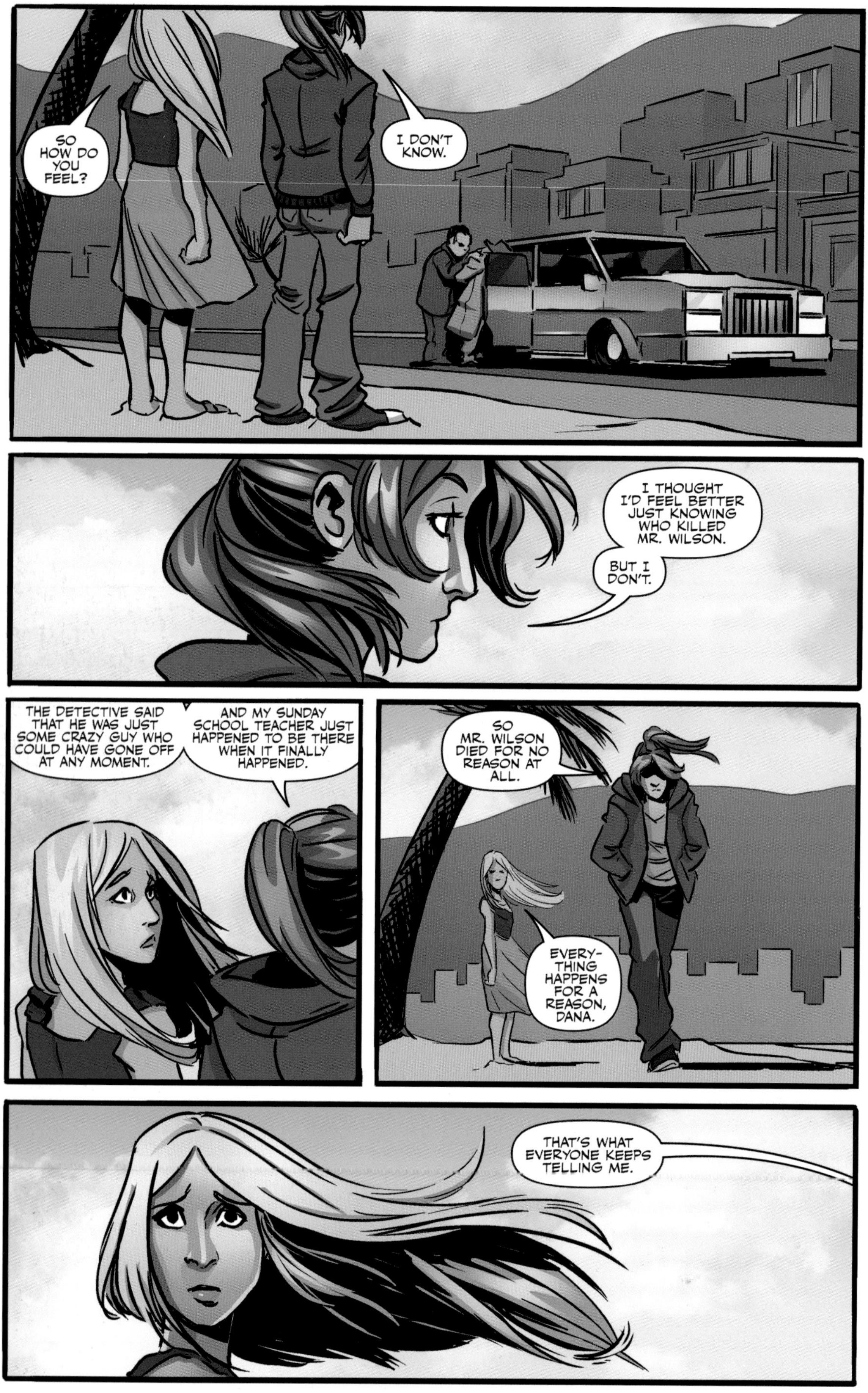
SO HOW DO YOU FEEL?
I DON'T KNOW.
I THOUGHT I'D FEEL BETTER JUST KNOWING WHO KILLED MR. WILSON.
BUT I DON'T.
THE DETECTIVE SAID THAT HE WAS JUST SOME CRAZY GUY WHO COULD HAVE GONE OFF AT ANY MOMENT.
AND MY SUNDAY SCHOOL TEACHER JUST HAPPENED TO BE THERE WHEN IT FINALLY HAPPENED.
SO MR. WILSON DIED FOR NO REASON AT ALL.
EVERY-THING HAPPENS FOR A REASON, DANA.
THAT'S WHAT EVERYONE KEEPS TELLING ME.

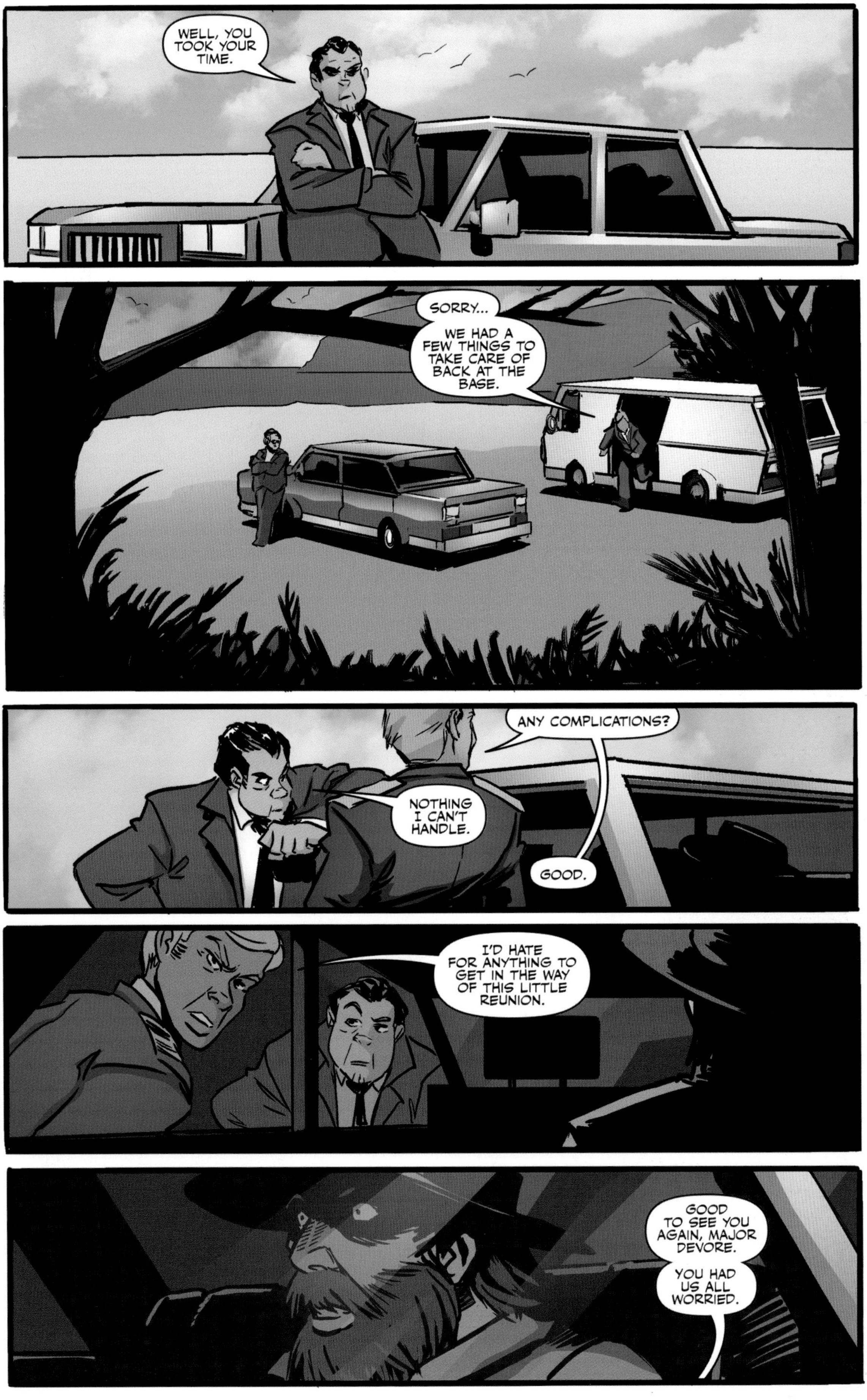
WELL, YOU TOOK YOUR TIME.
SORRY...
WE HAD A FEW THINGS TO TAKE CARE OF BACK AT THE BASE.
ANY COMPLICATIONS?
NOTHING I CAN'T HANDLE.
GOOD.
I'D HATE FOR ANYTHING TO GET IN THE WAY OF THIS LITTLE REUNION.
GOOD TO SEE YOU AGAIN, MAJOR DEVORE.
YOU HAD US ALL WORRIED.

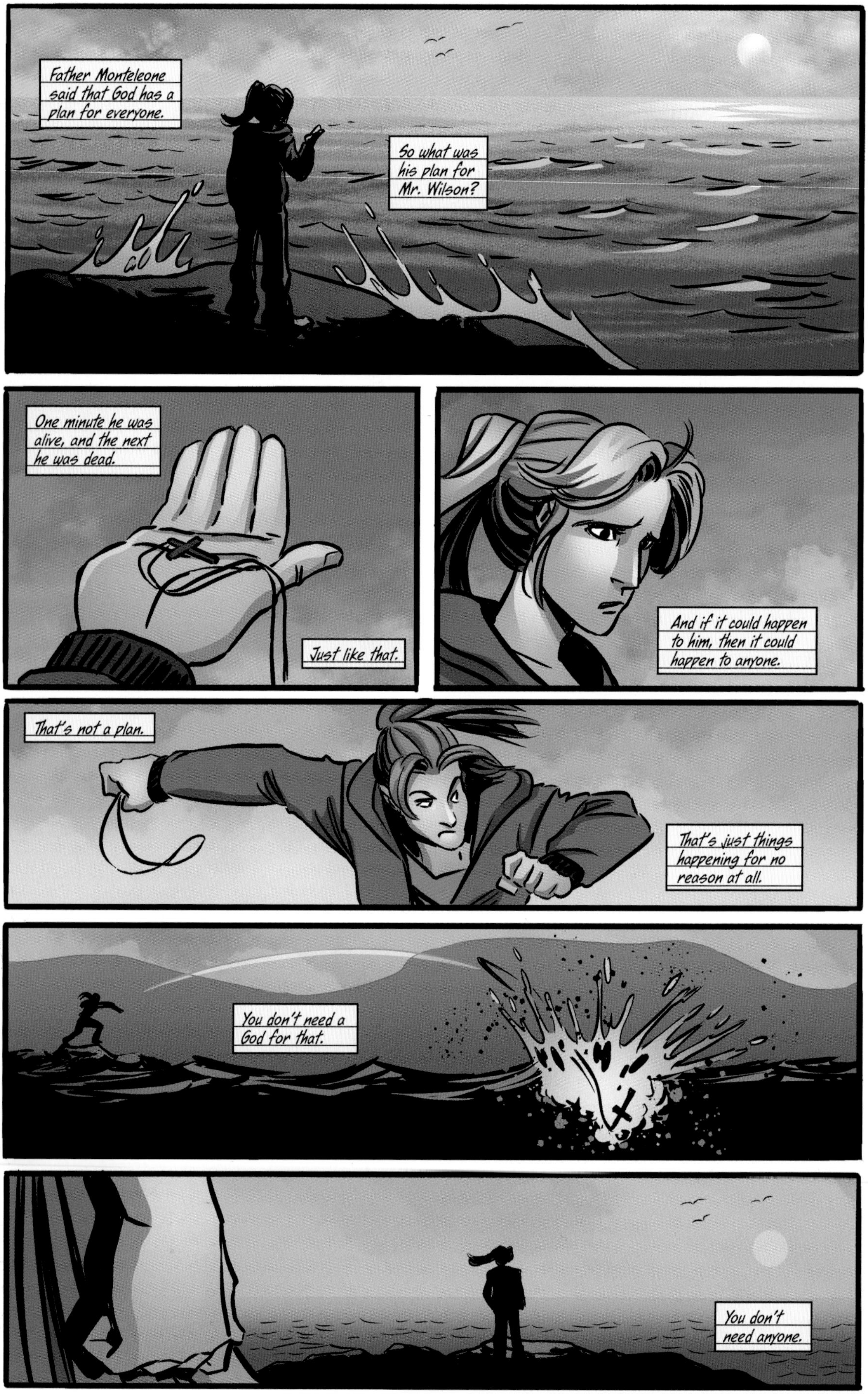
Father Monteleone said that God has a plan for everyone.
So what was his plan for Mr. Wilson?
One minute he was alive, and the next he was dead.
Just like that.
And if it could happen to him, then it could happen to anyone.
That's not a plan.
That's just things happening for no reason at all.
You don't need a God for that.
You don't need anyone.

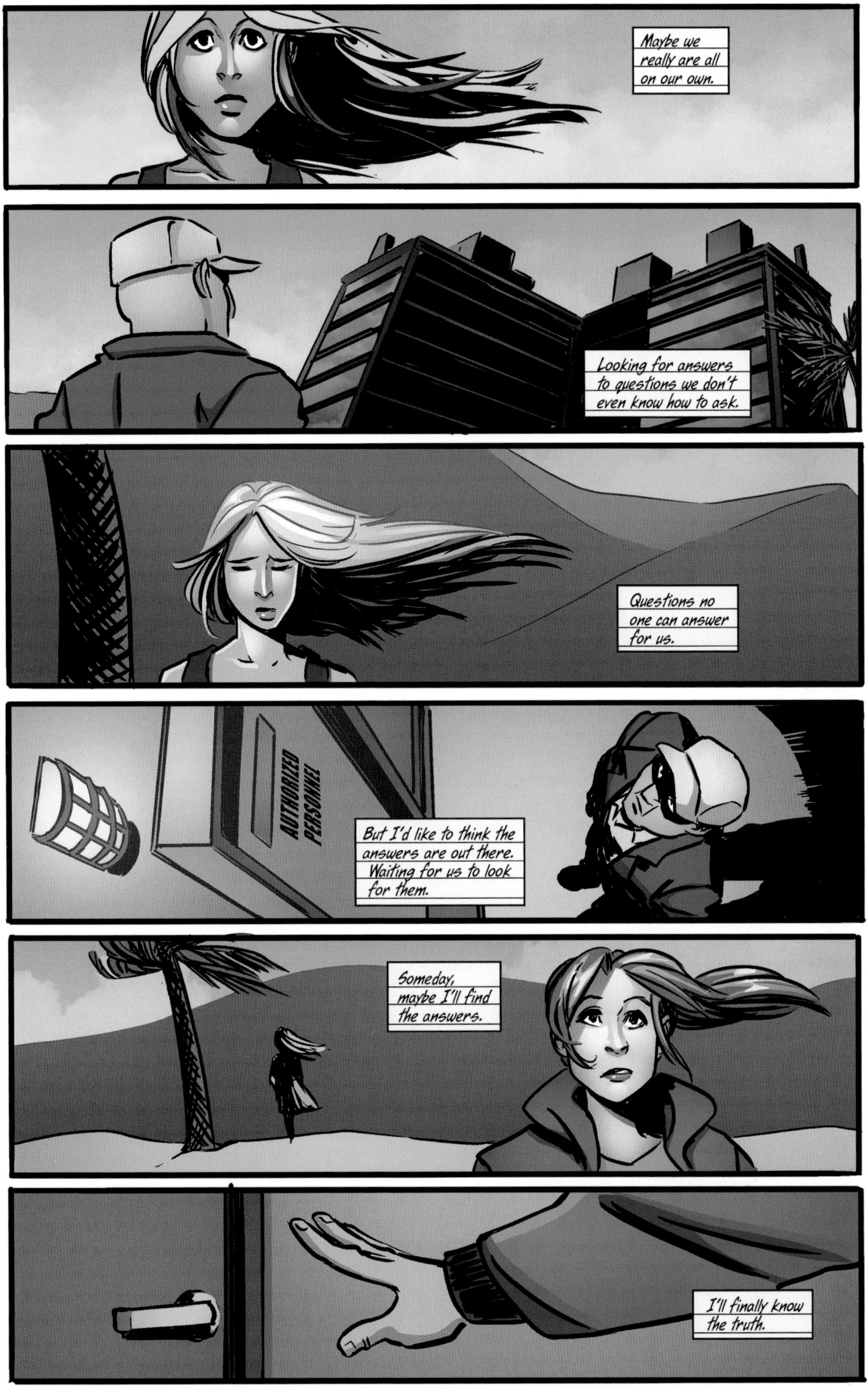
Maybe we really are all on our own.
Looking for answers to questions we don't even know how to ask.
Questions no one can answer for us.
AUTHORIZED PERSONNEL
But I'd like to think the answers are out there. Waiting for us to look for them.
Someday, maybe I'll find the answers.
I'll finally know the truth.

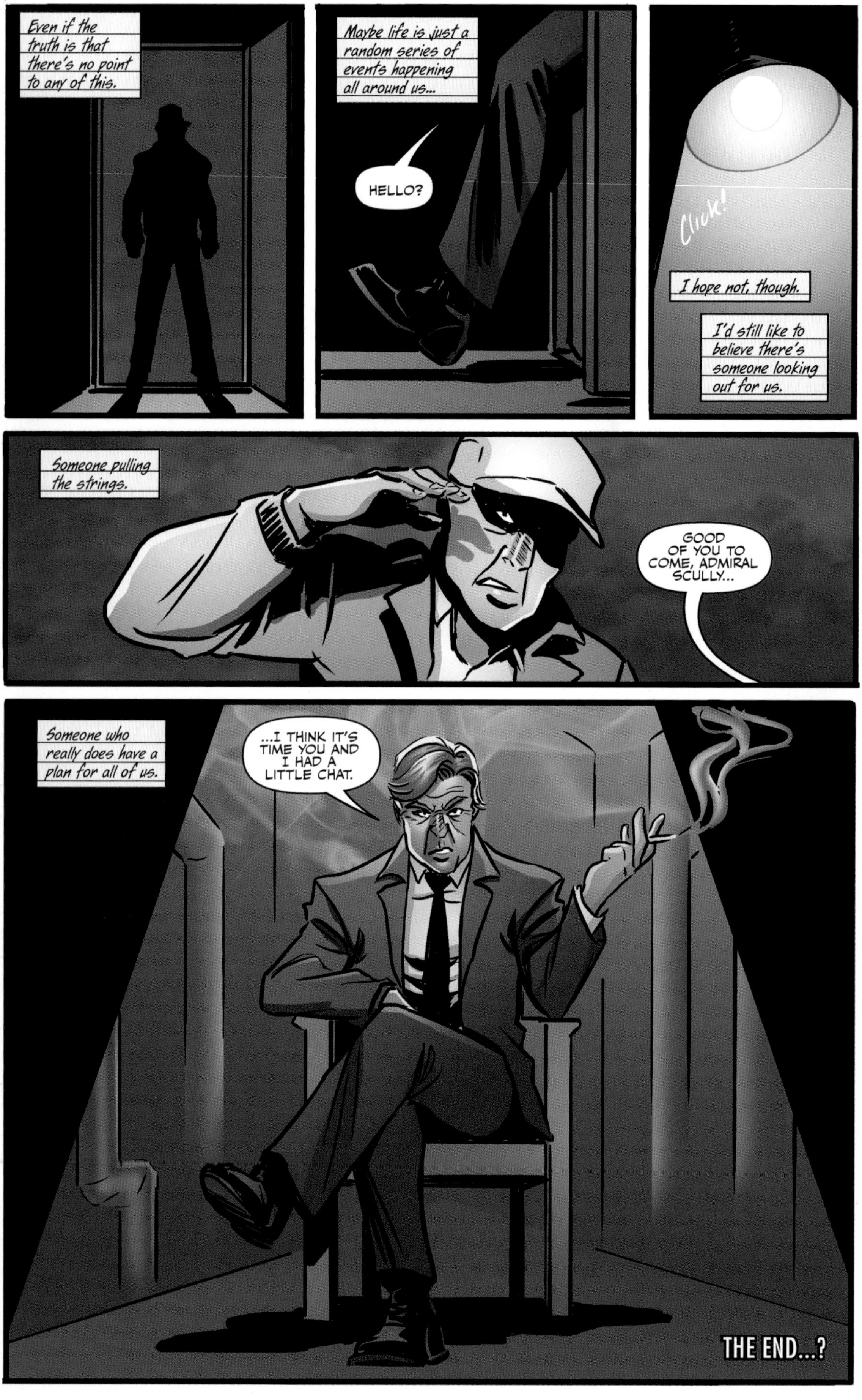

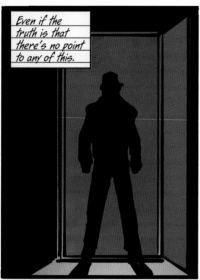

Even if the truth is that there's no point to any of this.
Maybe life is just a random series of events happening all around us...
HELLO?
Click!
I hope not, though.
I'd still like to believe there's someone looking out for us.
Someone pulling the strings.
GOOD OF YOU TO COME, ADMIRAL SCULLY...
Someone who really does have a plan for all of us.
...I THINK IT'S TIME YOU AND I HAD A LITTLE CHAT.
THE END...?

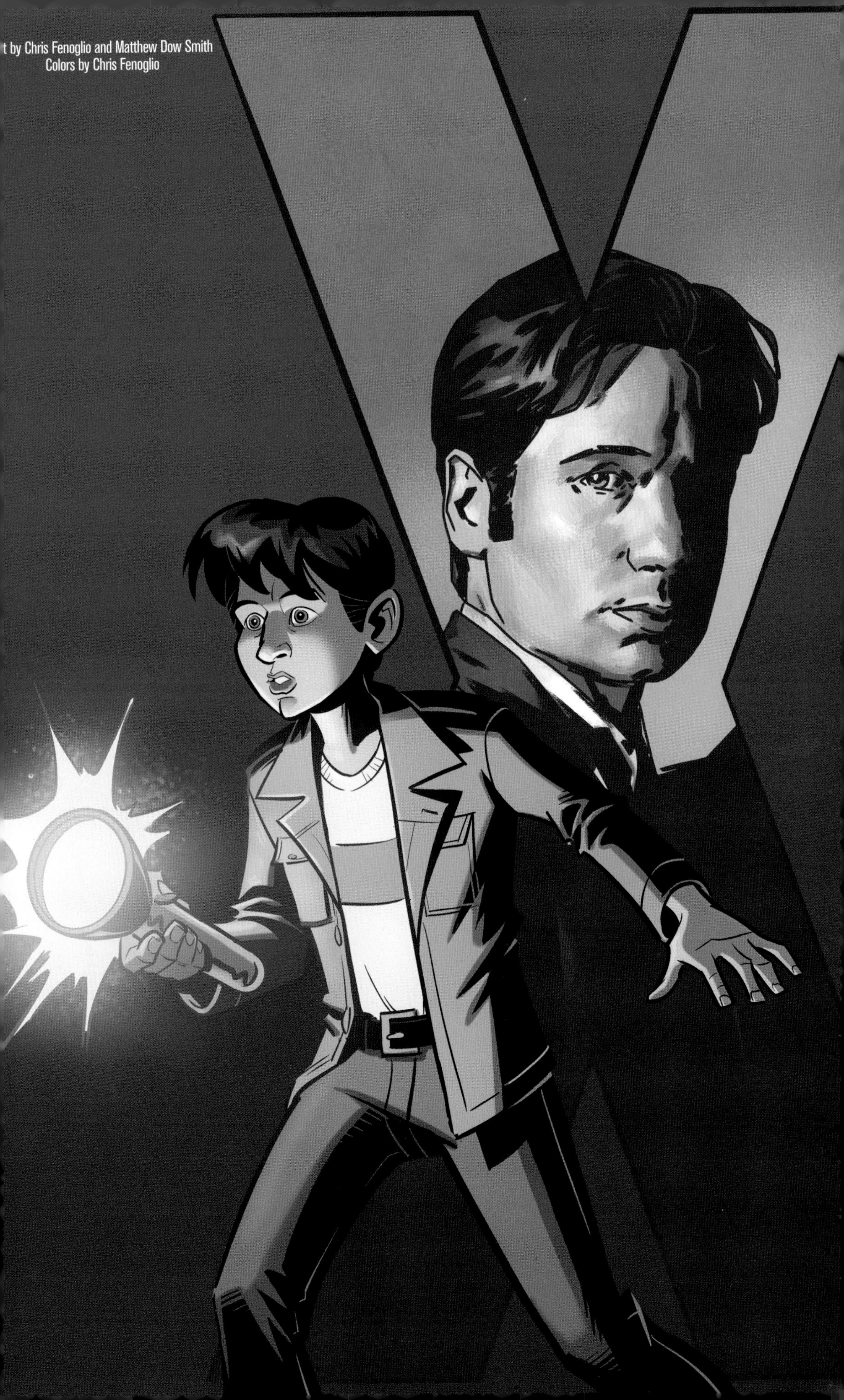

t by Chris Fenoglio and Matthew Dow Smith
Colors by Chris Fenoglio

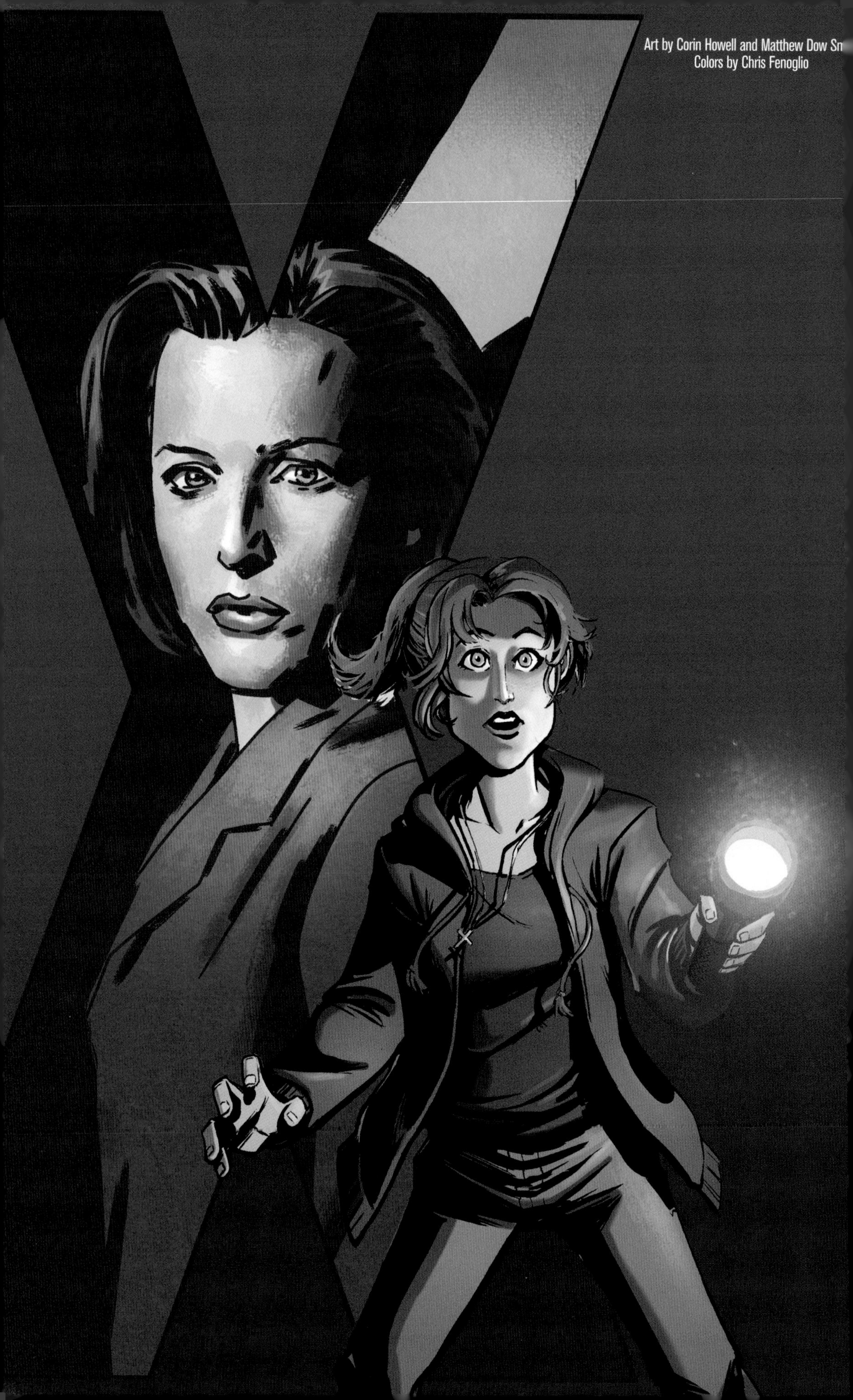

Art by Corin Howell and Matthew Dow Sn
Colors by Chris Fenoglio

Artwork by Chris Fenoglio

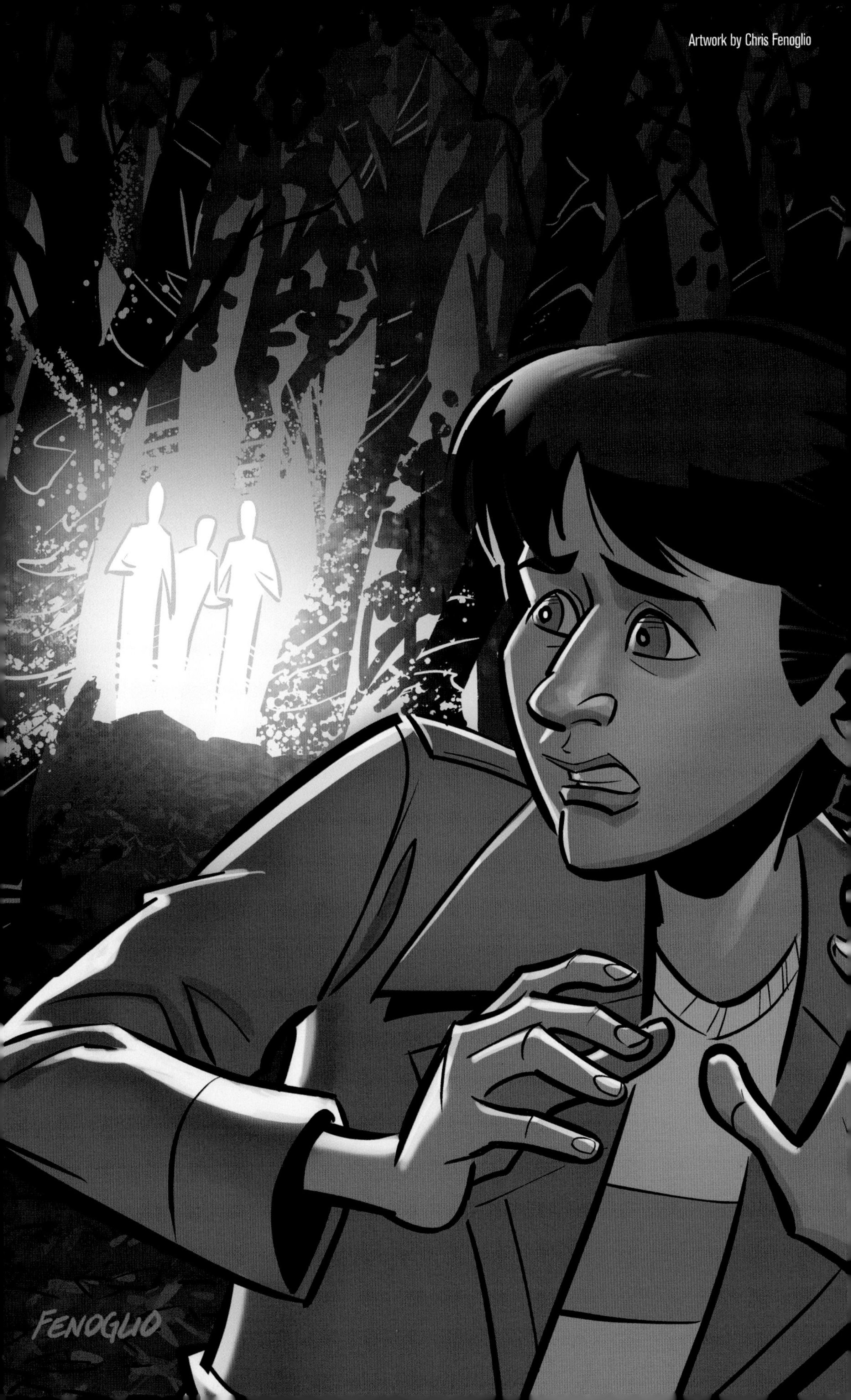
FENOGLIO

Art by Corin Howell
Colors by Chris Fenoglio

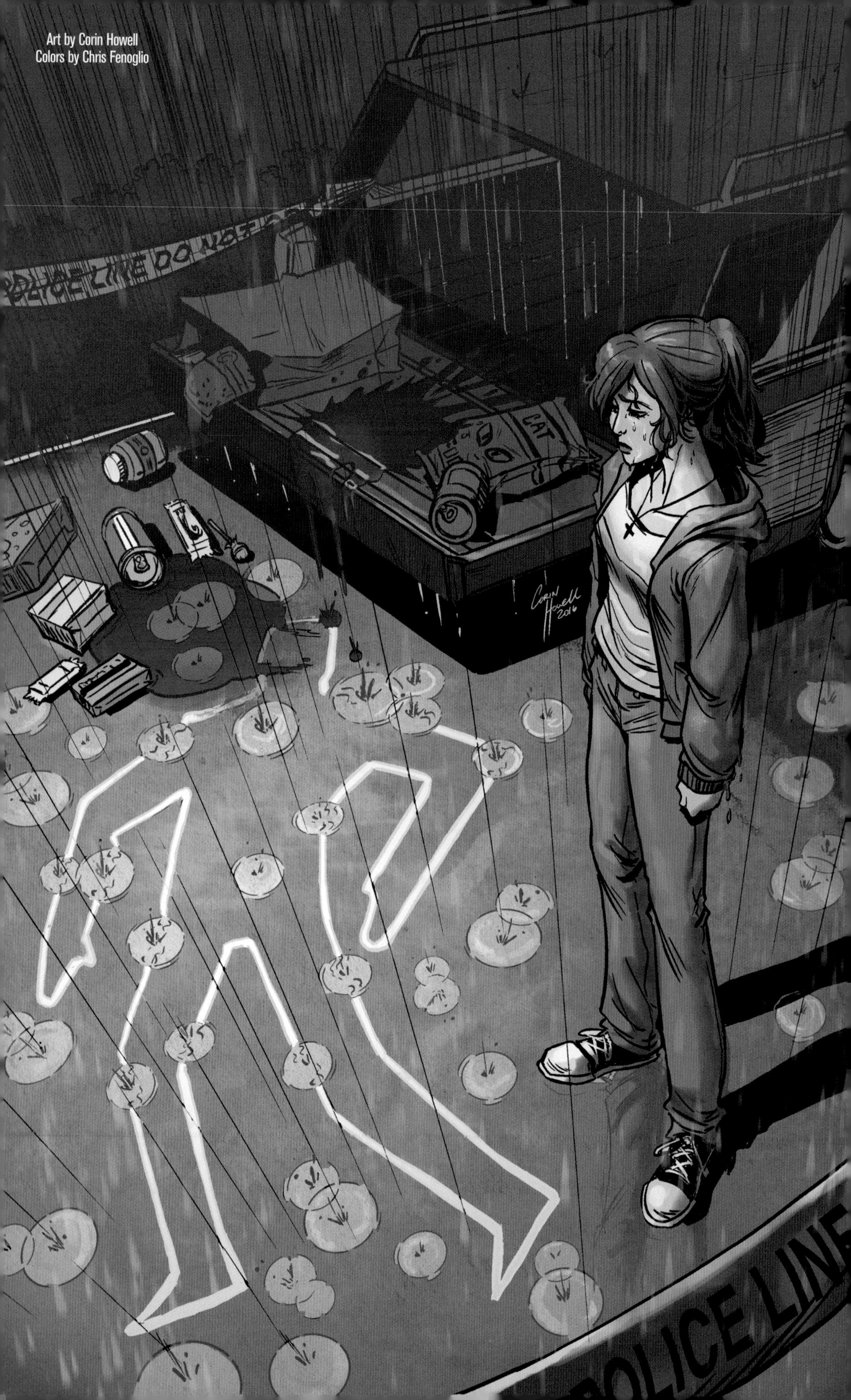

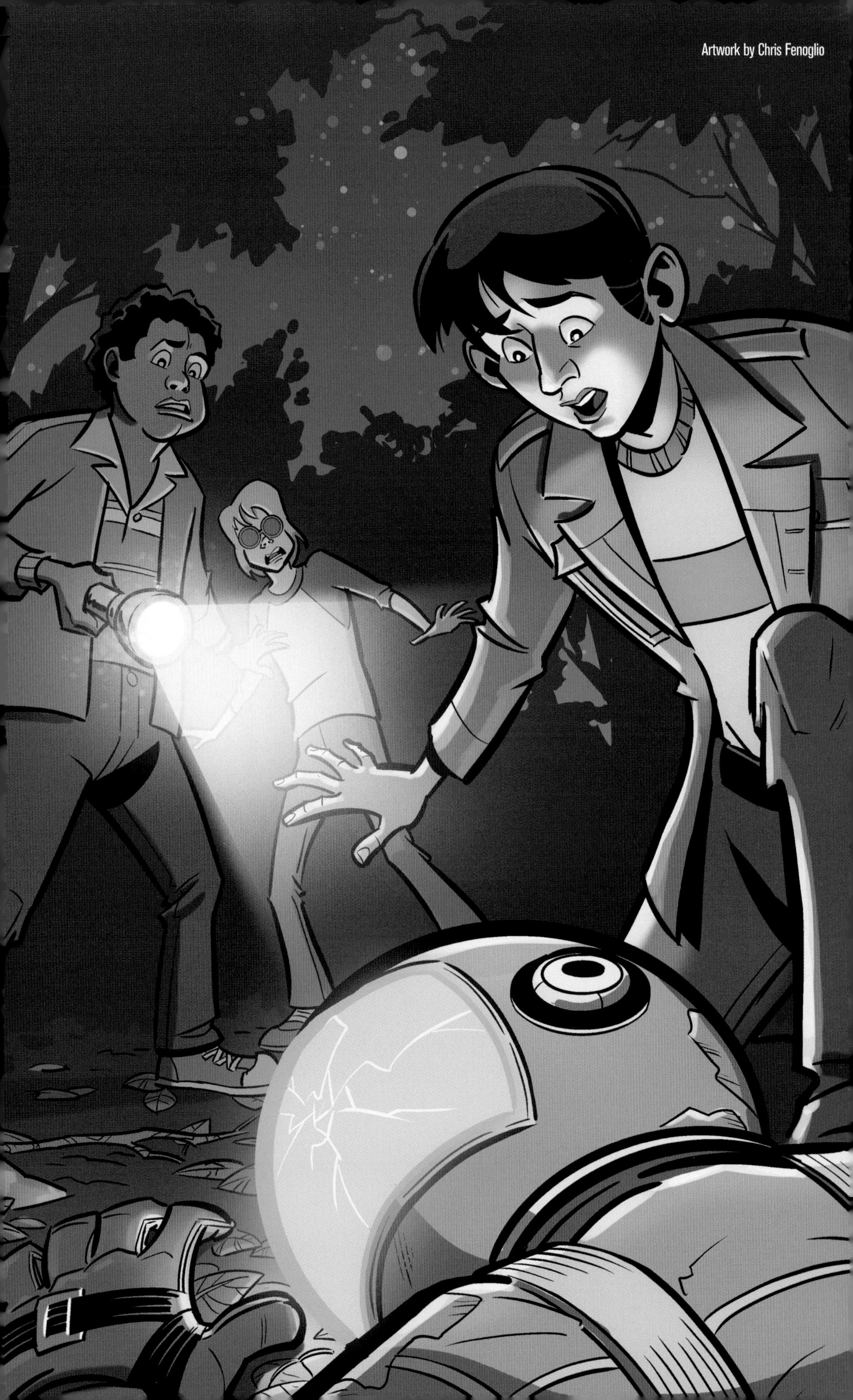

Artwork by Chris Fenoglio

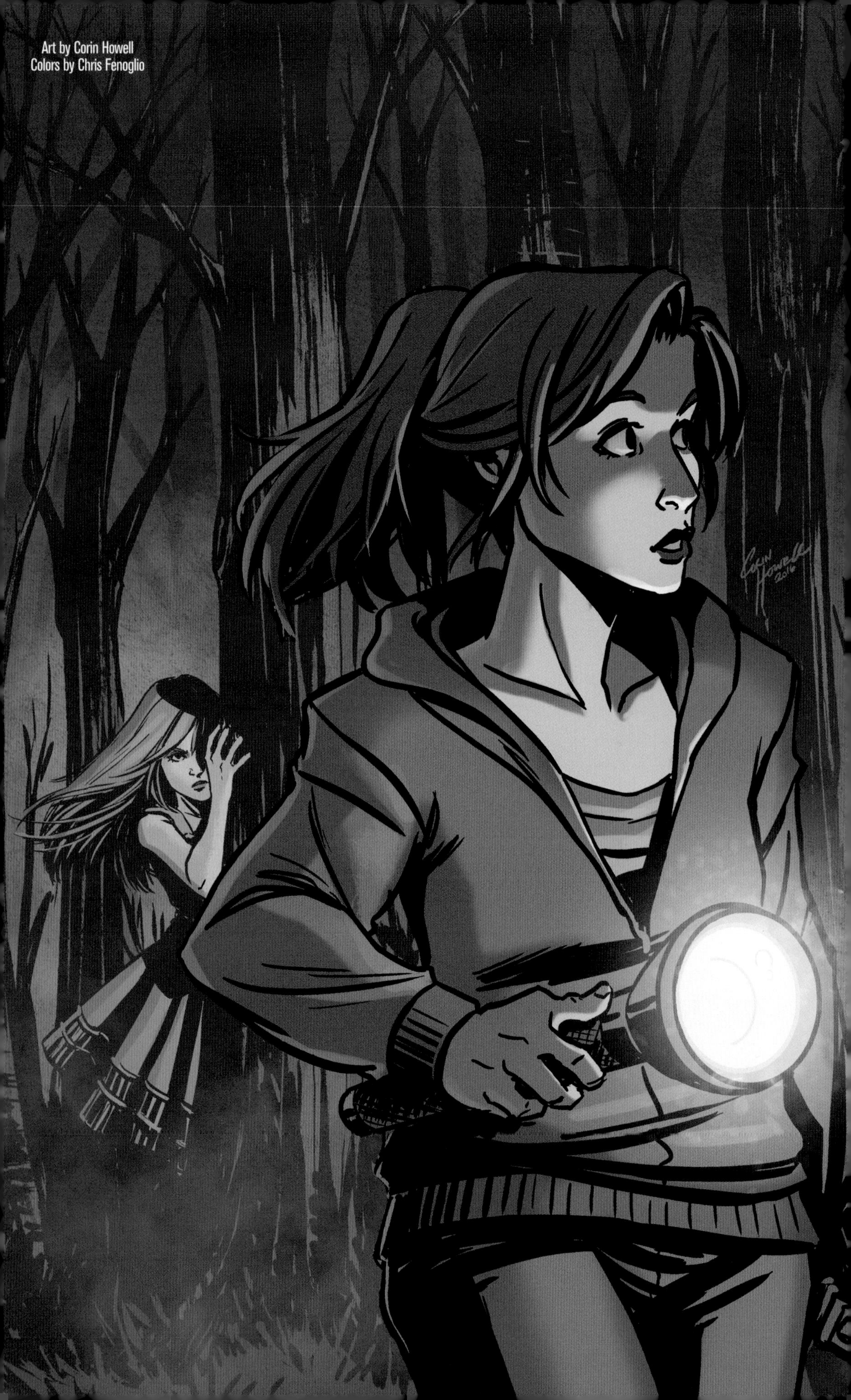
Corin Howell 2016

Art by Corin Howell
Colors by Chris Fenoglio

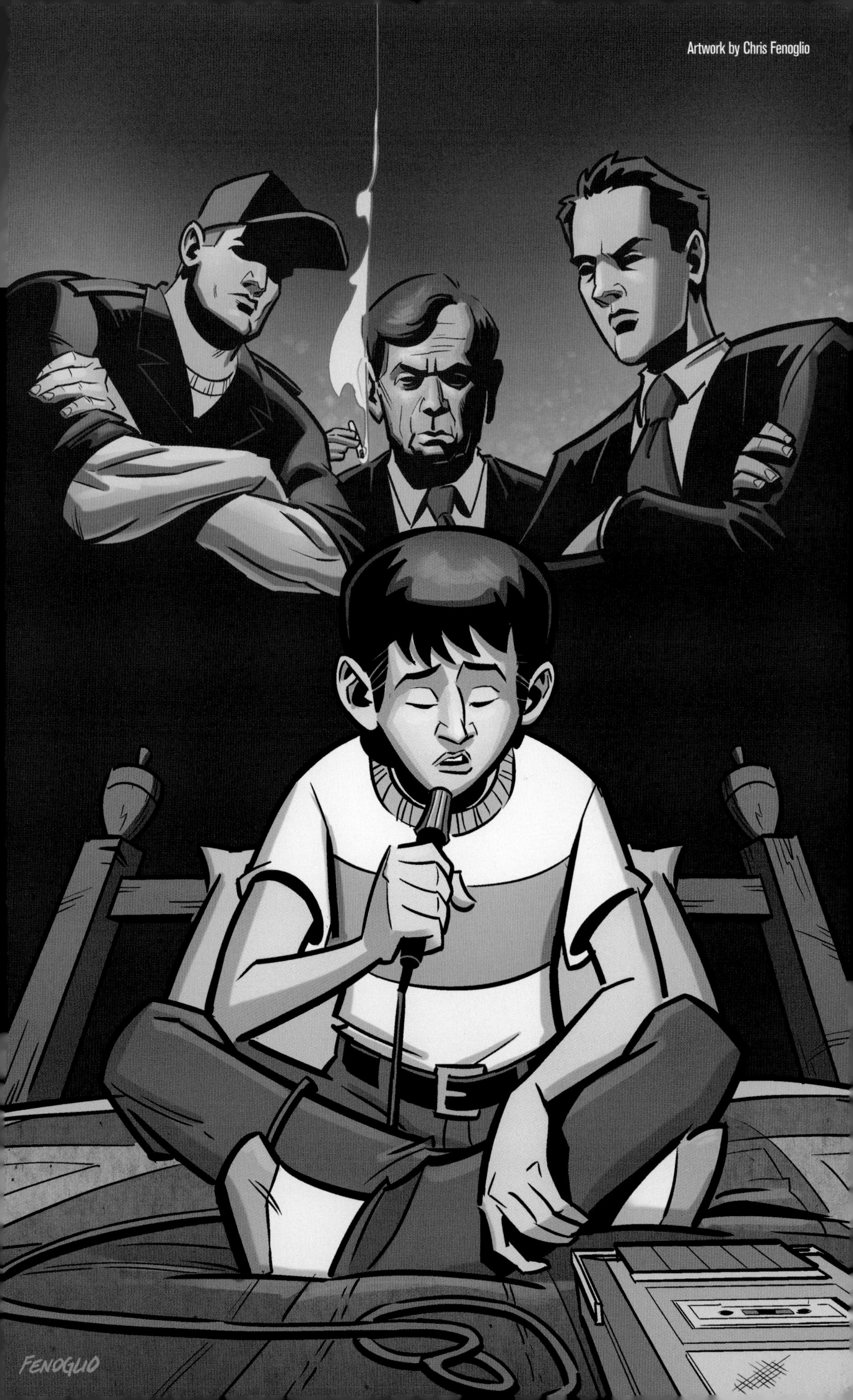
FENOGLIO
Artwork by Chris Fenoglio

Art by Corin Howell
Colors by Chris Fenoglio

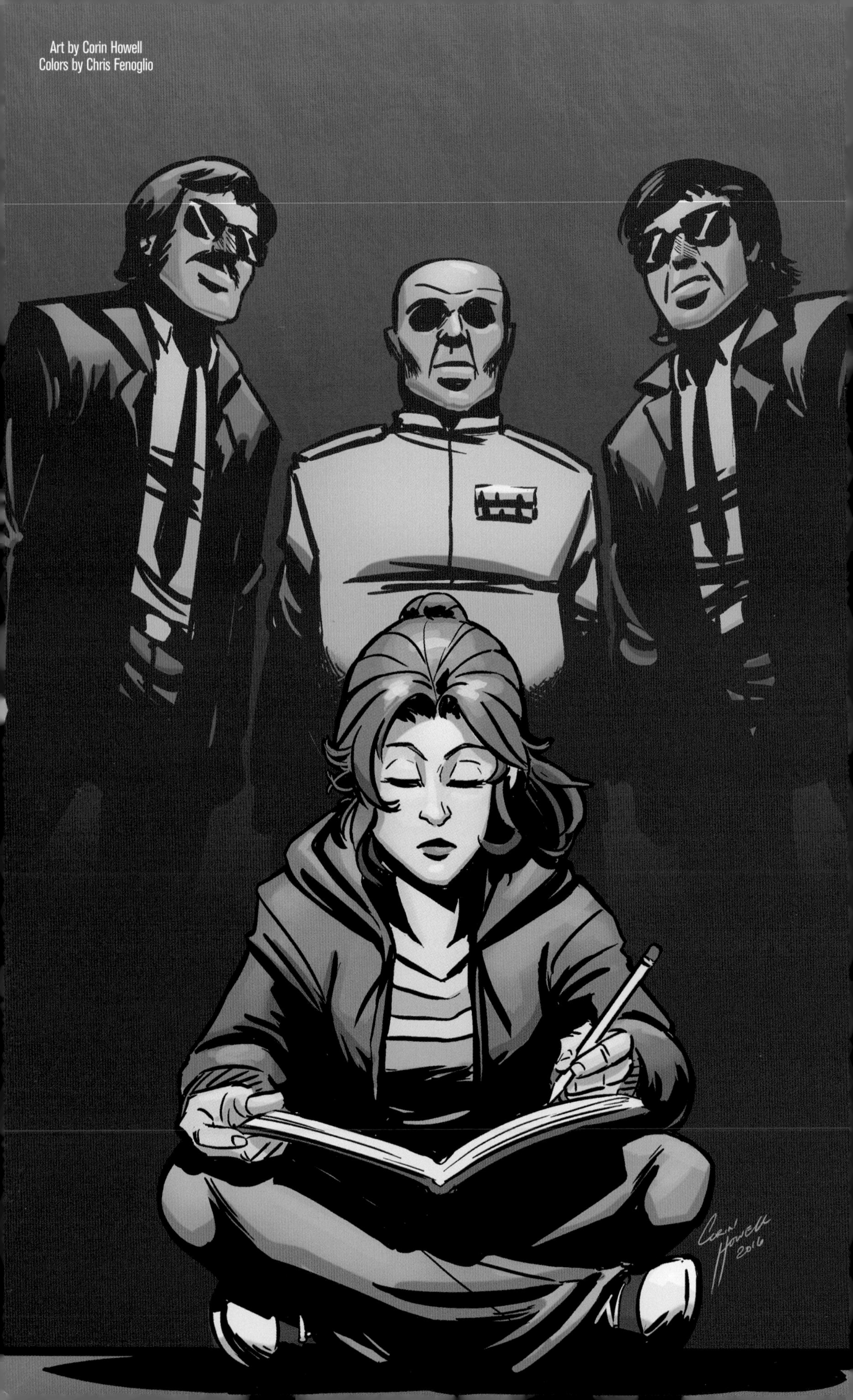
Corin Howell 2016

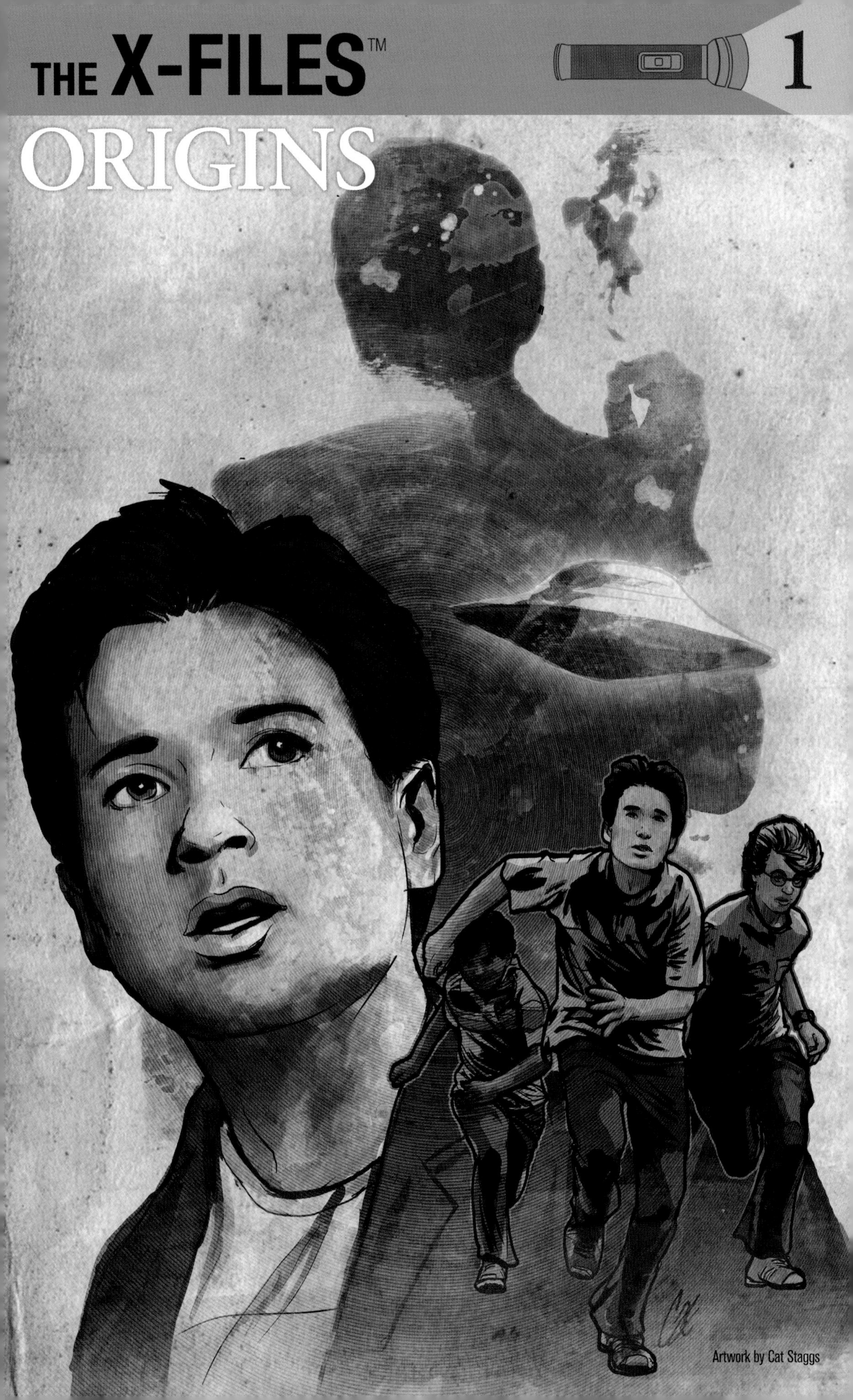
THE X-FILES™
1
ORIGINS
Artwork by Cat Staggs

THE X-FILES™ 1

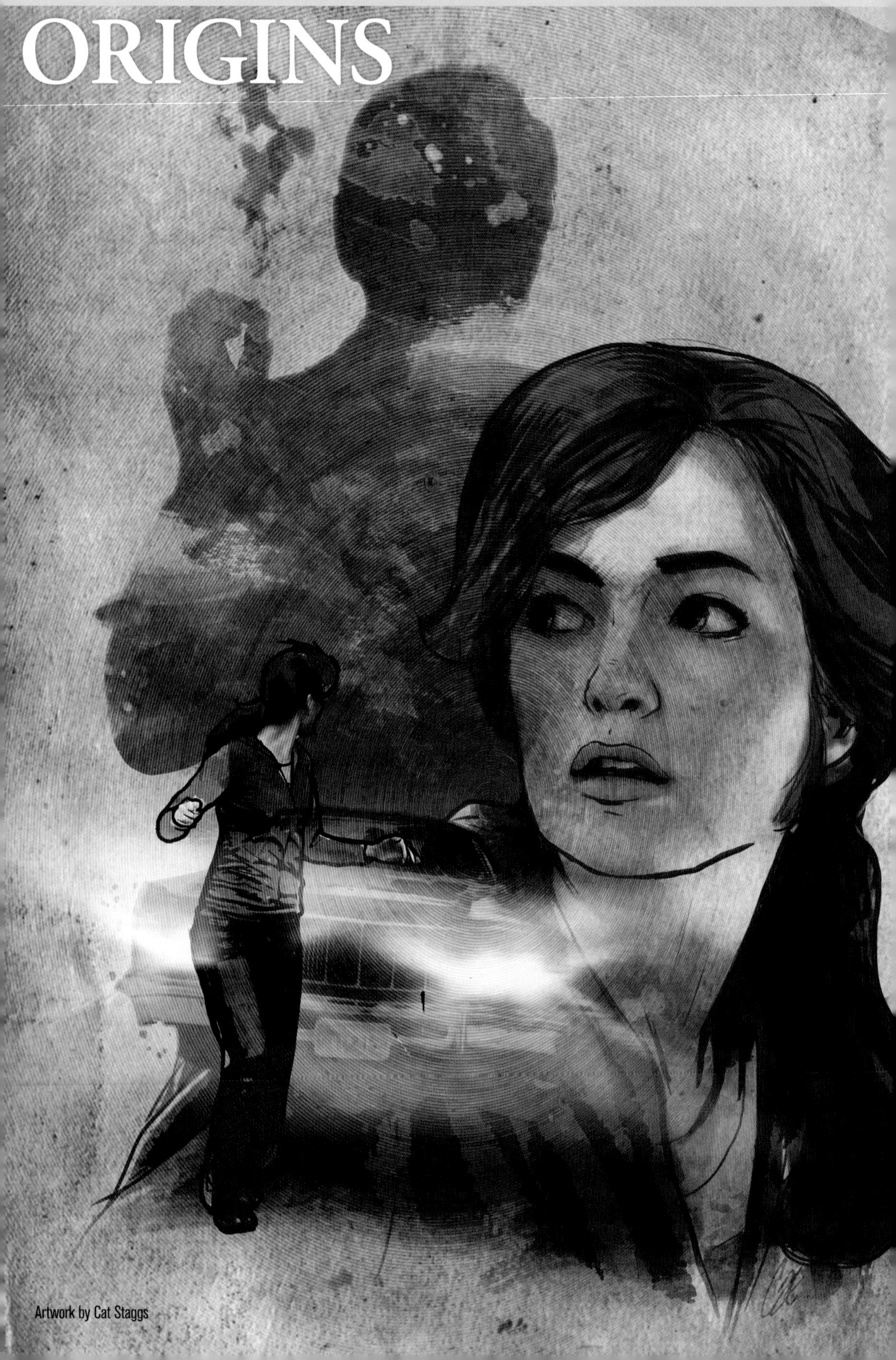
ORIGINS

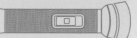

Artwork by Cat Staggs

THE X-FILES™ 2

ORIGINS

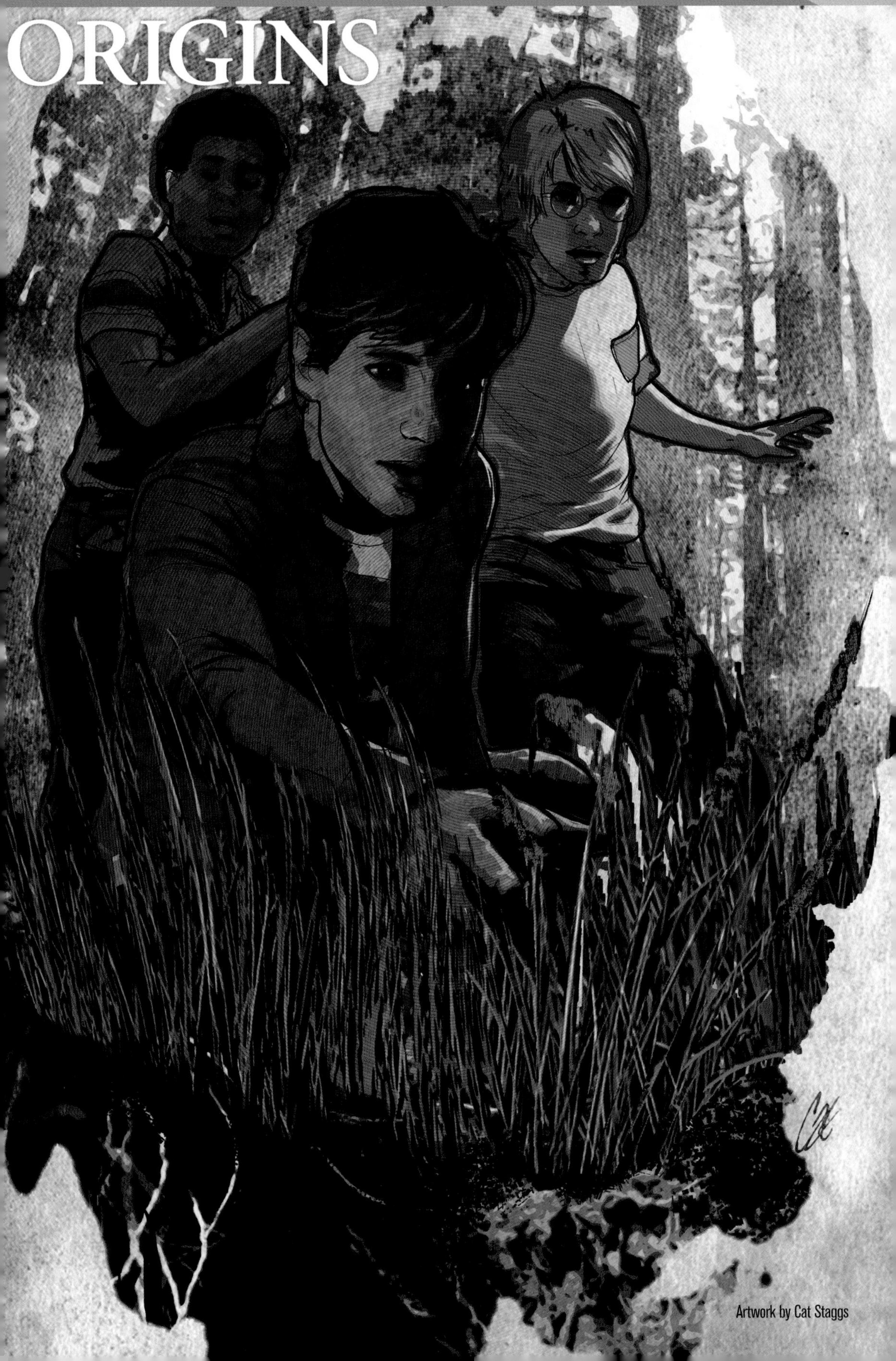

Artwork by Cat Staggs

THE X-FILES™ 2

ORIGINS

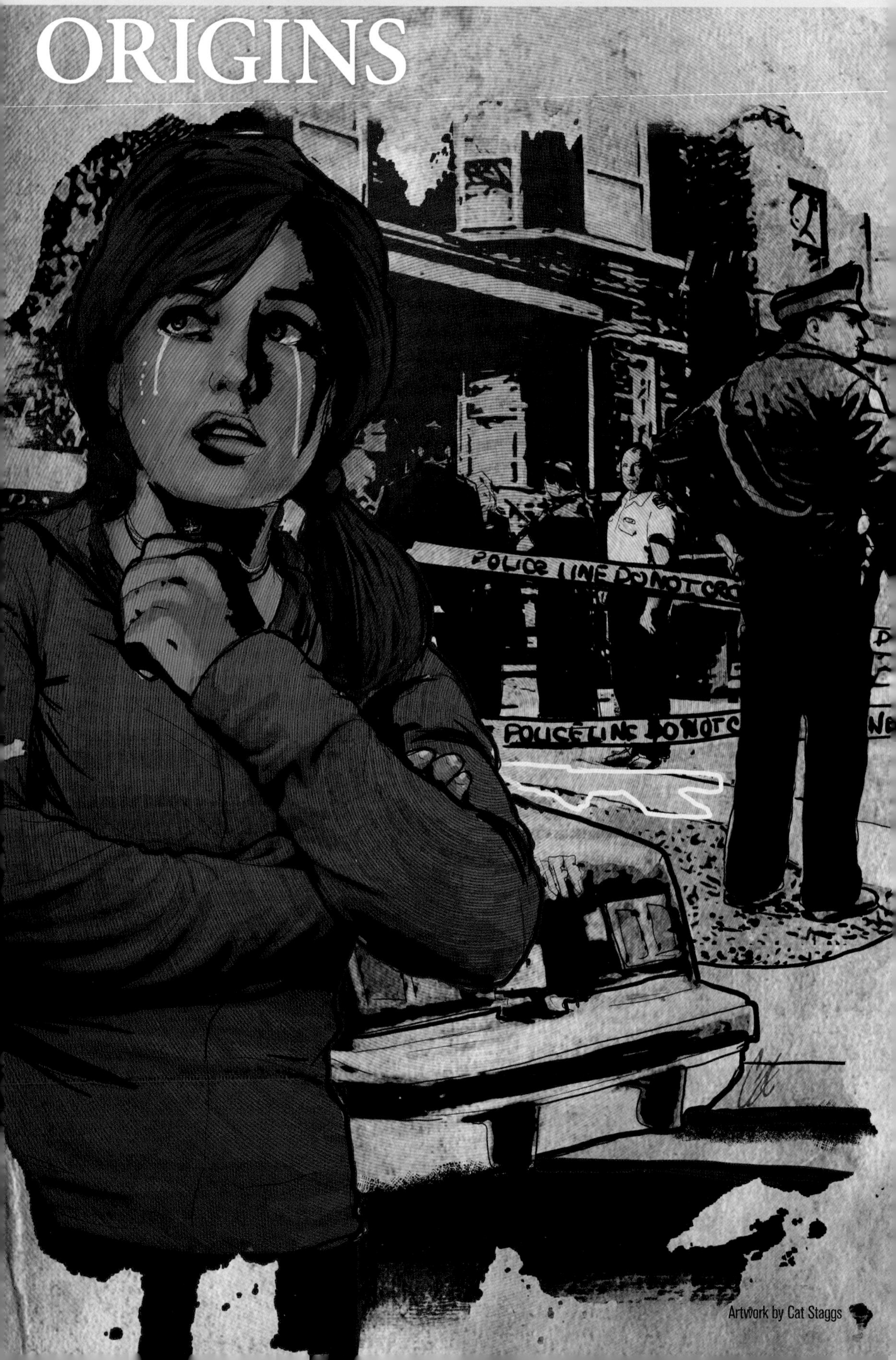
POLICE LINE DO NOT
POLICE LINE DO NOT

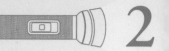

Artwork by Cat Staggs

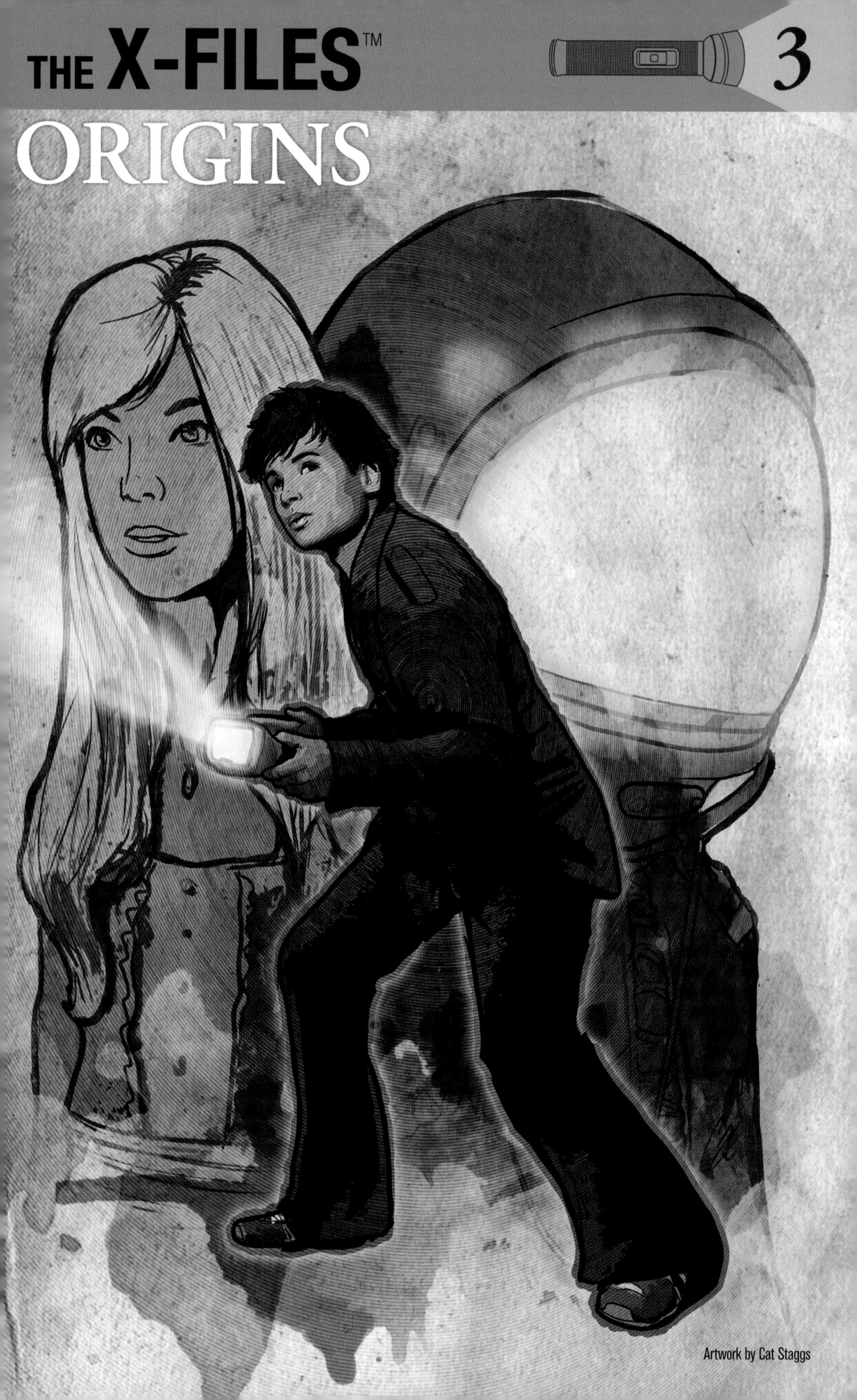
THE X-FILES™
3
ORIGINS
Artwork by Cat Staggs

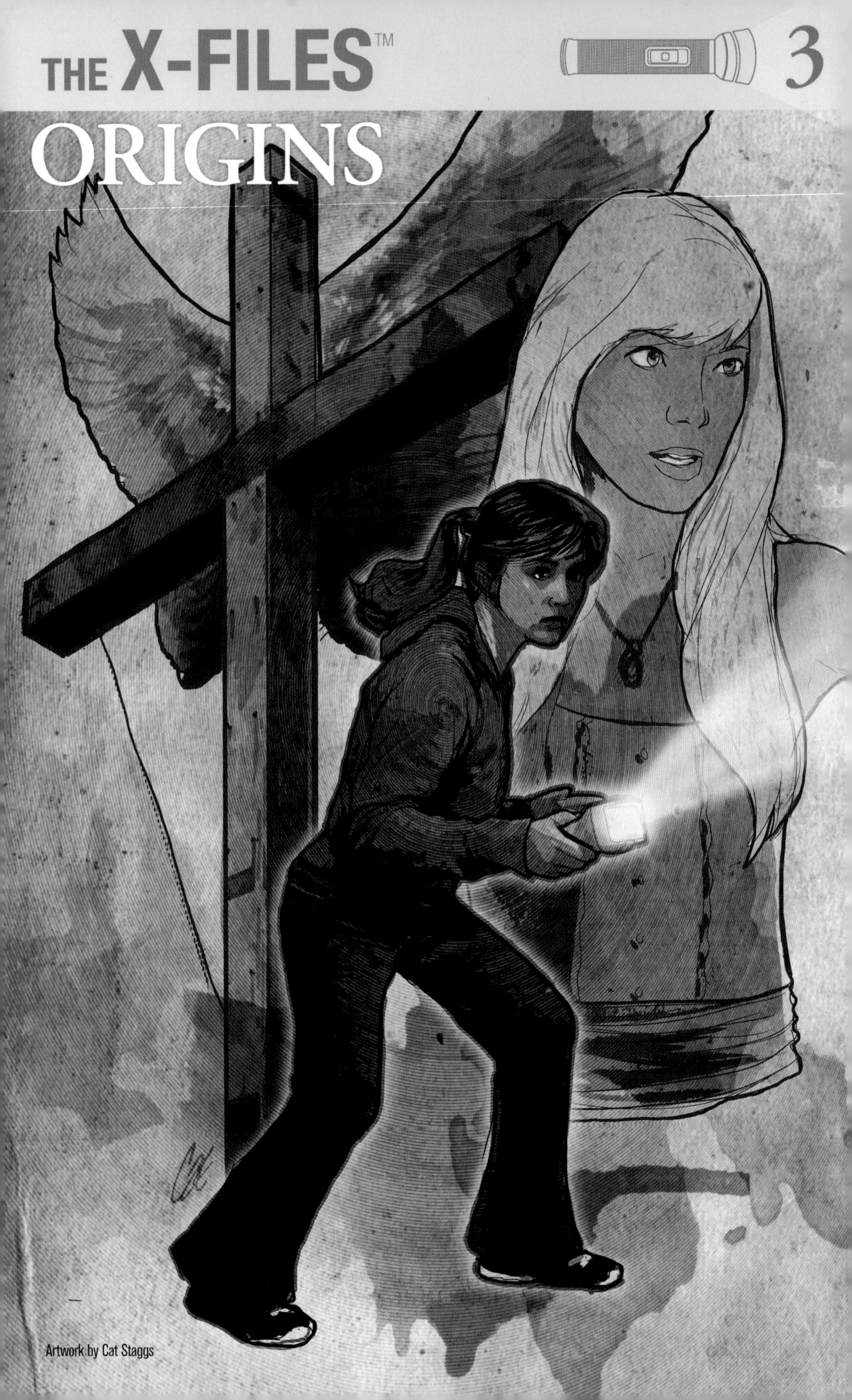
THE X-FILES™
3
ORIGINS

Artwork by Cat Staggs

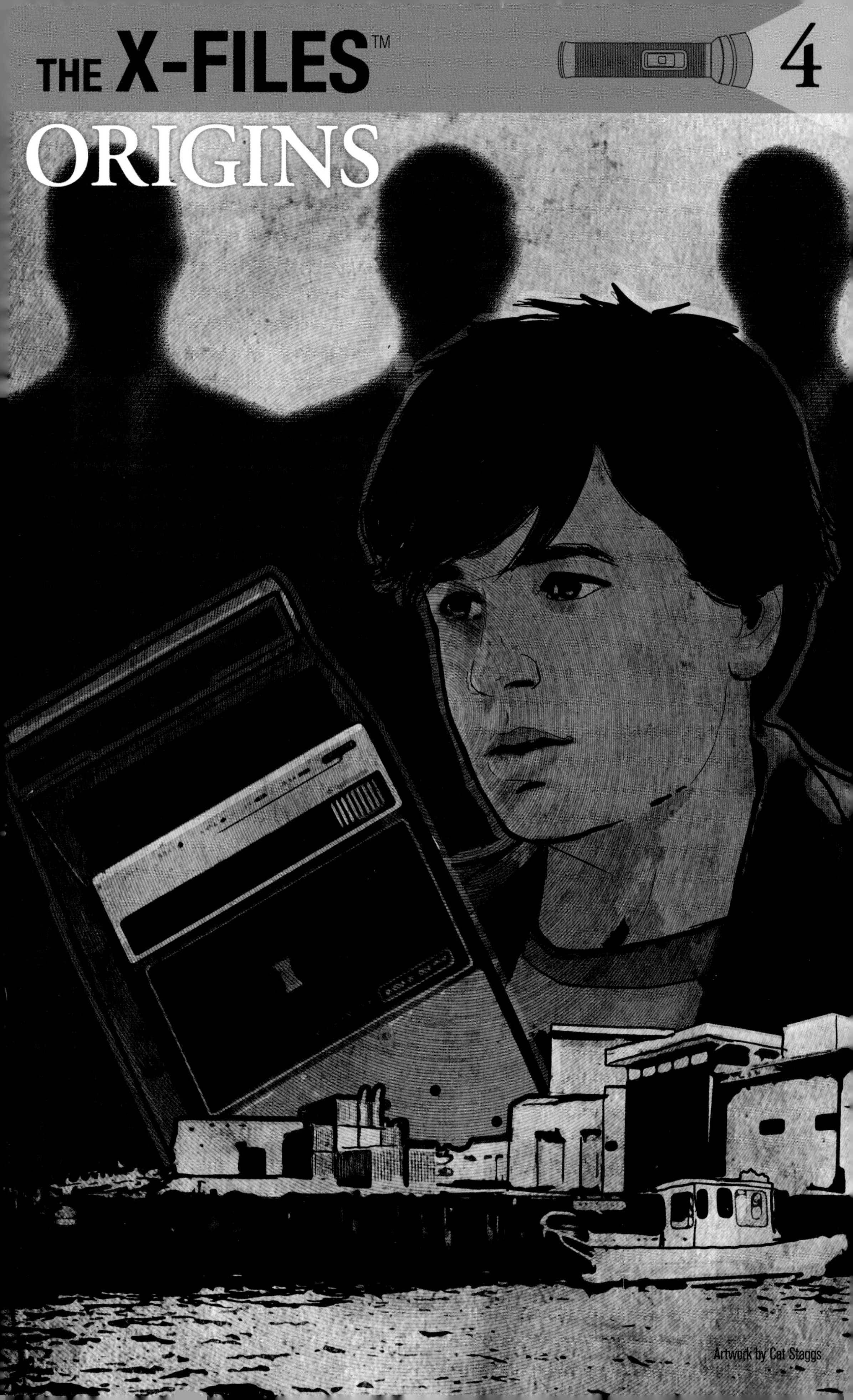
THE X-FILES™
4
ORIGINS
Artwork by Cat Staggs

THE X-FILES™ 4
ORIGINS

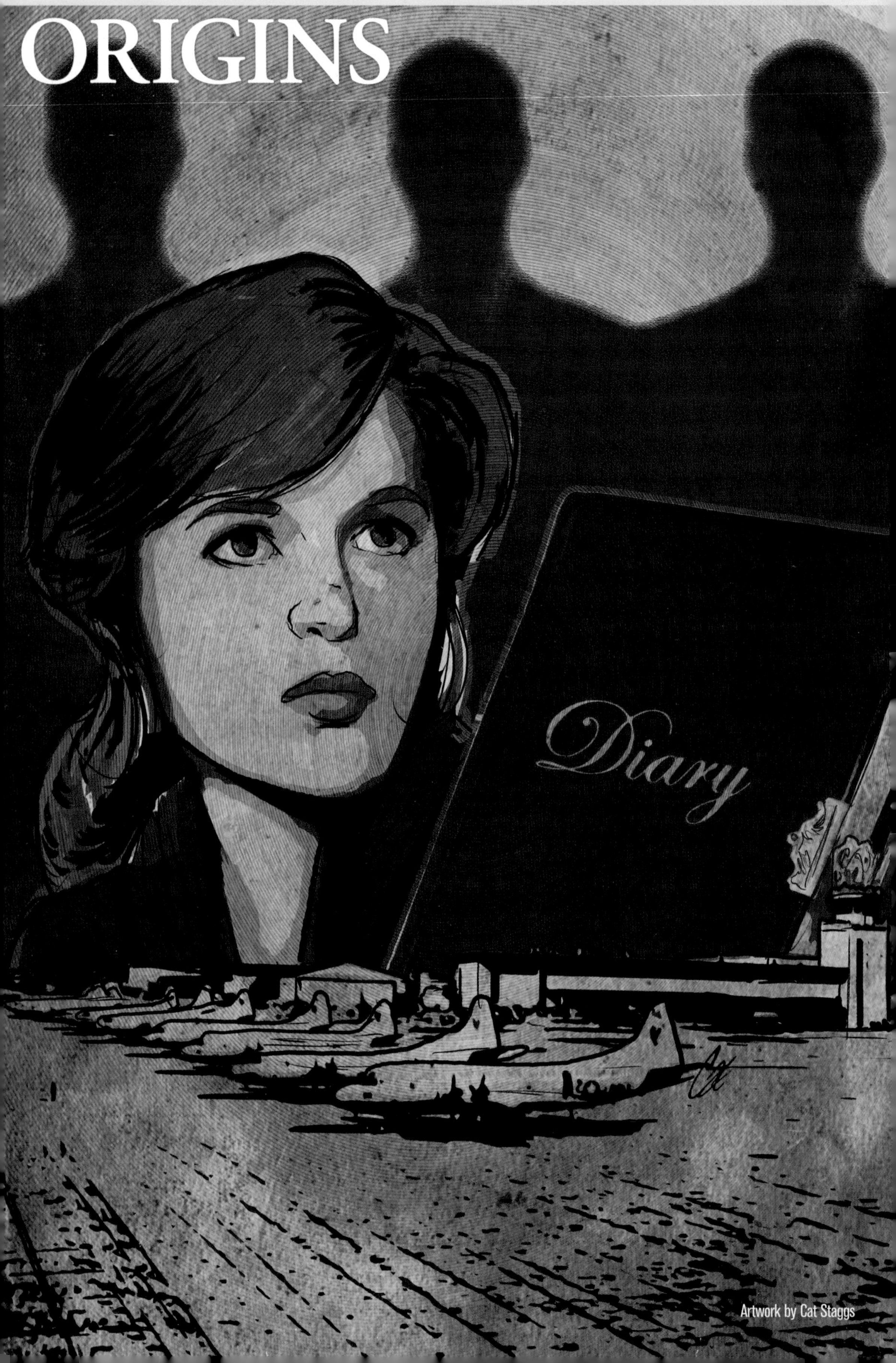
Diary

Artwork by Cat Staggs

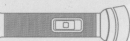